D0908826

AGS®

Math for the World of Work

by
Kathleen M. Harmeyer

AGS®
American Guidance Service, Inc.
Circle Pines, Minnesota 55014-1796
800-328-2560

About the Author

Kathleen M. Harmeyer, M.S., an award winning instructor, has taught mathematics for the Baltimore County Public Schools, University of Maryland, and Baltimore City Community College. As a mathematics specialist for the Maryland State Department of Education, Ms. Harmeyer assisted in the development of the objectives for the Maryland Functional Mathematics Test. She is currently President of ExperTech, an educational technology firm, and Associate Professor in the Math/Computer Science/Internet and Multimedia Technology Department at The Community College of Baltimore County.

Content Reviewer

Keith Harmeyer
Principal, Loch Raven High School
Baltimore, Maryland

Photo Credits: Cover photos: (top left) © Larry Gatz/Image Bank, (top right) © Gabriel M. Covian/Image Bank, (bottom left) © Romilly Lockyer/Image Bank, (bottom right) © China Tourism Press/Image Bank; pp. 6 (top), 150— © Jon Riley/Stone; p. 6 (bottom right)— © Peter Mason/Stone; pp. 6 (bottom left), 29, 112, 140, 211— © Walter Hodges/Stone; pp. 17, 98— © Jeff Greenberg/Unicorn Stock; p. 18— © Index Stock; p. 32— © Charles Thatcher/Stone; p. 38— © Roy Botterell/Stone; p. 49— © Rachel Epstein/PhotoEdit; p. 52— © Stephen Simpson/FPG International; pp. 54, 194— © Roger Ressemeyer/Corbis; p. 62— © David Young-Wolff/PhotoEdit; p. 73— © Dennis O'Clair/Stone; p. 76— © Don Klumpp/Image Bank; pp. 79, 168— © Ed Pritchard/Stone; p. 85— © American Stock/Archive Photos/Image Bank; p. 107— © Shambroom/PhotoEdit; pp. 113, 263— © Romilly Lockyer/Image Bank; p. 116— © Harry Bartlett/FPG International; p. 129— © David Frazier/Stone; p. 134— © Telegraph Colour Library/FPG International; p. 137— © Jon Feingersh/Stock Market; pp. 148, 156, 175, 178, 191, 214, 243— © Superstock; p. 153— © Pablo Corral/Corbis; p. 162— © Colin Garrett/Corbis; p. 171— © David K. Crow/PhotoEdit; p. 180— © Brian Blauser/Stone; p. 187— © Spencer Grant/PhotoEdit; p. 197— © Janis Burger/BURGE/Bruce Coleman, Inc.; pp. 201, 241— © Aneal F. Vohra/Unicorn Stock; p. 203— © David S. Hwang; p. 221— © Jamey Stillings/Stone; p. 225— © Bruce Ayres/Stone; p. 228— © Jeff Scheid/Liaison Agency; p. 231— © R. W. Jones/Corbis; p. 246— © Will & Deni McIntyre/Photo Researchers; p. 249— © Mark C. Burnett/Photo Researchers

Publisher's Project Staff

Director, Product Development: Karen Dahlen
Senior Editor: Patrick Keithahn
Assistant Editor: Emily Kedrowski
Development Assistant: Bev Johnson
Design Manager: Nancy Condon

Desktop Publishing Manager: Lisa Beller
Designer: Daren Hastings
Purchasing Agent: Mary Kaye Kuzma
Executive Director of Marketing: Matt Keller
Marketing Manager: Brian Holl

Editorial and production services provided by The Mazer Corporation and Fox Run Press. Special thanks to Glenn Austin for his review of this textbook.

Printed in the United States of America

ISBN 0-7854-2697-3

Product Number 93400

A 0 9 8 7 6 5 4 3 2 1

Contents

How to Use This Book: A Study Guide

Welcome to *Math for the World of Work*. Why do you need to know math for your job? The work world uses addition, subtraction, multiplication, and division for most calculations. Businesses use math to calculate wages, salaries and benefits, costs of production and selling, and administrative costs. They use fractions, decimals, and percents to decide whether to raise wages and prices. They use ratios and proportions to calculate amounts of increase or decrease.

Knowing how to estimate an answer, solve problems, and use technology will help you as an employee or as an employer. When you look for a job, you will know how to compare wages and salaries, and what benefits to look for. When you find a job, you will know what part of your wages is take-home pay. When you shop, you will be able to calculate the prices of discounted items. You will know what expenses businesses have, and how they calculate their profits. More importantly, knowing how to solve math problems prepares you to enter the world of work and be a valuable part of a business.

How to Study

- Plan a regular time to study.
- Choose a quiet desk or table where you will not be distracted. Find a spot that has good lighting.
- Gather all the books, pencils, paper, and other equipment you will need to complete your assignments.
- Decide on a goal. For example: "I will finish reading and taking notes on Chapter 1, Lesson 1, by 8:00."
- Take a five- to ten-minute break every hour to keep alert.
- If you start to feel sleepy, take a short break and get some fresh air.

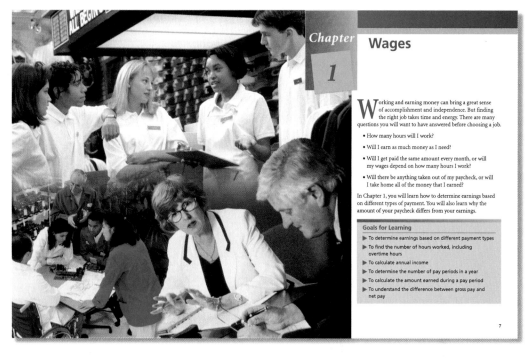

Chapter 1 — Wages

Working and earning money can bring a great sense of accomplishment and independence. But finding the right job takes time and energy. There are many questions you will want to have answered before choosing a job.

- How many hours will I work?
- Will I earn as much money as I need?
- Will I get paid the same amount every month, or will my wages depend on how many hours I work?
- Will there be anything taken out of my paycheck, or will I take home all of the money that I earned?

In Chapter 1, you will learn how to determine earnings based on different types of payment. You will also learn why the amount of your paycheck differs from your earnings.

Goals for Learning

- ► To determine earnings based on different payment types
- ► To find the number of hours worked, including overtime hours
- ► To calculate annual income
- ► To determine the number of pay periods in a year
- ► To calculate the amount earned during a pay period
- ► To understand the difference between gross pay and net pay

7

Before Beginning Each Chapter

- Read the chapter title to learn what the chapter is about.
- Study the Goals for Learning. The Chapter Review and tests will ask questions related to these goals.
- Look at the Graphic Organizers. Diagrams are another way to organize the information in the chapter.
- Look at the Chapter Review. The questions cover the most important information in the chapter.

Note these features:

Did You Know?—Interesting facts related to the topic being studied

Humor on the Job—Humorous stories related to the world of work

Technology Connection—Solve problems using a calculator and find information on the Internet

Try This—New ways to think about problems and solve them

Writing About Mathematics—Opportunities to write about problems and alternate solutions

Bold type

Words seen for the
first time will appear
in bold type

Glossary

Words listed in this
column are also
found in the glossary

Using the Bold Words

Knowing the meaning of all the boxed words in the left column will help you understand what you read.

These words appear in **bold type** the first time they appear in the text and are defined in the paragraph.

Her full weekly earnings are her **gross pay**.

All of the words in the left column are also defined in the **glossary**.

Gross pay—Full earnings before deductions (p. 10)

What to Do With a Word You Do Not Know

When you come to a word you do not know, ask yourself these questions:

- **Is the word a compound word?**
  Can you find two words within the word? This could help you understand the meaning. For example: *output.*

- **Does the word have a prefix at the beginning?**
  For example: *bimonthly.* The prefix *bi-* means "two," so this word refers to something that happens every two months.

- **Does the word have a suffix at the end?**
  For example: *quarterly, -ly.* This means occurring every quarter.

- **Can you identify the root word? Can you sound it out in parts?** For example: *ex port.*

- **Are there any clues in the sentence that will help you understand the word?**

Look for the word in the margin box, glossary, or dictionary.

If you are still having trouble with a word, ask for help.

Taking Notes in Class

As you read, you will be learning many new facts and ideas. Writing these key ideas down will help you remember them. Your notes will be useful when preparing for projects and class discussions and also when studying for tests.

There are many ways to take notes. You may want to try several methods to decide which one works best for you.

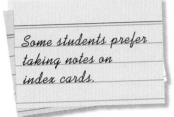

Some students prefer taking notes on index cards.

Others jot down key ideas in a spiral notebook.

1. Always write the main ideas and supporting details.

2. Using an outline format will help save you time.

3. Keep your notes brief. You may want to use abbreviations to speed up your note-taking.

    For example:
    - feet → ft.
    - and → +
    - dollars → $
    - United States → US
    - Social Security → SS

    Use the same method and abbreviations all the time. Then when you study for a test, you will know where to go to find the information you need to review.

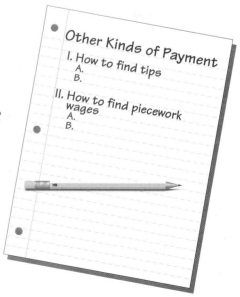

Using an Outline

You may want to outline each lesson using the main ideas. An outline will help you remember the main points of the lesson. Here is an example of an outline.

Using Graphic Organizers

You can use the Graphic Organizers to show how the main topics of each chapter are related. Here are examples of Graphic Organizers.

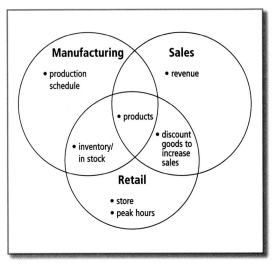

Test-Taking Tips

To help you take tests, read the *Test-Taking Tips* with each Chapter Review.

Test-Taking Tip | Read a problem thoroughly before you begin to solve it. After you complete your work, read the problem again to be sure your answer makes sense.

Here are other useful Test-Taking Tips:

Use your time wisely. Find out if the questions are all worth the same number of points. If they are, the easy questions will count the same as the hard ones. In this case, don't get stuck working too long on one question. Keep moving. Plan so that you will have time to complete the test.

Read each question twice. Read first to get the big idea. Then read the question again to gather the specific numbers and information you need to solve the problem.

Make a plan for solving the problem. Decide where to start, what information to use, and how to use it. Make notes about your plan so you don't forget or get lost in the middle of solving the problem.

Problem-Solving Strategies

Following these steps will help you to solve math problems in this textbook.

1. Read

- Read the problem to discover what information you need.
- Make sure you understand the business concepts.
- Study the problem to decide if you have all the necessary information and if there is information you do not need.
- Begin thinking about the steps needed to solve the problem.

2. Plan

Think about the steps you will need to do to solve the problem. Decide if you will use mental math, paper and pencil, or a calculator. Will you need to draw a picture? Are measurements in the same units? Will you use a formula? Will you need to do more than one step?

These strategies may help you find a solution:

- ☑ Reword the problem
- ☑ Draw a picture
- ☑ Estimate your answer
- ☑ Write an equation
- ☑ Divide the problem into smaller parts
- ☑ Make a chart or graph
- ☑ Use a formula
- ☑ Work backward

3. Solve

- Follow your plan and do the calculations.
- Make sure to label your answer correctly.

4. Reflect

- Reread the problem.
- Does your answer make sense?
- Did you answer the questions?
- Check your work to see if your answer is correct.

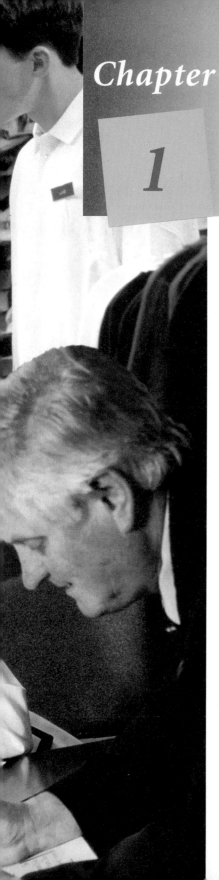

Chapter

1

Wages

Working and earning money can bring a great sense of accomplishment and independence. But finding the right job takes time and energy. There are many questions you will want to have answered before choosing a job.

- How many hours will I work?

- Will I earn as much money as I need?

- Will I get paid the same amount every month, or will my wages depend on how many hours I work?

- Will there be anything taken out of my paycheck, or will I take home all of the money that I earned?

In Chapter 1, you will learn how to determine earnings based on different types of payment. You will also learn why the amount of your paycheck differs from your earnings.

Goals for Learning

▶ To determine earnings based on different payment types
▶ To find the number of hours worked, including overtime hours
▶ To calculate annual income
▶ To determine the number of pay periods in a year
▶ To calculate the amount earned during a pay period
▶ To understand the difference between gross pay and net pay

Hourly rate

Amount of money paid for each hour of work

Wage

Money paid for hourly work

People who earn an **hourly rate** earn the same amount of money for each hour they work. The money they earn for hourly work is their **wages**. Calculate wages by multiplying the hourly rate by the number of hours worked.

EXAMPLE

Petra earns $7.50 per hour. She works $10\frac{1}{2}$ hours a week. What are her weekly wages?

hourly rate × hours worked = wages

Estimate:
$7.50 is between $7 and $8. $10\frac{1}{2}$ hours is about 10 hours. Her weekly wages are between $7 × 10 = $70 and $8 × 10 = $80.

To rewrite $\frac{1}{2}$ as a decimal, divide numerator by denominator. $\frac{1}{2} = 1 \div 2 = .5$ $10\frac{1}{2} = 10.5$

$7.50 per hour × $10\frac{1}{2}$ hours = wages

$$
\begin{array}{r}
7.50 \leftarrow 2 \text{ decimal places} \\
\times \quad 10.5 \leftarrow 1 \text{ decimal place} \\
\hline
3750 \\
0000 \\
+ 75000 \\
\hline
78.750 \leftarrow 3 \text{ decimal places}
\end{array}
$$

Petra's weekly wages are $78.75. The answer is close to the estimate.

The number of decimal places in the product is the same as the total number of decimal places in the factors.

Exercise A Find the weekly wages for each employee.

Employee	Hourly Rate	Hours Worked	Weekly Wages
1. Elaine	$8.00	40	_____
2. Miko	$9.25	40	_____
3. Tony	$6.90	25	_____
4. Michael	$8.00	$14\frac{3}{4}$	_____
5. Kareem	$10.40	$15\frac{1}{4}$	_____

The amount of money earned in a year is **annual wages**. A **living wage** is the annual wage needed to provide necessary goods. In 1998 a family of four earning below $17,000 a year did not earn a living wage. Families not earning a living wage may receive government help. If an employee works the same number of hours each week, this is how to find annual wages: Multiply weekly wages by the number of weeks worked in a year. There are 52 weeks in a year. We will use 50 to estimate the number of weeks in a year. To estimate the number of hours worked in a year, multiply the number of hours worked each week by 50.

EXAMPLE Darryl is an electrician. He works 38 hours a week. His hourly rate is $22.50. Estimate his annual wages.

Use 40 to estimate 38. Use $20 to estimate $22.50. 40 hours a week × 50 weeks = 2,000 hours worked in a year

$20 per hour × 2,000 hours = $40,000

Darryl's estimated annual wages are $40,000.

Exercise B Estimate the annual wages for each employee.

Employee	Hourly Rate	Hours Worked Each Week	Annual Wages
1. Lily	$7.00	40	_____
2. Max	$8.50	30	_____
3. Tim	$7.25	10	_____
4. Yoshitaka	$9.65	32	_____
5. Kathy	$10.80	41	_____
6. Carol	$11.15	12	_____
7. Stephen	$8.40	27	_____
8. August	$12.50	37	_____
9. Taylor	$6.95	10	_____
10. Anna	$8.75	38	_____

Most full-time workers work 40 hours a week.

40 hours a week × 50 weeks worked a year = 2,000 hours worked a year

$10 per hour × 2,000 hours = $20,000
$20 per hour × 2,000 hours = $40,000
$30 per hour × 2,000 hours = $60,000

Do you see a pattern? To estimate the annual wages of a full-time employee, double the hourly rate, then write three zeros.

Exercise C   Estimate the annual wages for each full-time employee.

Employee	Hourly Rate	Estimated Annual Wages
1. Hunter	$8.00	_____
2. Stella	$17.00	_____
3. Scott	$23.00	_____
4. Colleen	$12.50	_____
5. Kelsey	$17.50	_____

Deductions

Money withheld from gross pay

Gross pay

Full earnings before deductions

Take-home pay/ net pay

Amount a worker receives after deductions are subtracted from gross pay

Ellen works 20 hours a week. She earns $10.00 per hour. Her full weekly earnings are her **gross pay**, which is $200.00. However, her paycheck is only for $140.80. Why? Her employer subtracted **deductions** for income taxes, health insurance, social security, and a uniform fee. The amount of money a worker actually receives after all deductions have been subtracted from the gross pay is called **take-home pay**, or **net pay**.

GROSS PAY	NET PAY	DEDUCTIONS	
$ 200.00	$ 125.50	Federal Income Tax	$ 37.20
		Social Security	15.30
		State Income Tax	9.50
		Health Insurance	10.00
		Uniform Fee	2.50
		Total Deductions	$ 74.50

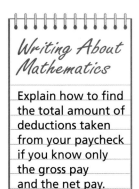

Writing About Mathematics

Explain how to find the total amount of deductions taken from your paycheck if you know only the gross pay and the net pay.

Be sure you line up the decimal points when you add or subtract.

EXAMPLE Mary earns $550.00. These deductions are subtracted from her gross pay:

> Taxes: $58.19
> Retirement account: $50.00
> Insurance: $23.10
> Union dues: $9.40

Find the total deductions. Then subtract the total from Mary's pay to find her net pay.

Step 1 Add to find the total deductions.

```
$  58.19   Taxes
    50.00   Retirement account
    23.10   Insurance
+    9.40   Union dues
$140.69   Total deductions
```

Step 2 Subtract the deductions from the gross pay.

```
$550.00   Gross pay
-140.69   Deductions
$409.31   Net pay
```

Mary's net pay is $409.31.

Exercise D Find the net pay.

| GROSS PAY | DEDUCTIONS | | | NET PAY |
	Taxes	Retirement Account	Insurance	
1. $265.00	$35.00	$26.00	$15.00	_____
2. $450.00	$47.00	$45.00	$22.90	_____
3. $315.25	$47.90	$22.50	$19.00	_____
4. $303.60	$64.25	$15.80	$23.55	_____
5. $389.75	$71.55	$28.55	$32.70	_____

TRY THIS...

For each problem above, start with gross pay. Subtract taxes. Then subtract retirement account. Then subtract insurance. Compare your answers to the answers above.

A.M.
The hours before noon

P.M.
The hours after noon

Time card
Record of the number of hours an employee works each day

Employees earning an hourly rate are paid for the number of hours they work. For example, most hourly employees do not get paid for time on lunch break. Employees use **time cards** to record the number of morning, or A.M. hours, and the number of afternoon, or P.M. hours, actually worked each day.

EXAMPLE   Cora starts work at 9:00 A.M. She goes to lunch at 11:45 A.M. and returns at 1:00 P.M. She leaves work at 5:30 P.M. How many hours does Cora work?

Step 1 Find the number of hours worked before lunch and after lunch. Subtract the earlier time from the later time.

11:45 A.M. (later time)   5:30 P.M. (later time)
− 9:00 A.M. (earlier time)   −1:00 P.M. (earlier time)
2:45 = 2 hr., 45 min.   4:30 = 4 hr., 30 min.

Step 2 Find the total hours worked.

2 hours, 45 minutes
+4 hours, 30 minutes
6 hours, 75 minutes

To simplify a fraction, divide numerator and denominator by the same factor.

Step 3 Rename 6 hours, 75 minutes.

75 min. = 60 min. + 15 min. = 1 hr., 15 min.
6 hr., 75 min. = 7 hr., 15 min.

Step 4 Write 15 minutes as a fraction of 1 hour.

$$\frac{15 \text{ min.}}{60 \text{ min.}} \quad \frac{\text{Minutes worked}}{\text{Minutes in one hour}} \quad \frac{15 \div 15}{60 \div 15} = \frac{1}{4}$$

Cora works $7\frac{1}{4}$ hours.

Use the Least Common Denominator (LCD) to add fractions. To change an improper fraction to a mixed number, divide the numerator by the denominator. Then simplify the fraction part.

One week Cora worked $8\frac{1}{2}$ hours on Monday, $7\frac{3}{4}$ hours on Tuesday, and $5\frac{1}{4}$ hours on Thursday. How many hours did she work that week?

$$8\frac{1}{2} = 8\frac{2}{4}$$
$$7\frac{3}{4} = 7\frac{3}{4}$$
$$+ 5\frac{1}{4} = 5\frac{1}{4}$$
$$20\frac{6}{4} = 20 + 1\frac{2}{4} = 21\frac{1}{2}$$

Cora worked $21\frac{1}{2}$ hours that week.

Exercise A Below is Ben's time card for one week. Find the number of hours Ben worked each day.

EMPLOYEE NAME: Ben McKee					
Day	In	Out	In	Out	Daily Hours
1. Mon.	8:00 A.M.	12:00 P.M.	1:00 P.M.	5:00 P.M.	____
2. Tues.	8:00 A.M.	12:30 P.M.	1:00 P.M.	4:00 P.M.	____
3. Wed.	9:00 A.M.	12:30 P.M.	1:00 P.M.	4:45 P.M.	____
4. Thurs.	8:00 A.M.	12:30 P.M.	1:00 P.M.	6:15 P.M.	____
5. Fri.	8:15 A.M.	12:30 P.M.	1:30 P.M.	5:45 P.M.	____

When there are not enough minutes to subtract from, rename 1 hour as 60 minutes.

EXAMPLE Patsy started work at 8:45 A.M. She went to lunch at 12:15 P.M. How many hours did she work?

$$
\begin{array}{r}
11{:}75 \\
\cancel{12{:}15} \\
-\ 8{:}45 \\
\hline
3{:}30
\end{array}
$$

Subtract the earlier time from the later time. Rename 1 hour as 60 minutes. Add 60 minutes to 15 minutes.

Patsy worked 3 hours, 30 minutes, or $3\frac{1}{2}$ hours.

When there are not enough hours to subtract from, rename the hours using a 24-hour clock.

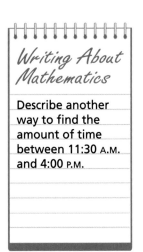

Writing About Mathematics

Describe another way to find the amount of time between 11:30 A.M. and 4:00 P.M.

EXAMPLE Samantha works from 11:00 A.M. to 4:00 P.M. How many hours does she work?

Rename 4:00 using the 24-hour clock.
To use the 24-hour clock, add the 12 morning hours to the afternoon hours. Here are some examples:

1:00 P.M. → 1:00 + 12:00 = 13:00
8:00 P.M. → 8:00 + 12:00 = 20:00
12:00 midnight → 12:00 + 12:00 = 24:00

$$
\begin{array}{r}
4{:}00 \\
-11{:}00
\end{array}
\quad \text{Add 12 hours.} \rightarrow \quad
\begin{array}{r}
16{:}00 \\
-\ 11{:}00 \\
\hline
5{:}00
\end{array}
$$

Samantha works 5 hours.

Exercise B Find the number of hours worked each day. Rename hours and minutes if necessary. Then find the total number of hours worked for the week.

Day	In	Out	In	Out	Daily Hours
1. Mon.	9:00 A.M.	1:00 P.M.	—	—	_____
2. Tues.	8:30 A.M.	12:00 P.M.	12:30 P.M.	4:45 P.M.	_____
3. Wed.	7:30 A.M.	12:00 P.M.	1:00 P.M.	5:00 P.M.	_____
4. Thurs.	10:00 A.M.	2:30 P.M.	3:30 P.M.	8:15 P.M.	_____
5. Fri.	6:30 A.M.	11:00 A.M.	11:30 A.M.	5:15 P.M.	_____

Total hours worked for the week: _____

Double time

Payment of 2 times the regular hourly rate

Overtime

Working time beyond a regular 40-hour week

Time and a half

Payment of 1.5 times the regular hourly rate

Sometimes employees work more than 40 hours a week. Time worked over 40 hours or on Sundays and holidays is **overtime**.

Workers often earn one and one half times the hourly rate, or **time and a half**, for working over 40 hours on regular workdays, Monday–Saturday.

Workers usually earn two times the hourly rate, or **double time**, for working on Sundays and holidays.

| EXAMPLE | Cary earns $7.00 per hour. What are his overtime rates? |

Time and a half

$\begin{array}{r} \$\ \ 7.00 \leftarrow 2 \text{ decimal places} \\ \times \quad 1.5 \leftarrow 1 \text{ decimal place} \\ \hline 3500 \\ +\ 7000 \\ \hline \$10.500 \leftarrow 2 + 1 = 3 \text{ decimal places} \end{array}$

Double time

$\begin{array}{r} \$\ \ 7.00 \leftarrow 2 \text{ decimal places} \\ \times \quad \ \ 2 \leftarrow 0 \text{ decimal place} \\ \hline \$14.00 \leftarrow 2 + 0 = \\ 2 \text{ decimal} \\ \text{places} \end{array}$

Cary's time-and-a-half rate is $10.50 per hour.
His double-time rate is $14.00 per hour.

To calculate wages for both regular and overtime hours:
- Find the number of regular hours worked. Find the number of overtime hours worked.
- Multiply regular hours times rate to find regular wages. Multiply overtime hours times rate to find overtime wages.
- Add regular and overtime wages to find total wages.

| EXAMPLE | Roberto's hourly rate is $6.50. He works 45 hours. He earns time and a half for overtime hours. What are his total wages? |

Step 1
```
  45  Hours worked
 -40  Regular hours
   5  Overtime hours
```

Step 4
```
$ 9.75  Rate
×    5  Hours
$48.75  Overtime wages
```

Step 2
```
$  6.50  Rate
×    40  Hours
$260.00  Regular wages
```

Step 5
```
$260.00  Regular wages
+ 48.75  Overtime wages
$308.75  Total wages
```

Step 3
```
$ 6.50  Hourly rate
× 1.5   Time and a half
 3250
+6500
$9.750  Overtime rate
```

Roberto's total wages are $308.75.

Exercise C Find the total wages. Use time and a half for overtime hours worked Monday through Saturday and double time for hours worked on Sundays and holidays.

HOURS WORKED		REGULAR HOURS	OVERTIME HOURS		HOURLY RATE	TOTAL WAGES
Mon.–Sat.	Sun. & Holidays		Time and a Half	Double Time		
1. 24	0	_____	_____	_____	$5.50	_____
2. 50	0	_____	_____	_____	$9.00	_____
3. 35	4	_____	_____	_____	$8.35	_____
4 46	2	_____	_____	_____	$10.70	_____
5. 55	6	_____	_____	_____	$7.90	_____

Exercise D Calculate yearly income. Use time and a half for the overtime rate.

Employee	Hourly Rate	Hours per Week	Weeks Worked	Yearly Income
1. Sarah	$8.25	40	50	_____
2. Colin	$11.50	32	50	_____
3. Tanner	$9.75	44	48	_____
4. Pam	$12.00	48	36	_____
5. Hideko	$5.15	42	50	_____

Tip
Extra money given for good service

Some employees receive money from their customers in addition to wages from their employer. For example, customers give food servers money for providing fast and polite service. The money that a customer gives directly to a worker is a **tip**. Tips can be additional payment for a service, and may be expected.

Other examples of workers who receive tips include cab drivers, hairstylists, and hotel bellhops. Some workers earn more money from tips than from their hourly wages.

EXAMPLE Kimo drives a cab. He earns $6.25 per hour. One week he worked 30 hours and received $250.00 in tips. What was his total income for the week?

Step 1
$ 6.25   Hourly rate
×   30   Hours worked
$187.50   Hourly wages

Step 2
$187.50   Hourly wages
+250.00   Tips
$437.50   Total income

Kimo's total income for the week was $437.50.

Exercise A   Find the total income for each person.

Name	Hours Worked	Hourly Rate	Tips Received	Total Income
1. Frank	35	$7.50	$189.00	_____
2. Carrie	40	$5.00	$148.00	_____
3. Jerome	25	$6.40	$164.00	_____
4. Jeff	58	$5.35	$312.00	_____
5. Emma	15	$7.15	$48.50	_____

Did You Know?

Want an office job where you can climb up in the world?

Try the World Trade Center in New York City. It has 110 stories and stands 1,368 feet high.

There are actually two "twin" towers, but the second tower is smaller than the first by 6 feet.

Percentage

An amount calculated by multiplying a percent by a number

To change a percent to a decimal, move the decimal point 2 places to the left and remove the percent symbol.

A tip may be a percent of the price, or a **percentage**. A standard tip is 15% to 20%. Many workers depend on tips as part of their earnings.

EXAMPLE   Karen styles hair. She charges $30.00 for a haircut. One customer gave her a 15% tip. How much did Karen earn for the haircut?

Step 1   Calculate the amount of the tip.

Change 15% to a decimal.   15.% = .15

Multiply the price of the haircut by the decimal.

$$
\begin{array}{ll}
\$30.00 \rightarrow & .15 \\
\times\ .15 & \times\ 30 \\
\hline
& \$4.50 \quad \text{Amount of tip}
\end{array}
$$

Step 2   Add the price of the haircut and the tip.

$$
\begin{array}{ll}
\$30.00 & \text{Haircut} \\
+\ 4.50 & \text{Tip} \\
\hline
\$34.50 & \text{Total amount earned}
\end{array}
$$

With tip, Karen earned $34.50.

PROBLEM SOLVING

Exercise B   Solve.

1. Harper delivers pizza for $5.75 per hour. One week he worked 25 hours and received $97.25 in tips. What were Harper's total earnings for the week?

2. Megan is a cab driver. She earns $7.00 per hour. Last week she worked 35 hours and received $280.00 in tips. What was her total income for the week?

3. Janice cleans and sets tables. She earns $6.50 per hour, plus 10% of the waiters' tips. If the waiters' tips are $350.00 during her 6-hour shift, how much does Janice earn?

4. Ken is a hairstylist. He earns $28.00 per haircut. On Monday he gave 7 haircuts and earned $225.40. Did he earn 15% in tips?

Piecework

Work paid according to the number of units completed

Sometimes a worker's pay depends on how much work is produced. For example, a worker at a bottling plant may be paid a certain amount for each crate of bottles that she loads onto a delivery truck. Payment based on the amount of work produced is called **piecework**.

EXAMPLE   Jana loads crates of fruit juice on delivery trucks. She earns $.80 for each crate of juice that she loads. How much does she earn if she loads 200 crates?

$$
\begin{array}{rl}
\$ \quad .80 & \text{Piecework rate} \\
\times \quad 200 & \text{Number of crates loaded} \\
\hline
\$160.00 & \text{Total earned}
\end{array}
$$

Jana earns $160.00 for loading 200 crates on trucks.

Exercise C   Find the wages for each employee.

Employee	Units Completed	Piecework Rate	Wages
1. Bruce	340	$.40	_____
2. Suki	210	$.50	_____
3. Sandy	840	$.15	_____
4. Carl	124	$.80	_____
5. Taylor	48	$2.50	_____

Exercise D   Find the weekly totals and the wages for each employee.

Employee	DAILY PRODUCTION					Weekly Total	Piecework Rate	Wages
	M	Tu	W	Th	F			
1. Geraldo	8	9	8	7	10	_____	$4.25	_____
2. Jack	9	7	10	6	8	_____	$5.15	_____
3. Hannah	12	18	13	10	19	_____	$1.80	_____
4. Deborah	23	30	25	32	20	_____	$.75	_____
5. Paco	4	3	8	5	6	_____	$6.80	_____

Some people earn an hourly rate plus extra money based on the amount of work they produce.

EXAMPLE Tony sells patio tables at craft fairs. He earns $8.00 per hour plus $20.00 for each table he sells. One weekend he works 20 hours and sells 18 tables. How much does Tony earn?

Step 1 Find Tony's wages.

$$
\begin{array}{ll}
\$\ 8.00 & \text{Rate} \\
\times\quad 20 & \text{Hours} \\
\hline
\$160.00 & \text{Wages}
\end{array}
$$

Step 2 Find piecework earnings.

$$
\begin{array}{ll}
\$\ 20.00 & \text{Piecework rate} \\
\times\quad 18 & \text{Tables sold} \\
\hline
\$360.00 & \text{Piecework earnings}
\end{array}
$$

Step 3 Find total earnings.

$$
\begin{array}{ll}
\$160.00 & \text{Wages} \\
+360.00 & \text{Piecework earnings} \\
\hline
\$520.00 & \text{Total earnings}
\end{array}
$$

Tony earns $520.00.

PROBLEM SOLVING

Exercise E Solve.

1. Grace sells trips to Florida. She earns $10.50 per hour plus $120.00 for each trip she sells. During a 40-hour week she sold 3 trips. How much did she earn?

2. Tasha recruits volunteers for a food pantry. She earns $7.80 per hour plus $32.00 for every 8 volunteers she recruits. One month she worked 93 hours and recruited 64 volunteers. How much did she earn?

3. A job stuffing envelopes pays either $10.50 per hour or $.02 per envelope. If Pam can stuff 500 envelopes per hour, which pay plan should she choose?

4. Tanner paints pottery. He earns $7.00 per hour plus $.50 for each piece of pottery over 50 that he paints in a day. He worked 10 hours on Monday and earned $76.50. How many pieces of pottery did he paint?

The United States Congress passed a law naming the least hourly rate most workers can be paid. This hourly rate is called the **minimum wage**. The minimum wage can be changed by Congress if the cost of living increases, so full-time workers earn a living wage.

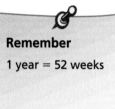

Remember

1 year = 52 weeks

EXAMPLES In 2000 the minimum wage was $5.15 per hour. Find the annual income of a full-time employee who earns the minimum wage.

40 hours per week × 52 weeks = 2,080 hours
Full-time workers work 2,080 hours in a year.

$ 5.15   Minimum wage
× 2,080   Hours worked in a year
$10,712.00   Annual income

The annual income of a full-time worker earning the minimum wage is $10,712.00.

Carla works at a fast-food restaurant and earns $5.15 per hour minimum wage. If she works 15 hours a week, what is her annual income?

Step 1   Find the number of hours worked in a year.

52   Weeks worked per year
× 15   Hours worked per week
780   Hours worked in a year

You can estimate Carla's annual income first. Then compare the answer with your estimate.

Step 2   Multiply to find the annual income.

$ 5.15   Minimum wage
× 780   Hours worked in a year
$4,017.00   Annual income

Carla's annual income is $4,017.00.

Exercise A Each person earns $5.15 per hour minimum wage. Find each annual income.

Employee	Hours Worked per Week	Annual Income
1. Estell	25	_____
2. John	30	_____
3. Robert	40	_____
4. Jackson	20	_____
5. Kris	35	_____
6. Nancy	12	_____
7. Evan	32	_____
8. Van	38	_____
9. Carol	18	_____
10. Mandy	26	_____

Annually
Once a year

Bimonthly
Every two months

Biweekly
Every two weeks

Quarterly
Every quarter of a year, or every three months

Salary
Payment of a fixed amount of money at regular intervals

Semimonthly
Twice a month

Not all wages are based on the number of hours an employee works. Some people earn a fixed amount of money, or **salary**, that does not depend on how many hours they work. People earning a salary usually are not paid overtime. Professionals and managers often earn a salary.

The pay period for people earning salaries varies from company to company. Salaries can be paid weekly, **biweekly** (every two weeks), **semimonthly** (twice a month), **bimonthly** (every two months), monthly, **quarterly** (four times a year), or **annually** (once a year).

EXAMPLE   Elaine is paid semimonthly. How many times a year does she get paid?

Elaine is paid twice a month. There are 12 months in a year.

$$
\begin{array}{rl}
12 & \text{Months in a year} \\
\times\ 2 & \text{Pay periods per month} \\
\hline
24 & \text{Pay periods per year}
\end{array}
$$

Elaine is paid 24 times a year.

Exercise B Find the number of pay periods per year for each employee.

Employee	How Often Paid	Pay Periods per Year
1. Doug	Weekly	_____
2. Brent	Biweekly	_____
3. Katrina	Quarterly	_____
4. Janice	Monthly	_____
5. Jerry	Semimonthly	_____

JANUARY						
Sunday	Monday	Tuesday	Wednesday	Thursday	Friday	Saturday
					1	2
3	4	5	6	7	8	9
10	11	12	13	14	15	16
17	18	19	20	21	22	23
24/31	25	26	27	28	29	30

FEBRUARY						
Sunday	Monday	Tuesday	Wednesday	Thursday	Friday	Saturday
	1	2	3	4	5	6
7	8	9	10	11	12	13
14	15	16	17	18	19	20
21	22	23	24	25	26	27
28						

MARCH						
Sunday	Monday	Tuesday	Wednesday	Thursday	Friday	Saturday
	1	2	3	4	5	6
7	8	9	10	11	12	13
14	15	16	17	18	19	20
21	22	23	24	25	26	27
28	29	30	31			

APRIL						
Sunday	Monday	Tuesday	Wednesday	Thursday	Friday	Saturday
					1	2	3
4	5	6	7	8	9	10
11	12	13	14	15	16	17
18	19	20	21	22	23	24
25	26	27	28	29	30	

Highlighted dates are paydays. ■ semimonthly ■ bimonthly ■ quarterly ■ biweekly

A job seeker who knows the annual salary a job pays can find the monthly gross pay. The monthly gross pay is the annual salary divided by the number of pay periods per year.

> **EXAMPLE** Aretha's salary is $38,500.00 per year. She is paid bimonthly. How much does she earn each pay period? Round to the nearest cent.
>
> Divide yearly earnings by number of pay periods per year. Bimonthly payments are made $12 \div 2 = 6$ times each year.
>
> $\$38,500.00 \div 6 = \$6,416.66\overline{6} \approx \$6,416.67$
>
> Aretha earns $6,416.67 each pay period.

Look at the thousandths place.

$6 \geq 5$

Round the hundredths place up.

Exercise C   Find the number of times per year that each worker is paid. Then find the amount earned during each pay period. Round to the nearest cent.

Employee	Annual Salary	How Often Paid	Pay Periods per Year	Earnings per Pay Period
1. Kevin	$26,000.00	Weekly	_____	_____
2. Teresa	$42,000.00	Monthly	_____	_____
3. Tammy	$18,600.00	Semimonthly	_____	_____
4. Helene	$64,000.00	Biweekly	_____	_____
5. Ming	$58,550.00	Bimonthly	_____	_____

Technology Connection

Compare Wages On-line

Searching for a job on the Internet is fast and simple. Most job-related Web sites have information about thousands of jobs and list the wages offered. Now that you have learned about hourly wages and salary, you can compare wages for different types of jobs.

Search the Web sites below, or find a Web site yourself. Find three jobs paying hourly wages and three paying a salary. Then calculate the annual income for each. Answer the following questions for each job listing.

Job Title: _____

Hourly wage or salary? _____

How much? _____ per _____

Estimated annual income: _____

Which is greater, the annual incomes of the jobs offering an hourly wage, or the annual incomes of the jobs offering a salary?

Suggested Web sites:
    www.career.com
    www.bestjobsusa.com
    www.ajb.org
    www.americanjobs.com
    www.Jobs.Internet.com

Commission
Payment of a percentage of total sales

Rate of commission
The percent used to compute commission

Wages of salespeople are often based on how much they sell. Salespeople who earn a **commission** earn a percentage of their total sales. The percent used to compute a commission is the **rate of commission**. The purpose of a commission is to encourage salespeople to sell more goods or services.

Move the decimal point 2 places to the left and remove the percent symbol. Write a zero to make 2 places to the left of the decimal point.

EXAMPLE Terrell sells a $150,000 life insurance policy. His rate of commission is 1.5%. What is Terrell's commission?

Commission = Sales × Rate of commission
= $150,000 × 1.5%

Change the percent to a decimal.

1.5% = 01.5% = .015

Multiply.

$ 150,000   Amount of sale
×   .015   Rate of commission
$2,250.00   Commission

Terrell's commission for selling the policy is $2,250.

Exercise A Find the amount of commission earned by each salesperson.

Salesperson	Amount of Sales	Rate of Commission	Amount of Commission
1. Voeung	$8,500	3.5%	_____
2. Will	$34,000	2.5%	_____
3. Mari	$12,600	1.8%	_____
4. Julia	$64,200	12%	_____
5. Elliot	$6,785	30%	_____
6. Carlotta	$92,100	8.5%	_____
7. Edmond	$375,800	7%	_____
8. Nick	$5,950	6.5%	_____
9. Victoria	$24,500	25%	_____
10. Scott	$1,028	5%	_____

If you know the amount of commission and the rate of commission, you can find the total amount of sales.

To divide $3,000 by .08:
1. Count the two decimal places in .08.
2. Write $3,000 with two decimal places as $3,000.00.
3. Move the decimal point two places to the right for both .08 and $3,000.00.
4. Divide.

EXAMPLE Ashley sells automobiles. She earns an 8% commission on each car she sells. She wants to earn about $3,000 a month. What must her total monthly sales be in order to earn $3,000? Round to the nearest dollar.

Total sales = Income needed ÷ Commission rate

= $3,000 ÷ 8%

= $3,000 ÷ .08

$$\frac{37,500.}{.08 \overline{)\$3,000.00}}$$

Ashley needs to have total sales of $37,500 in order to earn $3,000.

Exercise B Find the total sales needed to reach each income goal. Round to the nearest dollar.

Salesperson	Income Goal	Rate of Commission	Total Sales Needed to Reach Goal
1. Saritha	$2,500	5%	_____
2. Carl	$6,000	7%	_____
3. Joseph	$16,000	10%	_____
4. Alan	$35,000	12%	_____
5. Cameron	$1,200	7.5%	_____
6. Hillary	$50,000	25%	_____
7. Steve	$4,500	12.5%	_____
8. Kevin	$25,000	18%	_____
9. Suni	$80,000	33%	_____
10. Zach	$3,800	15%	_____

Sometimes salespeople are paid a salary plus commission.

EXAMPLE Megan sells hot tubs for a weekly salary of $270. She also earns a
commission of 12% on her total sales. Last week she sold $8,000 in
hot tubs and supplies. What was her income for the week?

Step 1
```
$ 8,000  Total sales
×    .12  Rate of commission
$960.00  Commission
```

Step 2
```
$  270  Weekly salary
+  960  Commission
$1,230  Total income
```

Megan earned $1,230 last week.

SALES/CUSTOMER SERVICE
International packaging manufacturer is seeking to add a position to our Sales and Customer Service Dept. Candidate must have excellent sales service experience, a positive attitude, self-motivation, and a strong desire to excel. Packaging/printing background a plus! Salary, bonuses, and benefits. Call Linda at 555-7949.

SALES PROFESSIONAL
Company seeking full time and part time sales professionals. Candidates need to be self starters, outgoing, and a team player. Base + commission.

SALES POSITION
Local retailer seeks sales representative. Position pays a base salary plus commission. Qualified applicants must have sales experience, good communication skills and reliable transportation. Mileage + expenses reimbursed. Full benefits include health and dental. Call 555-4387 to apply. EOE

SALES REPRESENTATIVE
Fortune 500 company seeks sales representative to maintain local clients and to open new accounts. Base salary plus commission. Sales experience and good verbal and written skills required. Expense account + car + full

SALES EXECUTIVE
Exceptional opportunity!!! Well-established employee owned firm is expanding. Required: 5-15 yrs. outside sales experience in forms, printing, office furniture, and copiers ideal. Full 100% paid health, dental, lucrative pension program. Call Matt at 555-8537.

New Sales Position
Immediate opening for an entry-level sales position. We offer an established, local territory with minimal travel, excellent benefits, company car, commissions and growth opportunities. Please call Al at 555-9925 for more information and

Exercise C Find commission and total earnings.

	Total Sales	Rate of Commission	Salary Earned	Commission	Total Earnings
1.	$50,000	10%	$1,000	_____	_____
2.	$32,000	5%	$1,250	_____	_____
3.	$120,000	7.5%	$1,400	_____	_____
4.	$542,300	2.5%	$42,000	_____	_____
5.	$425,000	9.25%	$32,000	_____	_____

Higher commission rates do not always mean greater earnings. The commission earned from a low percentage of a high sales figure may be more than the commission earned from a higher percentage of a lower sales figure.

EXAMPLE John sells printing machines for a 15% commission. He sold 3 machines for a total of $250,000. Ruth sells real estate for an 8% commission. She sold 3 houses for a total of $500,000. Whose commission is greater?

Use the formula: Commission rate × Total sales = Commission

John's Commission		**Ruth's Commission**	
$250,000	Total sales	$500,000	Total sales
× .15	Commission rate	× .08	Commission rate
$ 37,500	Commission	$ 40,000	Commission

Each made 3 sales last month. John's rate of commission, 15%, is greater than Ruth's rate of commission, 8%. However, Ruth's commission, $40,000, is greater than John's commission, $37,500.

PROBLEM SOLVING

Exercise D   Solve.

1. Which is more, 11% of $1,000 or 15% of $800? How much more?

2. Which is more, 40% of $1,500 or 25% of $2,500? How much more?

3. Job A pays a 12% commission on average annual sales of $60,000. Job B pays a 10% commission on average annual sales of $80,000. Which job pays more?

4. Raul sells $4,500 in copier parts. His commission rate is 20%. Hue earns a 10% commission selling a $12,000 copier. Whose commission is greater? How much greater?

5. Howie earns an 8% commission on sales of $9,000. Jocelyn earns a 12% commission on sales of $5,000. Who earns more in commissions? How much more?

Bonus

Bonus

Money given an employee in addition to earned wages or salary

Some employees are paid a salary and are given a **bonus**. A bonus is extra money paid to an employee for helping the company do unusually well. For example, a salesperson may receive a bonus for total sales of more than $1,000,000. Bonuses are usually paid on a quarterly or annual basis.

EXAMPLE   Chang sells seeds to farmers. He earns a yearly salary of $55,000. If he sells more than $500,000 in seeds in a year, he is paid an annual bonus. The amount of his bonus is 25% of the total sales over $500,000. Chang sells $650,000 of seeds. What is his total income?

Step 1   Find the amount of sales on which the bonus is figured.

$650,000   Total sales
−500,000   Sales on which no bonus is paid
$150,000   Sales on which bonus is paid

Step 2   Write the percent as a decimal.

25% = 25.% = .25

Step 3   Multiply to find the bonus amount.

$ 150,000
×   .25
$37,500.00

Step 4   Add to find Chang's total income.

$55,000   Annual salary
+$37,500   Annual bonus
$92,500   Total income

Chang's total income is $92,500.

Exercise E   Find the total income for each employee.

Salary	Bonus	Total Sales	Total Income
1. $65,000	12% of sales over $120,000	$150,000	_____
2. $24,000	40% of sales over $100,000	$240,000	_____
3. $65,000	8% of total sales	$52,000	_____
4. $44,000	16% of sales over $100,000	$98,000	_____
5. $35,000	35% of sales over $85,000	$242,000	_____

Raise or Bonus?

Would you rather get a raise of $1,000 or a bonus of $1,000? It may sound like a simple question. But think some more.

At the Morton Widget Company, all of the full-time workers earn $26,000 a year. The accountant had an idea that would save the company some money.

"Let's not give the workers raises of $1,000. Instead, let's give each worker a cash bonus of $1,000," he suggested to the boss.

The workers heard about the plan. Some thought it was a great idea.

"I'd love to get a check for $1,000 right now," said Hal. "A raise of $1,000 would be spread out over a whole year. We would hardly notice it."

"I'm not so sure," Tina replied. "In the long run, you'll lose money."

For Discussion

1. If everyone gets the raise, what is the new annual salary?

2. What did Tina mean? Why did Tina think taking a bonus instead of a raise might cost her money in the long run? Explain.

3. If you were working at Morton, would you agree with Hal or Tina? Why?

4. What are some advantages of the bonus plan to the workers? What are some disadvantages?

5. What is the main advantage of the bonus plan to the company? How might the plan be risky? Explain.

Write the letter of the best answer to each question.

1. An employee who is paid semimonthly is paid _____ times
   a year.

   a. 6   **b.** 12   **c.** 24   **d.** 26

2. The annual income of a person who earns a biweekly salary
   of $1,860 is _____ .

   a. $18,600   **b.** $22,320   **c.** $44,640   **d.** $48,360

3. If you earn an annual salary of $51,038.00 and are paid
   weekly, you earn _____ each pay period.

   a. $453.00   **b.** $471.12   **c.** $981.50   **d.** $1,963.00

Complete the time card for Mae Li. Find the number of hours
worked each day and the total hours worked for the week.

	Day	In	Out	In	Out	Hours
4.	Mon.	9:00 A.M.	12:30 P.M.	1:00 P.M.	5:00 P.M.	
5.	Wed.	8:45 A.M.	12:15 P.M.	1:45 P.M.	6:00 P.M.	
6.	Fri.	7:30 A.M.	12:00 P.M.	12:30 P.M.	4:15 P.M.	
7.					**Total hours worked:**	

Solve problems 8–15.

8. Mae Li earns $11.50 per hour. What is her gross pay for the
   week? Use her time card above.

9. The following deductions are taken from Mae Li's gross pay.
   What is her net pay for the week?

Social Security	$18.06
Federal Income Tax	$24.15
Health Insurance	$9.50
Retirement Account	$25.00

10. Carlton earns $10 per hour. He is paid time and a half for overtime. If he works 45 hours in a week, what are his weekly wages?

11. What are the monthly wages of a manager who earns an annual salary of $27,600?

12. The piecework rate of a garment worker is $.80 for each decal sewn on a jacket. If he sews 120 decals on jackets, how much does he earn?

13. A salesperson earns $45,000 a year plus a 10% commission on sales. If she has sales of $350,000, what is her annual income?

14. Julio needs to earn $2,700 a month. He earns a 12% commission on his total sales. What must his monthly sales be to reach his income goal?

15. Janice earns $8.25 per hour plus tips delivering flowers. She worked 26 hours last week and received $82 in tips. What were her total earnings?

| Test-Taking Tip | When you multiply to find an answer, use division to check your work. For example, when you multiply 200 × .4 = 80, check that 80 ÷ .4 equals 200 or that 80 ÷ 200 = .4. |

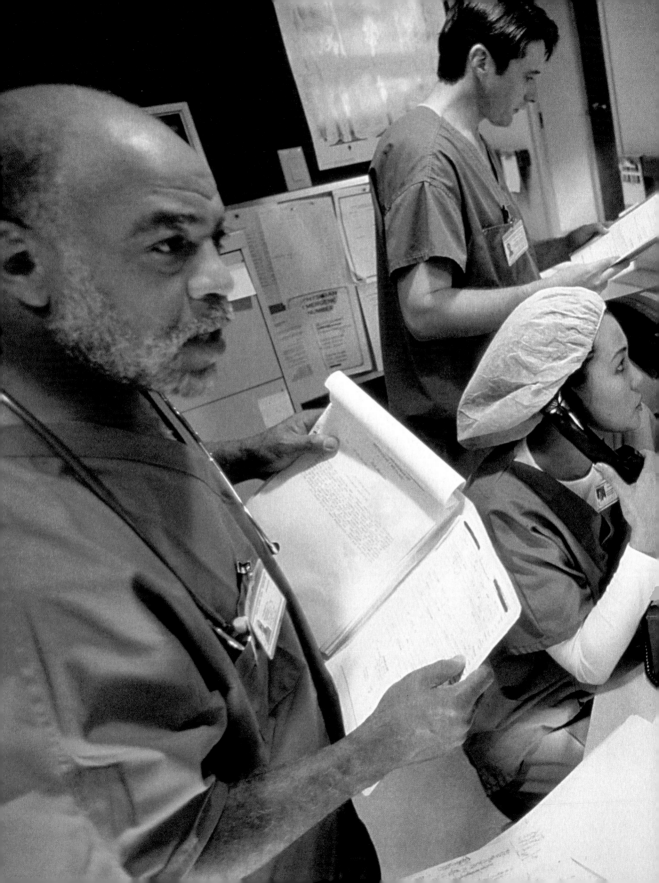

Chapter

2

Benefits

Have you ever heard the expression "Money isn't everything"? Well, this is especially true in the world of work. Many employers offer benefits to their employees in addition to an hourly wage or salary. These benefits can come in the form of health insurance, life insurance, profit-sharing plans, stock options, and more. Employers offer benefits as a way to attract and keep the best employees. As an employee, you will need to know what your benefits are and understand how they work.

In Chapter 2, you will learn about several common types of benefits that companies offer to employees. You will also learn the mathematical skills necessary to calculate the values of different kinds of benefits.

Goals for Learning

▶ To compute an employee's share of major medical claims

▶ To understand life insurance and calculate benefits

▶ To estimate Social Security benefits at retirement

▶ To define pension and estimate its value at retirement

▶ To calculate employee and company contributions to a 401(k) plan

▶ To distinguish between profit-sharing and stock-option plans, and calculate the value of each

Benefit

Portion of medical expenses covered by an insurance policy

Co-payment

Fixed amount or percentage the insured pays for certain medical services

Coverage

Specific services paid by the insurance company

Insured

Person whose costs are covered by an insurance policy

Premium

Amount paid for insurance coverage

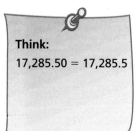

Think:
17,285.50 = 17,285.5

Employers often provide health insurance for their employees. Usually employees pay only a part of the **premium**, which is the price of the insurance, and the employer pays the rest. Health insurance plans vary, but all tell what services they pay for, which is also known as the **coverage**. The **insured** is the employee whose covered medical costs are paid by the insurance company.

In addition to the insurance premium, some plans require the insured to pay a percentage of the medical expenses. The part that the insured pays is called the **co-payment**. The amount of the medical expense paid by the insurance company is called the **benefit**.

EXAMPLE   Kendra's health insurance pays 80% of her medical bills, and she pays the remaining 20%. Kendra has an operation. Her hospital bills total $12,580.00. Doctors' bills are $4,575.00. Her medicines cost $130.50. What is Kendra's co-payment?

Step 1   Find Kendra's total medical expenses.

$12,580.00   Hospital bills
  4,575.00   Doctors' bills
+   130.50   Medicines
$17,285.50   Total medical expenses

Step 2   Multiply to find 20% of $17,285.50.

$17,285.50
×   .2   20% written as a decimal
$ 3,457.10   Amount Kendra pays

Kendra's co-payment is $3,457.10.

Step 3   Estimate to check the answer.

$12,580.00 → $13,000
  4,575.00 →   5,000
    130.50 → +   0
                 $18,000

$18,000 × .2 = $3,600
The estimate is close to $3,457.10.

Find the benefit the insurance company pays by subtracting the co-payment from the total medical expenses.

EXAMPLE What is the benefit paid by Kendra's insurance company?

$17,285.50   Total medical expenses
− 3,457.10   Kendra's co-payment
$13,828.40   Amount of benefit

The insurance company pays $13,828.40 of Kendra's medical expenses.

Exercise A   Each employee's co-payment is 20% of costs. Find the co-payment and benefit amounts.

Employee	Hospital Bills	Doctors' Bills	Medicines	Co-payment	Benefit
1. Alex	$8,600.00	$1,200.00	$85.00		
2. Elija	$0	$925.00	$30.00		
3. Roberto	$47,835.00	$0	$264.00		
4. Gina	$98,424.00	$4,560.00	$835.00		
5. Joe	$29,582.00	$128.25	$480.25		
6. Ellen	$21,909.00	$0	$1,503.00		
7. Greg	$15,014.68	$153.90	$81.42		
8. Tanner	$12,689.75	$892.50	$653.50		
9. Pearl	$1,592.85	$45.10	$18.35		
10. Celia	$105,023.60	$1,362.85	$0		

Humor on the Job

Gina went to bed uncertain whether tomorrow was a holiday. At 2 A.M., she decided to telephone her boss.

"Yes, Gina, you have to come to work later today," came the sleepy and unwelcome reply.

"OK. Thanks, boss. I'm very sorry I bothered you at 2 A.M."

"Oh, that's OK. I had to get up to answer the phone anyway."

Deductible

Money the insured pays before benefit coverage begins

Out-of-pocket expense

Total amount an insured pays for medical expenses

In some insurance plans, the insured pays all medical bills up to a fixed amount each year before the insurance company pays anything. This amount is called a **deductible**. Once the insured has spent the deductible amount for medical expenses, the only other medical cost for the rest of the year is the co-payment. The total amount the insured pays for medical expenses is the **out-of-pocket expense**.

 Susan's health insurance policy has a $500 deductible. Her co-payment is 20% of medical expenses after the deductible has been paid. If Susan has $3,800 in medical expenses, how much does she pay?

$3,800	Total medical expenses
− 500	Deductible
$3,300	Amount subject to 20% co-payment

$3,300	
× .2	Co-payment percent written as decimal
$660.0	Co-payment

Deductible + Co-payment = Out-of-pocket expense

↓   ↓   ↓

$500   + $660   = $1,160

Susan pays $1,160 for her medical expenses.

Think:

660.0 = 660

PROBLEM SOLVING

Exercise B   Solve.

1. Ashley has a $500 deductible and 20% co-payment on her health insurance. Last year she had $6,890 in medical bills. What was Ashley's out-of-pocket expense?

2. Candy has a $2,000 deductible and no co-payment on her health insurance. If she has a $4,820 hospital bill, what is the amount of her benefit?

3. Byron's co-payment is 20% for doctors' visits and 15% for medicines. His doctors' bills are $285, and medicines cost $38. How much does Byron pay?

4. If you have medical expenses of $8,359 in 1 year, which is cheaper, a $500 deductible and 20% co-payment, or a $1,000 deductible and 10% co-payment?

Beneficiary

Person(s) named to receive money when the insured dies

Life insurance

Insurance coverage that pays money to a beneficiary when the insured dies

Employers may provide a **life insurance** benefit for employees. Life insurance pays money to someone named in the insurance contract when the insured dies. The named person is the **beneficiary**. There can be several beneficiaries. The beneficiary is often someone who depends on the employee's earnings.

Employers usually pay for life insurance only as long as the employee works for the company. The amount of the benefit often equals a percentage of the employee's annual salary.

EXAMPLE The Heartland Company provides its employees with life insurance coverage. The table below shows the benefit as a percentage of the employee's annual salary, dependent on the employee's age at the time of death.

Employee's Age	Coverage Level
55 or under	100%
56–64	75%
65–69	55%
70–74	45%
75 or over	40%

JP Insurance   Form No. LF-001234

COMPANY NAME

COMPANY STREET ADDRESS   CITY   STA

EMPLOYEE NAME (LAST, FIRST, MI)

EMPLOYEE STREET ADDRESS

OCCUPATION/JOB TITLE

ENROLLMENT FOR INSURANCE

EMPLOYEE COVERAGE REQUESTED:
☐ Life / Accidental Death & Dismemberment   ☐ Life only
☐ Major Medical only
☐ Major Medical / RX Card

DEPENDENTS

DEPENDENTS

BENEFICIARY DESIGNATION

Ellen Wood

EMPLOYEE SIGNATURE

Jackson Wood

Jackson works for The Heartland Company. He earns $40,000 a year. If he dies at age 58, how much will his beneficiary receive from his life insurance?

Because Jackson is between 56 and 64 years old, his beneficiary will receive 75% of his annual salary.

$ 40,000   Annual salary
×   .75   Coverage percent as a decimal
$30,000.00   Life insurance benefit

Jackson's beneficiary will receive $30,000 upon his death.

Exercise A Find the life insurance benefit for each employee. Use the coverage levels for The Heartland Company on page 37.

Employee	Age at Death	Annual Salary	Benefit
1. T. Smith	51	$52,000	_____
2. M. Garcia	71	$72,000	_____
3. G. Sharp	55	$43,800	_____
4. B. Chang	56	$38,000	_____
5. F. Young	80	$120,000	_____

Life expectancy table

Statistics that predict how long a person is expected to live, based on date of birth and gender

Insurance companies gather statistics to help them predict how long people will live. Those statistics are then used to make a **life expectancy table** like the one below. These tables show how long a person is expected to live, based on the person's year of birth and gender. Insurance companies use this information to decide how much premium to charge people of different ages for life insurance coverage.

Year of Birth	Total	Male	Female
1900	47.3	46.3	48.3
1940	63.0	60.8	65.2
1970	70.9	67.1	74.7
1980	73.8	70.0	77.5
1981	74.1	70.4	77.8
1982	74.5	70.9	78.1
1983	74.6	71.0	78.1
1984	74.7	71.2	78.2
1985	74.7	71.2	78.2
1986	74.8	71.3	78.3
1987	75.0	71.5	78.4
1988	74.9	71.5	78.3
1989	75.1	71.7	78.5
1990	75.3	71.8	78.8
1992	75.5	72.1	78.9
1994	75.7	72.4	79.0
1996	76.1	73.1	79.1
1998	76.7	73.9	79.4

SOURCE: National Center for Health Statistics, U.S. Dept. of Health and Human Services

Look at the digit to the right of the rounding place. If it is 5 or greater, add 1 to the digit in the rounding place. If it is less than 5, do not change the digit in the rounding place.

EXAMPLE   Gary is 14 years, 9 months old. He was born in 1986. According to the life expectancy table on page 38, how many more years is Gary expected to live? Find the row for 1986. Look across for the number in the "Male" column. The column lists 71.3 years.

Step 1   Estimate first.

14 years, 9 months ≈ 15 years   71.3 ≈ 71

Subtract.

```
 71   Life expectancy
-15   Gary's age
 56   Expected years left to live
```

Gary is expected to live **about 56** years more.

Step 2   Change 71.3 years to years and months.
71.3 yr. = 71 yr. + .3 of a yr.
1 yr. = 12 mo. → .3 of a yr. × 12 mo. = 3.6 mo.

Since 3.6 ≈ 4, 71.3 years is about 71 years, 4 months.

```
       70        16
       7̶1̶ years, 4̶ months   Life expectancy
     -14 years, 9 months   Age now
       56 years, 7 months   Expected years left to live
```

Someone like Gary is expected to live 56 years, 7 months longer. The answer is about the same as the estimate, so it is reasonable.

PROBLEM SOLVING

Exercise B   Use the life expectancy table on page 38 to solve.

1. How much greater is the life expectancy of a male born in 1998 than that of a male born in 1900?

2. How much longer is a person born in 1990 expected to live than a person born 50 years earlier?

3. If you are a 16 year, 2 month old female born in 1987, how much longer are you expected to live?

4. How much greater is the difference between male and female life expectancy in 1998 than the difference in 1900?

Actuary

Person who calculates premiums and benefits using statistics and probabilities

Contribution

Social Security tax paid to a Social Security account

Retire

Voluntarily stop full-time work permanently

Social Security

Federal program that provides retirement benefits to all U.S. citizens over age 62 who have paid into the program

In addition to paying income tax, most workers pay **Social Security** tax on earnings. Social Security is a federal program that pays benefits to workers who have paid Social Security taxes. A worker pays half the Social Security tax owed. The employer pays the other half. These taxes are **contributions** to the worker's Social Security account.

Some or all of Social Security taxes are paid to workers when they **retire**, or voluntarily stop full-time work. The amount of monthly benefit is based on the worker's average monthly pay over a 35-year period, with a maximum monthly benefit. The monthly benefit is less if the worker retires early.

Actuaries are people who use formulas and statistics to calculate premiums and benefits. You can estimate the Social Security retirement benefit using this formula relating monthly benefit B to total contributions C:

$$B \approx .015C$$

EXAMPLE   Jana paid $50,000 in Social Security taxes over a 35-year period. Her monthly retirement benefit will be about $1\frac{1}{2}$% of the total contributions. Estimate her monthly Social Security retirement benefit.

Jana's contribution + Employer's contribution = Total

↓		↓	↓
$50,000	+	$50,000	= $100,000

	$ 100,000	Total contribution
×	.015	Benefit percent as a decimal
	$1,500.00	Estimated monthly benefit

If Jana retires at age 65, she will receive about $1,500 every month until she dies.

Think:

.015 = .01500

.015 × 100,000 =

.01500.

Exercise A Use the formula $B \approx .015C$ to estimate each monthly benefit. Round to the nearest dollar.

Employee Contribution	Employer Contribution	Total Contribution	Retirement Benefit (based on $1\frac{1}{2}\%$)
1. $60,000	_____	_____	_____
2. $25,000	_____	_____	_____
3. $42,500	_____	_____	_____
4. $64,280	_____	_____	_____
5. $31,492	_____	_____	_____

TRY THIS...

Go to the Web site *http://www.ssa.gov/ OACT/COLA/benefit Ex.html* to get an estimate of Social Security benefits for the employees in problems 1–5. Enter age *25*, the *Employee Contribution* from each problem, and check *today's dollars.* How do these estimates compare to the estimates you calculated?

Writing About Mathematics

If you live long enough, you will receive more in Social Security benefits than you paid in. Explain how to find the "break even" point.

Sometimes retirees receive more benefits than the total contributions paid by employers and employee.

EXAMPLE Derek retires at age 66. The total contribution to his Social Security was $64,500. His monthly retirement benefit is $968. If Derek lives to be 72, about how much more will he receive in Social Security benefits than was contributed?

Step 1 Find Derek's annual Social Security benefit.

$$\begin{array}{rl} \$ \quad 968 & \text{Monthly benefit} \\ \times \quad 12 & \text{12 months in a year} \\ \hline \$11,616 & \text{Annual Social Security benefit} \end{array}$$

Step 2 Find Derek's total Social Security benefits during his retirement.

Find the number of retirement years. $72 - 66 = 6$
Derek will receive retirement benefits for 6 years.

$$\begin{array}{rl} \$11,616 & \text{Annual Social Security benefit} \\ \times \quad 6 & \text{Years of retirement} \\ \hline \$69,696 & \text{Total Social Security benefits} \end{array}$$

Step 3 Find the difference.

$$\begin{array}{rl} \$ \ 69,696 & \text{Total Social Security benefits} \\ -64,500 & \text{Total Social Security contribution} \\ \hline \$ \ 5,196 & \text{Difference} \end{array}$$

Derek will receive $5,196 more from Social Security than he and his employers contributed.

Exercise B Complete. Use $1\frac{1}{2}\%$ of total Social Security contributions to calculate monthly benefit. Round money to the nearest dollar.

	Total Contribution	Monthly Benefit	Annual Benefit	Years of Retirement	Total Retirement Benefit	Benefits Greater or Less Than Contributions?
1.	$83,000	_____	_____	11	_____	_____
2.	$110,000	_____	_____	4	_____	_____
3.	$65,230	_____	_____	18	_____	_____
4.	$48,625	_____	_____	7	_____	_____
5.	$54,322	_____	_____	$5\frac{1}{2}$	_____	_____

Pension

Retirement income paid by a former employer

Pension plan

Money placed in a special account to be paid to employees when they retire

Social Security was never meant to be the only source of retirement income. Many employers have **pension plans** that invest money to give to employees when they retire. A **pension** is often a major source of retirement income. Employees usually pay no money into their pension plans. The longer they work for a company, the greater their pension benefits.

Pension plans vary. A company's Human Resource department provides employees with details about pension benefits.

A pension plan might calculate benefits using the following steps:
1. Find 60% of average monthly pay.
2. Find 50% of monthly Social Security benefit.
3. Subtract step 2 from step 1.
4. Divide years worked for the company (up to 35) by 35.
5. Multiply step 3 by step 4.

EXAMPLE   Midori works for the same company for 30 years and retires at age 65. Her average monthly pay was $2,500. Her Social Security benefit is $1,000 a month.

Use the steps above to calculate her monthly pension.

1. 60% × $2,500 average monthly pay	$1,500
2. 50% × $1,000 Social Security benefit	− 500
3. Difference	$1,000
4. 30 ÷ 35 ≈ .857	× .857
5. Multiply step 3 by step 4.	$ 857

Midori's monthly pension from her company is $857.

Exercise C Use steps 1–5 on page 42 to find each monthly pension benefit. Round decimals to the nearest thousandth. Round money to the nearest dollar.

Average Monthly Pay	Social Security Benefit	Years Worked	Years Worked Divided by 35	Monthly Pension Benefit
1. $3,000	$1,800	25	_____	_____
2. $2,800	$1,100	35	_____	_____
3. $4,200	$2,100	18	_____	_____
4. $3,675	$1,793	33	_____	_____
5. $3,675	$1,793	6	_____	_____

401(k) plan

Program in which employees can postpone receiving some of their salary until retirement

Balance

The value of a financial account

Defer

Postpone receiving part of one's salary until retirement by putting it into a 401(k) account

Ratio

Number relationship between two or more things

One way to save for retirement is to make yearly contributions to a **401(k) plan**. Employees whose companies offer 401(k) plans can put some of their salary into the 401(k) each year. This **defers** or postpones receiving those earnings until retirement. This also defers income tax on those earnings, so less tax is withheld from wages.

Money in a 401(k) account grows in value tax-free until it is paid out. The value of an account is also known as the **balance**. If 401(k) money is invested wisely, the balance at retirement may be much greater than the money originally invested.

Many employers match their employees' contributions to 401(k) accounts. Some contribute a percentage of the deferred earnings. Some make contributions based on the number relationship given by a **ratio**, such as 2:1 or 1:1. A 2:1 ratio means if you put $2 into your 401(k), your employer puts $1 into your 401(k).

Rosa puts $100 of her weekly pay into her 401(k). Her employer makes a 2:1 matching contribution. How much money is deposited into her 401(k) annually?

Rosa's Contribution	Employer's Contribution
$100 Weekly contribution × 52 Pay periods $5,200 Annual contribution	Write the ratio 2:1 as $\frac{2}{1}$. Write and solve a proportion. $$\frac{2}{1} = \frac{5,200}{x}$$ Find the cross products. $2x = 5,200$ Divide 5,200 by 2. $\quad 2,600$ $\qquad\qquad\qquad 2\overline{)5,200}$

Add the contributions.

$5,200   Rosa's contribution
+ 2,600   Employer's matching contribution
$7,800   Total 401(k) contribution

The total amount deposited in Rosa's 401(k) account annually is $7,800.

Exercise D   Complete to find each total annual 401(k) contribution.

	Earnings Deferred per Paycheck	Pay Schedule	Annual Employee Contribution	Employer Matching Plan	Employer Contribution	Total Annual Contribution
1.	$150	Biweekly	_____	4:1	_____	_____
2.	$275	Semimonthly	_____	2:1	_____	_____
3.	$306	Monthly	_____	1:1	_____	_____
4.	$872	Bimonthly	_____	2:1	_____	_____
5.	$185.50	Weekly	_____	4:1	_____	_____

Profit
Amount of money earned after paying all expenses

Profit sharing
Benefit that gives a portion of a company's profits to its employees

Some employers share the company's **profit** with employees. The profit is the company's earnings after expenses have been subtracted. This employment benefit is called **profit sharing**. A profit-sharing plan might give a percentage of the company's profit, if there is one, to employees.

EXAMPLE   The Baxter Company has a profit-sharing plan for its employees. It distributes 20% of its annual profits equally among 100 employees. If the company makes a profit of $1,000,000, how much does each employee receive in profit-sharing benefits?

Step 1   Find the amount of profit shared with employees.

$1,000,000   Annual profit
×   .2   Percent of profit shared as a decimal
$ 200,000   Profit shared with employees

Step 2   Divide to find each employee's share of company profits.

$200,000 ÷ 100 = $2,000

Each employee receives $2,000 of the company's profit.

Exercise A   Find the employee profit-sharing benefit for each company. Round to the nearest dollar.

Company	Annual Profit	Percent of Profit Shared	Number of Employees	Benefit per Employee
1. CRS Co.	$148,000	20%	10	_____
2. Pinebrook	$1,750,000	10%	320	_____
3. HealthTek	$920,000	8%	34	_____
4. Biotrend Inc.	$850,000	15%	200	_____
5. Johns & Co.	$4,850,000	15%	144	_____

TRY THIS...

For problems 1–5, divide the annual profit by the number of employees to find the company's profit per employee. Then multiply that by the percent of profit shared to find each employee's share. How do these answers compare to your answers?

Exercise options

Take advantage of stock options by actually buying the stock

Share

Equal parts into which a corporation's capital stock is divided

Stock

Part of a corporation that can be divided into shares and sold

Stock options

Shares of stock offered at a guaranteed price for a limited time

Value

The amount of money a share of stock is worth if it is sold

Some corporations issue certificates of ownership, or **stock**, to raise money. This allows buyers to own a part of the corporation called **shares**. Each share of stock has the same **value** because it can be sold for the same amount of money.

Corporations may offer employees **stock options** as a benefit. This benefit gives employees the right to buy shares of the corporation's stock within a given time, such as two years, at a given price.

An employee can **exercise options** by buying shares and immediately selling the stock if its value is greater than the price charged by the corporation. When the sale price is greater than the purchase price, the employee makes a profit.

EXAMPLE   Pam receives 1,000 stock options at a price of $28.25 per share guaranteed for three years. Two years later the stock's value is $38.50 per share. If she exercises her options and sells immediately, how much profit does Pam make on each share of stock? Estimate first.

Estimate	Actual	
$ 40	$ 38.50	Selling price
−30	−28.25	Purchase price
$ 10	$ 10.25	Profit per share

Pam's profit is $10.25 on each share. This is close to the estimate of $10 profit per share.

Exercise B   Estimate, then find the actual profit per share.

	Purchase Price	Selling Price	Estimated Profit	Amount of Profit
1.	$.80	$2.10	_____	_____
2.	$2.99	$12.01	_____	_____
3.	$10.10	$11.00	_____	_____
4.	$26.90	$38.45	_____	_____
5.	$41.30	$43.10	_____	_____

An employee may choose to exercise some or all of the stock options.

> **EXAMPLE** Blaise receives 500 stock options at a price of $12.45 per share. Two months later, the stock is selling for $18.60 per share. If Blaise exercises 250 of his stock options, how much profit does he make?
>
> **Step 1** Find profit on one share of stock.
>
> $ 18.60 Selling price
> −12.45 Purchase price
> $ 6.15 Profit per share
>
> **Step 2** Multiply to find total profit.
>
> $ 6.15 Profit per share
> ×   250 Shares exercised
> $1,537.50 Total profit
>
> Blaise makes a profit of $1,537.50.

Another way to solve the problem is to find the selling price and purchase price for 250 shares first.

Exercise C Find each profit.

	Purchase Price	Selling Price	Number of Options Exercised	Profit
1.	$9.00	$11.00	200	_____
2.	$22.00	$30.00	150	_____
3.	$1.50	$8.25	600	_____
4.	$6.00	$6.80	320	_____
5.	$3.92	$4.18	1,000	_____
6.	$11.08	$14.28	250	_____
7.	$9.88	$9.90	600	_____
8.	$36.45	$83.50	400	_____
9.	$1.05	$9.23	800	_____
10.	$18.14	$21.05	1,800	_____

Technology Connection

You can use a calculator to find the profit from exercising stock options. Use these steps:

Step 1 Key in the selling price.

Step 2 Press ⊟.

Step 3 Key in the purchase price.

Step 4 Press ⊨.

Step 5 Press ⊠.

Step 6 Key in the number of shares.

Step 7 Press ⊨.

EXAMPLES Purchase price: $1.35 per share
Number of shares: 600
Selling price: $8.96 per share
Press: *8.96* ⊟ *1.35* ⊨ ⊠ *600* ⊨
The display reads *4566.*
The profit is $4,566.

Purchase price: $15.96 per share
Number of shares: 1,000
Selling price: $16.45 per share
Press: *16.45* ⊟ *15.96* ⊨ ⊠ *1000* ⊨
The display reads *490.*
The profit is $490.

The Benefit of Benefits

Harry runs the Always Green Landscaping Company. He started out mowing just a few lawns. He was good with customers, so his business grew rapidly. First he hired one assistant, then another. Before long he had a crew of nine and a successful business. He paid his people well. They were good workers, and business was booming.

Then, in August came the shocker. First, Maria quit. A week later, Greg quit. This couldn't go on. He called a meeting of his staff.

"What's going on? I pay better than anyone," Harry asked.

"The truth is, boss, salary isn't the problem. You pay us well. But we don't get any benefits here," complained Alex, a good friend of both Maria and Greg.

He continued, "Maria and Greg took jobs at Mega Lawn-Chem Services. They make less per hour there, but they are getting all kinds of benefits. They get health insurance and life insurance. They even have a 401(k) plan."

Harry thought long and hard. It sounded as if Alex might be the next to leave. He had to do something quickly.

He thought of how he disliked doing paperwork. That's why he had resisted offering benefits. Handling insurance and 401(k) plans would mean even more time in the office. Then, the idea hit him.

"I'll hire an office manager to do all the paperwork and administer all the benefits. I'll be able to keep my people happy, and it will give me more time to work with them."

For Discussion

1. Explain why someone might leave one job for a similar job with lower pay.
2. When Harry decided to hire an office manager, he solved two problems at once. What were they?
3. What might be risky about Harry's decision?

Write the letter of the answer that best completes each sentence.

1. _____ is 15% of $84,652?

   a. $5,643.47   b. $12,697.80   c. $12,700   d. $15,872

2. The decimal .28654 rounded to the nearest thousandth is _____ .

   a. .286   b. .2865   c. .287   d. .29

3. $642.48 rounded to the nearest dollar is _____ .

   a. $640.00   b. $642.00   c. $642.50   d. $650.00

4. Anne buys 100 shares of stock for $2.38. She sells them for $5.16. Her profit per share is _____ .

   a. $2.78   b. $3.22   c. $5.16   d. $7.54

5. Vanessa has a 20% co-payment on her medical expenses. Her benefit for medical expenses of $4,780 is _____ .

   a. $956   b. $3,824   c. $4,800   d. $9,560

Solve problems 6–15.

6. Odessa defers $320.00 from each paycheck to a 401(k) plan. If she is paid monthly, what is her annual 401(k) contribution?

7. One year Leroy pays $7,230 in Social Security taxes. What is the total contribution to Leroy's Social Security account?

8. A life insurance benefit pays 80% of the insured's annual salary. How much will the beneficiary receive if the insured's annual salary is $67,500 at the time of death?

9. Tom has the following medical bills. If he has a 15% insurance co-payment, how much does he pay?
   Hospital: $52,578
   Doctor: $1,380
   Lab work: $3,243

10. Peggy's health insurance has a $250 deductible and 10% co-payment. She has medical bills totaling $1,248. What is Peggy's total out-of-pocket medical expense?

11. Kim contributes $125 monthly to her 401(k) account. Her company makes a 2:1 matching contribution. How much does Kim's company contribute annually to her 401(k) account?

12. Dixie's company gives her 120 stock options at a purchase price of $14.60 per share. She exercises all of them for $22.30 per share. What is Dixie's profit?

13. The total contribution to Todd's Social Security is $92,464. His monthly benefit is about 1.5% of the total contribution. About how much is Todd's *annual* Social Security benefit? Round to the nearest dollar.

14. Logan retires at age 65. He and his employer each paid $42,000 for his Social Security taxes. His monthly Social Security benefit is about $1\frac{1}{2}$% of the total contribution. If he lives to be 74 years old, how much more will Leroy receive in Social Security benefits than was paid in?

15. Tim is retiring after 28 years at XYZ, Inc. His average monthly pay was $4,000. His monthly Social Security benefit is $1,600. Use these steps to estimate Tim's monthly pension benefit.

    1. Find 80% of average monthly pay.
    2. Find 40% of Social Security benefit.
    3. Subtract step 2 from step 1.
    4. Divide years worked (up to 35) by 35.
    5. Multiply step 3 by step 4.

Test-Taking Tip   When solving problems having more than one step, check your work after each step. A small mistake in one step may cause a wrong final answer.

Kinds of Businesses

There are many different kinds of businesses. Some manufacture consumer goods. Some make products that are used to make other products. Some businesses sell the products either to other businesses or to the general public. Some businesses provide services. Whatever the kind of business, each needs to make a profit; that is, to earn more money than it takes to run the business. In order to do this, all businesses need to be skillfully managed.

In this chapter, you will learn about different kinds of businesses and what it takes to make each one successful. You will also practice the math skills used by businesses to operate smoothly and efficiently.

Goals for Learning

▶ To calculate a production schedule and determine the quantity of goods to produce

▶ To calculate sales needed to meet revenue goals

▶ To understand the relationship between price reductions and profits

▶ To determine the staffing needs of retail businesses

▶ To determine the amount of equipment and number of employees needed to meet customer expectations

▶ To calculate operating expenses and analyze fund-raising campaigns for nonprofit organizations

Production schedule

Plan showing how many goods to manufacture each day or week

Manufacturing businesses produce goods that are sold to other businesses. They produce their goods according to a **production schedule**. A production schedule is used to plan how many goods to manufacture each day or week. By following the schedule, the manufacturer can produce enough goods on time to meet customer demand.

EXAMPLE   The Outdoor Experience Company has to fill an order for 318 play sets in 3 months. The company can produce 12 play sets a day. It takes 1 week to ship the play sets to the customers. If the order needs to be received by the customer on February 13, when should production of the play sets begin?

Step 1   Find the number of play sets produced in a week.

12 sets per day × 5 work days per week = 60 sets per week

Step 2   Find the number of weeks needed to produce 318 sets.

318 sets ordered ÷ 60 sets per week = 5.3 weeks

.3 of a week × 5 work days = 1.5 days

Round 1.5 days to 2 days.

It will take about 5 weeks plus 2 work days to produce 318 play sets.

Step 3   Add shipping time.

5 weeks, 2 days + 1 week = 6 weeks, 2 days

Production should begin 6 weeks, 2 work days before February 13.

Use the calendar on the next page. Count back 6 weeks from February 13. This date is January 2. Because January 15 is a holiday, add another day to the 2 days. Count back 3 work days from January 2. Remember not to count January 1. This brings you to December 27.

Production needs to begin on December 27.

Outdoor Experience Company Production Schedule Calendar

SEPTEMBER

S	M	T	W	T	F	S
					1	2
3	4	5	6	7	8	9
10	11	12	13	14	15	16
17	18	19	20	21	22	23
24	25	26	27	28	29	30

OCTOBER

S	M	T	W	T	F	S
1	2	3	4	5	6	7
8	9	10	11	12	13	14
15	16	17	18	19	20	21
22	23	24	25	26	27	28
29	30	31				

NOVEMBER

S	M	T	W	T	F	S
			1	2	3	4
5	6	7	8	9	10	11
12	13	14	15	16	17	18
19	20	21	22	23	24	25
26	27	28	29	30		

DECEMBER

S	M	T	W	T	F	S
					1	2
3	4	5	6	7	8	9
10	11	12	13	14	15	16
17	18	19	20	21	22	23
24/31	25	26	27	28	29	30

JANUARY

S	M	T	W	T	F	S
	1	2	3	4	5	6
7	8	9	10	11	12	13
14	15	16	17	18	19	20
21	22	23	24	25	26	27
28	29	30	31			

FEBRUARY

S	M	T	W	T	F	S
				1	2	3
4	5	6	7	8	9	10
11	12	13	14	15	16	17
18	19	20	21	22	23	24
25	26	27	28			

MARCH

S	M	T	W	T	F	S
				1	2	3
4	5	6	7	8	9	10
11	12	13	14	15	16	17
18	19	20	21	22	23	24
25	26	27	28	29	30	31

APRIL

S	M	T	W	T	F	S
1	2	3	4	5	6	7
8	9	10	11	12	13	14
15	16	17	18	19	20	21
22	23	24	25	26	27	28
29	30					

MAY

S	M	T	W	T	F	S
	1	2	3	4	5	
6	7	8	9	10	11	12
13	14	15	16	17	18	19
20	21	22	23	24	25	26
27	28	29	30	31		

JUNE

S	M	T	W	T	F	S
					1	2
3	4	5	6	7	8	9
10	11	12	13	14	15	16
17	18	19	20	21	22	23
24	25	26	27	28	29	30

JULY

S	M	T	W	T	F	S
1	2	3	4	5	6	7
8	9	10	11	12	13	14
15	16	17	18	19	20	21
22	23	24	25	26	27	28
29	30	31				

AUGUST

S	M	T	W	T	F	S
			1	2	3	4
5	6	7	8	9	10	11
12	13	14	15	16	17	18
19	20	21	22	23	24	25
26	27	28	29	30	31	

Dates in red are holidays.

Exercise A   Find production time. Then use the calendar above to find each date production should begin. Allow 2 weeks' shipping time on all orders.

	Number Ordered	Number Produced per Day	Number Produced per Week	Production Time (weeks and days)	Delivery Date	Production Start Date
1.	1,250 swing sets	25	_____	_____	Apr. 30	_____
2.	320 bird baths	20	_____	_____	Nov. 15	_____
3.	825 lawn chairs	18	_____	_____	May 4	_____
4.	2,300 bird feeders	45	_____	_____	Dec. 1	_____
5.	830 patio tables	25	_____	_____	Feb. 6	_____

To follow a production schedule, manufacturers want to have all the materials needed to produce the goods **in stock**, or on hand. Ordering the correct amount of materials for production requires careful planning.

EXAMPLES The following materials are needed to make one pair of in-line skates:

> 2 boots
> 2 boot liners
> 10 wheels
> 8 buckles
> 1 brake

How many of each item is needed to manufacture 10 pairs of skates?

Multiply the amount needed for one pair by 10.

Boots: 2 per pair × 10 pairs = 20 boots
Boot liners: 2 per pair × 10 pairs = 20 boot liners
Wheels: 10 per pair × 10 pairs = 100 wheels
Buckles: 8 per pair × 10 pairs = 80 buckles
Brakes: 1 per pair × 10 pairs = 10 brakes

A manufacturer of in-line skates receives an order for 144 pairs of skates. There are 360 buckles in stock. How many more buckles are needed to complete production of 144 pairs of skates?

Step 1 Multiply to find the number of buckles needed to produce 144 pairs of skates.

> 144   Pairs of skates
> ×   8   Buckles per pair
> ———
> 1,152   Number of buckles for 144 pairs

Step 2 Subtract to find the number of buckles still needed.

> 1,152   Number of buckles for 144 pairs
> − 360   Buckles in stock
> ———
> 792   Buckles still needed

To complete production of 144 pairs of skates, 792 more buckles are needed.

Exercise B   Find the materials needed to manufacture each given number of pairs of skates.

Number of Pairs	Boots Needed	Boot Liners Needed	Wheels Needed	Buckles Needed	Brakes Needed
1	2	2	10	8	1
1. 25	_____	_____	_____	_____	_____
2. 520	_____	_____	_____	_____	_____
3. 1,650	_____	_____	_____	_____	_____
4. 3,740	_____	_____	_____	_____	_____
5. 10,432	_____	_____	_____	_____	_____

PROBLEM SOLVING

Exercise C   Solve. Use 2 boots, 2 boot liners, 10 wheels, 8 buckles, and 1 brake for each pair of skates.

1. There are 610 brakes in stock. How many more brakes are needed to complete production of 800 pairs of skates?

2. The manufacturer has 8,650 wheels in stock. How many pairs of skates can be made with 8,650 wheels?

3. A manufacturer has 250 wheels in stock. How many more wheels are needed to complete production of 60 pairs of skates?

4. There are 1,325 buckles in stock. How many more buckles are needed to make 166 pairs of skates?

5. A manufacturer receives an order for 375 pairs of skates. There are 400 boots, 800 boot liners, 4,000 wheels, 3,025 buckles, and 400 brakes in stock. How many more of which items are needed to fill the order?

Did You Know?

Manufacturing jobs accounted for 13% of all jobs in 1998. Economists expect 89,000 fewer manufacturing jobs in 2008 than there were in 1998. Manufacturing jobs are expected to account for just 12% of all jobs in 2008.

SOURCE: U.S. Bureau of Labor Statistics Data

Revenue

Total income earned by a company

Sales companies sell the goods that manufacturing companies produce to individuals or to other businesses. The price of goods and number of sales determine a company's **revenue**. Revenue is the total amount of money a company earns. To make sure that the company is successful and that it earns enough revenue, a sales company sets goals. If the goals are not reached, the company may not be able to pay all its expenses.

EXAMPLES   A copy machine company sets a goal of $500,000 in annual revenue. If each copier sells for $800, how many must be sold to reach the revenue goal?

Divide the revenue goal by the selling price of each copier.

$$
\begin{array}{r}
625 \\
\$800\overline{)\$500,000} \\
-480\ 0 \\
\hline
20\ 00 \\
-16\ 00 \\
\hline
4\ 000 \\
-4\ 000 \\
\hline
\end{array}
$$

The company must sell 625 copiers to meet its revenue goal.

To meet its annual sales goal of 625 copiers, the company sets a monthly sales goal. On average, how many copiers must be sold each month to reach the annual sales goal of 625 copiers?

Divide the annual sales goal by 12.

$$
\begin{array}{r}
52.08 \quad \text{Round to 53.} \\
12\overline{)625.00} \\
-60 \\
\hline
25 \\
-24 \\
\hline
1\ 00 \\
-96 \\
\hline
\end{array}
$$

Sales goals should all be rounded up. If the goal is rounded down, it will not be met. If the goal is rounded up, it will be exceeded. It is better to go over a sales goal than not to reach it. Why do you think that is?

The company must sell an average of 53 copiers each month to meet its sales goal.

Exercise A   Find the number of sales needed to meet each revenue goal.

	Annual Revenue Goal	Income from Each Sale	Annual Sales Goal	Monthly Sales Goal
1.	$75,000	$625	_____	_____
2.	$850,000	$400	_____	_____
3.	$425,000	$180	_____	_____
4.	$575,000	$3,800	_____	_____
5.	$1,000,000	$1,200	_____	_____

PROBLEM SOLVING

Exercise B   Solve.

1. A book publisher sets an annual revenue goal of $25,000,000. If the average book sale is $20, how many books must the publisher sell to reach the goal?

2. A tea exporting company has an annual revenue goal of $320,000. If it sells tea for $30 a box, how many boxes of tea must it sell to reach its revenue goal?

3. Ergo Chair Company has an annual revenue goal of $1,200,000. Its average chair sells for $625. If the company sells 1,824 chairs, by how much does the company miss reaching its goal?

4. A pool and spa company sells pools for an average of $3,420 and spas for an average of $1,860. Last year the company sold 430 pools and 1,342 spas. Did it reach its annual revenue goal of $4,000,000? By how much did it miss or exceed its goal?

5. In 2001 a real estate company had revenue of $3,250,000. In 2002 it increased its annual revenue goal by $650,000. Its average sale is $120,000. How many houses need to be sold to meet the new revenue goal?

TRY THIS...

Look at problem 5 in Exercise B. Do the problem again. This time, round the decimal down, not up. How does rounding the decimal down affect the annual revenue?

Discount

Reduce the selling
price of an item by a
fixed amount or
a percentage

Sometimes companies **discount** the price of an item to increase the number of sales. A discount reduces the price of an item and also reduces the amount of profit made on each item.

EXAMPLE The Johnson Coat Company sells full-length wool coats for $650.25. If it discounts the price of the coat 20%, what is the discounted price?

TRY THIS...

What is another
way to find the
discounted price?

Step 1   Find the amount of the discount.

$650.25   Regular price
×   .2   Percent of discount
$130.05   Amount of discount

Step 2   Subtract to find the discounted price.

$650.25   Regular price
−130.05   Amount of discount
$520.20   Discounted price

The discounted price of the coat is $520.20.

Writing About Mathematics

When the price of
an item is reduced
by 20%, does this
reduce the profit on
each item by 20%
also? Explain your
thinking. Provide
examples to support
your answer.

How does a discount affect the profit on the sale of each coat? The profit on each coat is reduced by the amount of the discount. By reducing the price of the coat 20%, the profit on each coat is reduced by $130.05.

Exercise C   Find each discounted price and the profit lost.

Regular Price	Discount Percent	Discount Price	Profit Lost
1. $60.00	20%	_____	_____
2. $120.00	30%	_____	_____
3. $15.50	10%	_____	_____
4. $2.80	25%	_____	_____
5. $745.00	15%	_____	_____

A company that has to sell many discounted items earns much less profit than expected. It may even have a loss.

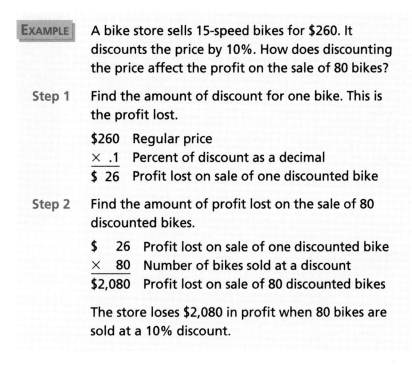

EXAMPLE   A bike store sells 15-speed bikes for $260. It discounts the price by 10%. How does discounting the price affect the profit on the sale of 80 bikes?

Step 1   Find the amount of discount for one bike. This is the profit lost.

$260   Regular price
× .1   Percent of discount as a decimal
$ 26   Profit lost on sale of one discounted bike

Step 2   Find the amount of profit lost on the sale of 80 discounted bikes.

$ 26   Profit lost on sale of one discounted bike
×   80   Number of bikes sold at a discount
$2,080   Profit lost on sale of 80 discounted bikes

The store loses $2,080 in profit when 80 bikes are sold at a 10% discount.

Exercise D   Find the total profit lost.

Regular Price	Discount Percent	Number of Discounted Items	Profit Lost
1. $50.00	10%	120	_____
2. $350.00	20%	70	_____
3. $130.00	15%	45	_____
4. $95.75	30%	210	_____
5. $8.95	60%	334	_____

Humor on the Job

"Hey, Jim!" called the boss, as Jim was wasting time by the water cooler.

"There's a very important job that needs to be done. I'd like you to give it a try."

"What job is that, boss?" Jim inquired.

"Your job!"

Peak hour
Time when stores have the most customers

Retail store
Business that sells items to the general public

Retail stores buy a variety of products that they sell to the general public. Retail businesses are very competitive, so it is important that stores provide good service to their customers. Retail stores make sure they hire enough employees to help customers during **peak hours** when the stores are busiest. This requires careful planning.

EXAMPLE

Foods Galore does not want its customers to wait in long lines. It plans to have 1 checkout clerk for every 15 shoppers. The manager has made a table to plan the employees' work schedules. The table shows the average number of customers in the store at different times. How many checkout clerks are scheduled to work Saturdays between 3 P.M. and 7 P.M.?

Shift	Hours	AVERAGE NUMBER OF CUSTOMERS		
		Mon.–Fri.	Sat.	Sun.
Shift 1	7 A.M.–11 A.M.	65	160	80
Shift 2	11 A.M.–3 P.M.	114	220	180
Shift 3	3 P.M.–7 P.M.	140	175	115
Shift 4	7 P.M.–10 P.M.	44	110	40

Step 1   Find the number of shoppers on Saturdays between 3 P.M. and 7 P.M. This is Shift 3. Find where the *Shift 3* row and the *Sat.* column meet. An average of 175 customers are in the store on Saturdays between 3 P.M. and 7 P.M.

Step 2   Divide to find the number of checkout clerks needed.

$$11.6 \quad \text{Round up to 12.}$$
$$15\overline{)175.0}$$

The manager schedules 12 checkout clerks to work between 3 P.M. and 7 P.M. on Saturdays.

Exercise A Use the table on page 62 to find the number of checkout clerks needed.

Shift	M	Tu	W	Th	F	Sa	Su
Shift 1	5	**1.** ___	5	5	**2.** ___	**3.** ___	6
Shift 2	8	8	**4.** ___	8	**5.** ___	15	**6.** ___
Shift 3	**7.** ___	10	10	10	10	**8.** ___	8
Shift 4	3	3	3	**9.** ___	3	**10.** ___	3

Inventory
Products available for sale

In addition to providing good customer service, retail stores must also offer a good selection of products for sale. The products a store has available for sale are its **inventory**. Deciding how much inventory to have is an important part of a retail business. Stores do not want a lot of items that do not sell fast.

One way to reduce inventory and increase sales is to offer discounts. If inventory that might not sell at the regular price can be sold at a discount, the store can still make a profit.

EXAMPLE   A sporting goods store wants to sell its bike inventory before winter. It usually sells about 40 bikes a month at the regular price. The store has an inventory of 110 bikes to sell in 2 months. It puts the bikes on sale at a 25% discount. In the past, reducing prices by 25% increased sales by about 40%. If this occurs, will the store sell all its bikes in 2 months?

Step 1   Find the number of additional sales expected at the discounted price.

    40   Average bike sales in 1 month
    ×.4   Percent of increased sales as a decimal
    16   Additional sales because of discount

Step 2   Add to find the total number of expected sales.

    40   Average monthly sales
    +16   Additional sales because of discount
    56   Expected number of bike sales in 1 month

Step 3   Multiply to find the total number of bikes sold in 2 months.

    56   Expected monthly bike sales
    × 2   Months
    112   Expected bike sales in 2 months

If the store sells the bikes at a 25% discount, it will sell its inventory in 2 months.

A store may make a greater profit selling more items at a discount than selling fewer items at the regular price.

EXAMPLE   Ted's Bike Store buys bikes for $39 and sells them for $220. Ted's can sell about 80 bikes a month at this price. If the price is discounted 25%, Ted's expects to sell all 120 bikes in inventory. How does the profit from selling 80 bikes at the regular price compare to the profit from selling 120 bikes at a 25% discount?

Step 1   Find the profit from selling 80 bikes for $220 each.

Price   −   Cost   =   Profit
↓   ↓   ↓
$220   − $39   = $181   Profit on 1 bike

Multiply profit on 1 bike by 80 bikes.

```
$   181   Profit on 1 bike
×    80   Number of bikes
$14,480   Profit on 80 bikes at regular price
```

Step 2   Find the price of 1 bike at a 25% discount.

```
$220   Regular price              $220   Regular price
×.25   Discount decimal          − 55   Discount
$ 55   Amount of discount         $165   Discounted price
```

Step 3   Find the profit from selling 120 bikes at a 25% discount.

Discounted price   −   Cost   =   Profit
↓   ↓   ↓
$165   − $39   = $126   Profit on 1 bike

Multiply profit on 1 bike by 120 bikes.

```
$   126   Profit on 1 discounted bike
×   120   Number of bikes
$15,120   Profit on 120 discounted bikes
```

Step 4   Subtract to compare profits. $15,120 − $14,480 = $640

The profit from selling all 120 bikes at a 25% discount is $640 more than the profit from selling 80 bikes at the regular price.

Exercise B   A jewelry store buys heart-shaped pendants for $420 each and sells them for $998 each. Solve.

1. The jewelry store sells about 20 pendants a week. When prices are discounted 50%, sales usually increase about 75%. At the discounted price, how many pendants does it expect to sell in a week?

2. What is the discounted price of each pendant?

3. What is the weekly profit from selling 20 pendants at the regular price? What is the weekly profit from selling the discounted pendants?

4. What is the difference in profit between selling the pendants at the regular price for 2 weeks and selling them at a discount for 2 weeks?

5. The store wants to sell its entire inventory of 100 heart-shaped pendants. If it discounts the pendants, can it sell all of them in 3 weeks? What profit will the store make on the sale of the discounted pendants?

Did You Know?

In 2000 the average retail hourly wage was about $9.40, and the average manufacturing hourly wage was about $14.30. This wage is more than 50% higher than the average retail wage.

SOURCE: U.S. Bureau of Labor Statistics Data

Service business

Company whose focus is service instead of a product

A **service business** sells a service, such as fixing computers, instead of a product. It makes a profit by charging enough for the service to more than cover expenses. Unlike a retail business, there is little, if any, inventory to manage. This kind of business manages equipment, supplies, and employees instead.

EXAMPLE   Jiffy Maid uses about 6 ounces of Super Suds to clean each house. How many houses can be cleaned with a 48-ounce can of Super Suds?

Divide ounces in 1 can by ounces used to clean 1 house.

$$\begin{array}{r} 8 \\ 6\overline{)48} \end{array}$$ Number of houses cleaned

Ounces for 1 house   Total ounces in 1 can

A 48-ounce can of Super Suds can clean 8 houses.

Jiffy Maid cleans about 350 houses per week. About how many 48-ounce cans of Super Suds are needed for 1 week's work?

Divide the number of houses cleaned per week by the number of houses cleaned with 1 can.

Step 1   Estimate using compatible numbers.

$350 \approx 320$ $320 \div 8 = 40$

OR

$8 \approx 9$ and $350 \approx 360$ $360 \div 9 = 40$

About 40 cans are needed for 1 week's work.

8 is a factor of 320, so 8 and 320 are compatible numbers. 9 is a factor of 360, so 9 and 360 are compatible numbers.

Step 2   Divide. Round to the nearest whole number.

$$\begin{array}{r} 43.7 \\ 8\overline{)350.0} \\ -32 \\ \hline 30 \\ -24 \\ \hline 6\,0 \end{array}$$

Houses cleaned with 1 can

Cans per week
Houses per week

$43.7 \approx 44$

Jiffy Maid needs about 44 cans of Super Suds per week. The answer is close to the estimate.

Exercise A Find the supplies used each week. Round to the nearest whole number.

Item	Average Amount Used	Houses Cleaned per Week	Amount Used per Week
1. 64-oz. bottle of glass cleaner	8 oz. per house	56	_____
2. Box of 100 cleaning wipes	8 wipes per house	225	_____
3. Toilet bowl freshener blocks	3 blocks per house	130	_____
4. 24-oz. bottle of furniture polish	2 oz. per house	173	_____
5. Vacuum bags	1 for every 5 houses	88	_____

Service businesses also need to know how many employees to send on a job.

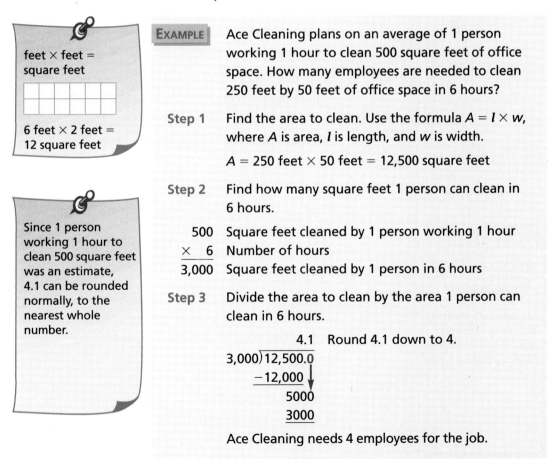

feet × feet = square feet

6 feet × 2 feet = 12 square feet

Since 1 person working 1 hour to clean 500 square feet was an estimate, 4.1 can be rounded normally, to the nearest whole number.

EXAMPLE Ace Cleaning plans on an average of 1 person working 1 hour to clean 500 square feet of office space. How many employees are needed to clean 250 feet by 50 feet of office space in 6 hours?

Step 1 Find the area to clean. Use the formula $A = l \times w$, where A is area, l is length, and w is width.

$A = 250$ feet $\times 50$ feet $= 12,500$ square feet

Step 2 Find how many square feet 1 person can clean in 6 hours.

500	Square feet cleaned by 1 person working 1 hour
× 6	Number of hours
3,000	Square feet cleaned by 1 person in 6 hours

Step 3 Divide the area to clean by the area 1 person can clean in 6 hours.

$$\begin{array}{r} 4.1 \\ 3,000\overline{)12,500.0} \\ -12,000 \\ \hline 5000 \\ 3000 \\ \hline \end{array}$$ Round 4.1 down to 4.

Ace Cleaning needs 4 employees for the job.

Exercise B   Find the number of employees needed to clean each area.

	Size (feet by feet)	Area Cleaned by 1 Person in 1 Hour	Time Available (hours)	Number of Employees
1.	140 by 160	400	8	_____
2.	50 by 160	250	8	_____
3.	70 by 330	550	6	_____
4.	20 by 731	210	7	_____
5.	60 by 910	600	6.5	_____

Companies often buy supplies in large quantities. They need to know how often the supplies are used up so they can plan when to replace them.

EXAMPLE	Ace Cleaning uses an average of 6 trash can liners for every 1,200 square feet of area cleaned. One week Ace Cleaning cleans a total area of 84,000 square feet. If liners are purchased in boxes of 80, how many boxes are used each week? Use a calculator.

Step 1   Find how many 1,200-square-foot areas are in 84,000 square feet.

Press: 84000   ÷   1200
The display reads: 70.

Step 2   Multiply the 70 areas by the number of liners used for each 1,200 square feet.

Press: 70   ×   6
The display reads: 420.

Ace Cleaning needs 420 liners to clean 84,000 square feet.

Step 3   Divide the number of liners needed for 84,000 square feet by the number of liners in each box to find the number of boxes needed.

Press: 420   ÷   80
The display reads: 5.25
Round 5.25 up to 6.

Ace Cleaning uses about 6 boxes of trash can liners per week.

Writing About Mathematics

Usually 5.25 rounds down to 5. Explain why in this example 5.25 rounds up to 6.

Exercise C   Find how many boxes of liners each company uses per week.

Company	Liners Used	Total Square Feet Cleaned Each Week	Liners in 1 Box	Boxes Used Each Week
1. Super Clean	10 per 800 square feet	36,000	50	____
2. Clean and Shine	4 per 750 square feet	82,500	40	____
3. AAA Cleaners	2 per 100 square feet	112,400	144	____
4. Professional O. C.	12 per 1,000 square feet	144,000	60	____
5. Office Maids	25 per 1,200 square feet	68,870	36	____

Technology Connection

Businesses of all kinds use computer technology to promote their products or services. It is a rare company that doesn't have a Web site for potential customers to visit.

Imagine that you own a service business. You want to develop a Web site to help find customers and build your business. Where do you start? How do you develop a Web site? If you need answers to these questions, there are several places to get help.

Searching the Internet is a good place to start. Web-page design companies specialize in developing Web sites for businesses. Many software programs also provide everything needed for "do it yourself." There are also classes offered, both on-line and in your community, that focus on Web-page design.

Investigate three different resources for developing a Web site for your service business. Briefly describe each resource, and discuss the advantages and disadvantages of each. Is one more expensive than the others? Does one take more time than the others? Will the resource produce quality results? Then choose a resource to design your Web site. Give reasons for your decision.

Some links to begin your search on the Internet are listed below. Look for Web-page design classes and software on the Internet as well.

http://www.homestead.com

http://www.web-space-station.com/indes.html

http://www.cool-page.com/index_nn4.html

http://www.squirrelnet.com

http://www.designing-solutions.com

http://www.ed2go.com (nationwide on-line education courses)

Lesson 5 — Nonprofit Businesses

Budget
Plan for managing income and expenses, usually for a set period of time

Donation
Contribution made without expectation of goods or services in return

Nonprofit business
Company that puts all its profit back into the company to further its cause

Not all companies are in business to make a profit. The purpose of a **nonprofit business** is to help a particular cause. All the money it is given in **donations** or that it earns is used to support its cause. Nonprofit businesses have many of the same expenses as other businesses. **Budgets** are plans that help them decide how much money they can spend for a cause and still meet all expenses.

EXAMPLE   Second Chance is a nonprofit business that gives care and shelter to homeless animals. The circle graph below shows its annual budget. The whole circle represents 100% of the budget. Each section shows a percentage of the budget. The key tells the expense each colored section represents. In 2002 Second Chance receives $800,000 from donations and fund-raising campaigns. How much money is budgeted in 2002 for care and shelter?

Second Chance Annual Budget

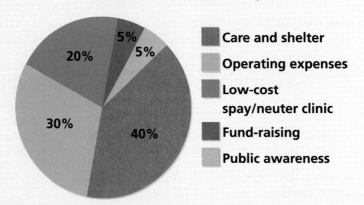

- Care and shelter
- Operating expenses
- Low-cost spay/neuter clinic
- Fund-raising
- Public awareness

The circle graph shows that 40% of the annual budget is for the care and shelter of animals.

$800,000   Income in 2002
×   .4   Percent for animal care as a decimal
$320,000   Budgeted amount for care and shelter in 2002

Second Chance budgets $320,000 in 2002 for the care and shelter of homeless animals.

Exercise A Use the Second Chance Annual Budget. Find each budgeted amount.

Income	Expense	Budgeted Amount
1. $1,000,000	Fund-raising	_____
2. $3,500,000	Care and shelter	_____
3. $875,000	Spay/neuter clinic	_____
4. $232,000	Operating expenses	_____
5. $180,000	Public awareness	_____

PROBLEM SOLVING

Exercise B Use the Second Chance Annual Budget to solve.

1. This year Second Chance has an income of $520,000. It spends $114,000 on the spay/neuter clinic. Is this amount over its budget for the clinic? If so, by how much?

2. Second Chance has income of $825,000 in 2001 and $1,000,000 in 2002. How much more money is available for public awareness in 2002 than in 2001?

3. One year Second Chance has an income of $950,000. How much money is available for the spay/neuter clinic and care and shelter combined?

4. Second Chance has income of $1,200,000 in 2001. The same year, it spends $72,000 for fund-raising and $46,000 for public awareness. Does the shelter go over its budget for fund-raising and public awareness combined? If so, by how much?

5. One year Second Chance spends $30,000 for operating expenses. This is exactly the budgeted amount for operating expenses. What is Second Chance's income that year?

TRY THIS...

Second Chance spends $200,000 for operating expenses. The income that year is $800,000. What percent of the budget is spent for operating expenses?

Nonprofit businesses need to raise money. Most of the money needed to run a nonprofit business comes from fund-raising campaigns.

Second Chance holds a concert to raise money. Volunteers sell 782 tickets that cost $40 each. How much money does the fund-raiser earn for the shelter before fund-raising expenses are paid?

Multiply the number of tickets sold by the price of 1 ticket.

```
    782   Number of tickets sold
×   $40   Price of 1 ticket
$31,280   Total amount from ticket sales
```

The fund-raiser earns $31,280 before expenses are paid.

Exercise C   Second Chance holds five fund-raisers. Find the amount of money raised by each fund-raising campaign.

Event	Cost	Number of Sales	Money Raised
1. Walk-a-thon	$40 per person	6,347	_____
2. Celebrity dinner	$200 a plate	864	_____
3. Cruise raffle	$60 a ticket	4,623	_____
4. Phone campaign	$30 membership fee	3,097	_____
5. Magazine sales	$25 per subscription	8,325	_____

PROBLEM SOLVING

Exercise D   Use the money raised in Exercise C to solve.

1. Which fund-raising event raised the most money?

2. How much more money did the walk-a-thon raise than the phone campaign?

3. If the fund-raising goal for all five events is $1,000,000, did the shelter reach its goal? How much over or under its goal was raised?

4. Suppose the fund-raising goal for all five events is $1,050,000. How many new members more than 3,097 are still needed to meet the fund-raising goal?

Help Wanted Ads

Fran found several "Help Wanted" ads over the Internet. She downloaded all the entry-level jobs. What a wide range in starting salaries! Some jobs required a college degree, some didn't. Some paid hourly wages, some paid salaries. She studied each ad.

PAINTER

Painter's assistant. Work outdoors. High school diploma necessary. $8.50 per hour to start.

ACCOUNTANT

Major firm. No experience necessary. College degree, accounting major. Starting salary: $40,000.

SALES

Retail position at major clothing outlet. Excellent benefits. Will train the right person. Good people skills. High school diploma necessary. Some college a plus. $11.00 per hour to start.

COMPUTER PROGRAMMER

College degree required. Math, science, or computer science major. The right person starts at $53,000.

APPRENTICE

Manufacturing firm has opening for beginner willing to learn computer-assisted design. High school diploma necessary, some college preferred. Algebra and geometry skills essential. $17.50 per hour to start. Possible advancement to $26.00 per hour in just two years.

Well-t
owne
Requ
sales
print
and
100%
lucrat
Call N

Nev
Imm(
entry
We (
local
trave
comp
and (
Pleas
for p

Fran looked over the ads. Then she decided that she had better start studying her math!

For Discussion

1. Arrange the jobs in order of starting annual salary, lowest to highest. For the jobs paying hourly, assume a 40-hour week.

2. Why do some jobs pay more than others? Discuss.

3. Which jobs require the most on-the-job training? the least? Explain.

4. Which jobs require the most math skills? the least? Discuss.

Write the letter of the answer that best completes each sentence.

1. If a manufacturing company produces 265 jewelry boxes a day, how many can it produce in 12 working days?
   a. 22   b. 23   c. 3,070   d. 3,180

2. If a car manufacturer produces 25 new cars per week, how long will it take to produce 180 new cars?
   a. $7\frac{1}{2}$ days   c. 7 weeks, 2 days
   b. 7 weeks, 1 day   d. 8 weeks

3. What is the least number of sales needed to reach a revenue goal of $11,000 if the average sale is $330?
   a. 30   b. 33   c. 34   d. 40

Solve problems 4–7.

4. A company uses an average of 125 rolls of masking tape per month painting houses. If it buys boxes of tape with 8 rolls to a box, how many boxes does it need to order each month?

5. A retail store reduces the price of dishwashers by 10%. If the regular price of the dishwashers is $580, what is the discount price?

6. By reducing the price of scooters, a sporting goods store hopes to increase sales by 40%. It sells an average of 70 scooters a month at the regular price. How many scooters does it hope to sell in a month at the discounted price?

7. A ski boot manufacturer uses 12 buckles for each pair of boots it makes. If it has 225 buckles in stock, how many complete pairs of boots can it make?

Complete the table. Find the number of monthly sales needed to meet the annual revenue goal.

	Annual Revenue Goal	Amount of Each Sale	Monthly Sales Goal
8.	$225,000	$1,250	
9.	$50,400	$140	
10.	$1,100,000	$1,820	

Solve problems 11–12.

11. It takes 1 hour for 1 worker to clean an area that is 20 feet by 30 feet. How many workers are needed to clean 18,400 square feet in 8 hours?

12. In March a nursery sold 130 apple trees that cost $20 each for the regular price of $32. In April it reduced the price to $24 and tripled its sales. What was each month's profit from the sale of apple trees? In which month was the profit greater?

Use the circle graph for problems 13–15.

Save the Whales Annual Budget

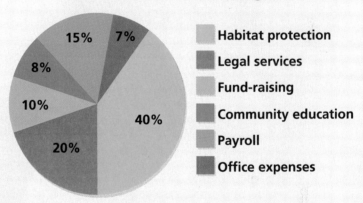

- Habitat protection
- Legal services
- Fund-raising
- Community education
- Payroll
- Office expenses

13. If $1,500,000 is raised in one year, how much money is budgeted for habitat protection?

14. In 2002 Save the Whales has $850,000 in income and spends $180,000 for legal services. How much more is spent for legal services than the budgeted amount?

15. How much more money is budgeted for fund-raising than for community education for each $500,000 received in donations?

Test-Taking Tip | Read a problem thoroughly before you begin to solve it. After you complete your work, read the problem again to be sure your answer makes sense.

Employment Application

LAST NAME	FIRST NAME				MIDDLE
STREET ADDRESS				HOME PHONE NO.	
CITY		STATE	ZIP CODE	FULL TIME ☐	PART T ☐
JOB APPLYING FOR					
EDUCATION	NAME AND ADDRESS			GRADUATE?	TYPE OF
High School					

Chapter

4

Human Resource Departments

The success of a company depends on its placing employees in jobs best suited for them. Employees who can use their skills and interests in their jobs are happy and productive. Most large companies have a Human Resource Department that is responsible for hiring employees. Human resource specialists may also handle employee benefits, establish fair pay rates, organize training programs, and resolve disagreements.

In this chapter, you will learn about several employment issues that involve human resource specialists. You will also use many of the same math skills that human resource specialists use to make decisions about employee-related issues.

Goals for Learning

▶ To determine staffing needs in different situations

▶ To compare unemployment figures for different parts of the country

▶ To calculate staff turnover in a large corporation

▶ To calculate raises based on employee performance

▶ To understand the relationships between poverty level and number of dependents, and inflation and cost of living increases

▶ To compare the costs of training and education with income potential

▶ To graph median incomes for various occupations

Staff

All the people employed by a company

One responsibility of the Human Resource Department is to oversee the hiring of **staff**. Staff are all the workers in a company. An overstaffed company has a greater payroll than is necessary. An understaffed company cannot meet its production goals.

EXAMPLE   ABC Manufacturing has a contract with a chain of retail stores to produce clothing. It agrees to provide the chain with 518,700 pairs of jeans over the next year. The plant is open 5 days a week. One worker can produce 15 pairs of jeans per day. What production staff is needed to meet the production goal?

Step 1   Find how many pairs of jeans need to be produced each day to meet the annual goal.

5 work days a week × 52 weeks a year = 260 work days a year

Divide 518,700 pairs by 260 days to find the pairs to produce each day.

```
            1,995   Pairs of jeans per day
   260)518,700
       −260
        258 7
       −234 0
         24 70
        −23 40
          1 300
         −1 300
```

Step 2   Find the number of workers needed. Since each worker produces 15 pairs daily, divide the daily production goal by 15.

1,995 ÷ 15 = 133

A production staff of 133 is needed to reach the annual production goal.

Step 3   Estimate. Round 518,700 to 500,000. Round 15 to 20. Round 52 to 50.

5 days a week × 50 weeks a year = 250 days a year
500,000 pairs ÷ 250 days = 2,000 pairs per day
2,000 pairs per day ÷ 20 = 100 workers

About 100 workers are needed, so the actual answer of 133 is reasonable.

Exercise A Find the production staff needed to meet each annual goal in 260 work days. Round decimals up to meet goals.

Clothing	Number Produced by 1 Worker in 1 Day	Annual Production Goal	Production Staff Needed
1. Blouse	30	312,000	_____
2. Tank top	50	949,000	_____
3. Dress	35	254,800	_____
4. Jacket	5	59,750	_____
5. Shirt	42	625,000	_____

Many companies have a **sales force**. A sales force is made up of employees who sell a company's products or services and find new customers. The size of the sales force usually depends on the number of potential customers in a given geographic area, or **territory**.

EXAMPLE   A company wants to expand its business into Minnesota. It would like a ratio of 1 salesperson to every 10,000 people in the territory. How many salespeople are needed for Minnesota?

Step 1   Use the table below to find the population of the territory.

The population of Minnesota is 4,775,508.

Step 2   Divide the population by 10,000 to find the number of salespeople needed.

$4,775,508 \div 10,000 = 477.5508$

Round up to have enough salespeople.

The company needs 478 salespeople for Minnesota.

To divide a whole number by 10; 100; 1,000; and so on, start at the far right of the number. Put a decimal point as many places to the left as there are zeros in the divisor.
Example:
$4,775,508 \div 10,000 = 477.5508$

SELECTED STATE POPULATION ESTIMATES			
State	**Population**	**State**	**Population**
Alaska	619,500	Minnesota	4,775,508
Arizona	4,778,332	Nebraska	1,666,028
California	33,145,121	New Jersey	8,143,412
Colorado	4,056,133	New Mexico	1,739,844
Connecticut	3,282,031	New York	18,196,601
Delaware	753,538	North Dakota	633,666
Florida	15,111,244	Oklahoma	3,358,044
Idaho	1,251,700	Oregon	3,316,154
Iowa	2,869,413	Pennsylvania	11,994,016
Kentucky	3,960,825	Texas	20,044,141
Louisiana	4,372,035	Wisconsin	5,250,446
Michigan	9,863,775	Wyoming	479,602

SOURCE: Population Estimates Program, Population Division, U.S. Census Bureau, Washington, D.C.

Exercise B Use the table on page 80 to find the sales force needed for each territory.

State	Salesperson-to-Population Ratio	Salespeople Needed for Territory
1. New Jersey	1 to 25,000	_____
2. Alaska	1 to 8,000	_____
3. California	1 to 30,000	_____
4. North Dakota	1 to 35,000	_____
5. Colorado	1 to 4,500	_____

PROBLEM SOLVING

Exercise C Use the table on page 80 to solve.

1. A company wants 1 salesperson for every 22,000 people in a territory. It has a sales force of only 32 people. For which states can the company supply a large enough sales force?

2. A company has a salesperson-to-population ratio of 1 to 21,000. Which states need a sales force of at least 800 people?

3. A company wants 1 salesperson for every 45,000 people in the territory of Iowa, Minnesota, and Wisconsin. How large a sales force is needed?

4. A company's salesperson-to-population ratio is 1 to 12,000. How much greater does a sales force in Pennsylvania need to be than a sales force in Connecticut?

5. Which territory needs a larger sales force, Wyoming with a salesperson-to-population ratio of 1 to 10,000, or New Mexico with a salesperson-to-population ratio of 1 to 30,000?

Did You Know?

The farming business in America has changed quite a bit over the last century. Before World War II, there were more than 6,000,000 farms. The average farm was less than 200 acres in size. Now, there are only about 2,000,000 farms, but the average farm now is about 500 acres in size.

Labor force

All people who are capable of working

Unemployed

Not working at a paying job

Unemployment rate

Percent that compares the number of workers who do not have a job to the labor force

The **labor force** is all people who are capable of working. Some workers do not have a paying job, or are **unemployed**. The **unemployment rate** is a percent that compares the number of people who are unemployed to the labor force. The unemployment rate varies from state to state and from year to year. The unemployment rate in the United States in 1999 was 4.2%, the lowest in 30 years. Between 1997 and 1999, the unemployment rate for the whole United States fell .7%. During that time, the unemployment rate increased in some states and decreased in others.

EXAMPLES

In 1997 the unemployment rate in Louisiana was 6.1%. By 1999 it had fallen to 5.1%. How much did the unemployment rate fall?

Subtract to find the difference.

6.1% − 5.1% = 1.0%

The unemployment rate fell 1%, or changed −1%.

A decrease, or negative change, in unemployment can be written as a negative percent. An increase in unemployment is written as a positive percent.

In 1999 the unemployment rate in Massachusetts was 3.2% when the Massachusetts labor force was 3,278,000 people. How many people were unemployed? Round to the nearest thousand.

Multiply to find 3.2% of 3,278,000.

```
  3,278,000   Labor force
×      .032   Unemployment rate as a decimal
  6556 000
 98340 000
104,896.000
```

104,896 rounded to the nearest thousand is 105,000.

About 105,000 people were unemployed in Massachusetts in 1999.

Exercise A Find the change in the unemployment rate between 1997 and 1999 for each state. Write + for an increase and − for a decrease.

State	Labor Force, 1999	Unemployment Rate, 1997	Unemployment Rate, 1999	Change in Rate
1. Alaska	315,000	7.9%	5.8%	_____
2. California	16,586,000	6.3%	5.9%	_____
3. Colorado	2,264,000	3.3%	3.8%	_____
4. Illinois	6,385,000	4.7%	4.5%	_____
5. Kansas	1,434,000	3.8%	3.8%	_____
6. Kentucky	1,970,000	5.4%	4.6%	_____
7. Maine	672,000	5.4%	4.4%	_____
8. Pennsylvania	5,969,000	5.2%	4.6%	_____
9. Texas	10,206,000	5.4%	4.8%	_____
10. Utah	1,084,000	3.1%	3.8%	_____

SOURCE: Bureau of Labor Statistics Data

PROBLEM SOLVING

Exercise B Use the table above to solve.

1. Which state had the greatest increase in its unemployment rate between 1997 and 1999?

2. Which state had the greatest decrease in its unemployment rate between 1997 and 1999?

3. Which state had no change in its unemployment rate between 1997 and 1999?

4. How many people were unemployed in California in 1999?

5. How many more people were unemployed in Illinois than in Pennsylvania in 1999?

Turnover

Number of employees who leave a company and are replaced

Hiring and training new employees costs money. A company's Human Resource Department plans for this expense. It estimates the number of employees who need to be replaced annually. It does this by calculating the average number of employees who left the company during a given time period. The rate at which employees leave a company and are replaced is called the **turnover** rate. Turnover rates are given as percents.

EXAMPLE

A restaurant chain employs about 36,500 people. In 5 years, 8,346; 8,052; 9,210; 7,998; and 6,544 employees left the company and were replaced. What was the average turnover rate?

Step 1   Find the average turnover per year. Add the 5 numbers. Then divide the sum by 5.

$$
\begin{array}{r}
8,346 \\
8,052 \\
9,210 \\
7,998 \\
+\ 6,544 \\
\hline
40,150
\end{array}
\qquad
\begin{array}{r}
8,030 \\
5\overline{)40,150} \\
-40 \quad\ \\
\hline
15 \\
-15 \\
\hline
00
\end{array}
$$

Step 2   Write the turnover rate as a fraction.

$\dfrac{8,030}{36,500}$ Average turnover
Number of employees

Step 3   Divide to represent the fraction as a decimal.

$$
\begin{array}{r}
.22 \\
36,500\overline{)8,030.00} \\
-7300\ 0 \\
\hline
730\ 00 \\
-730\ 00 \\
\hline
\end{array}
$$

Step 4   Write the decimal as a percent.

Move the decimal point to the right two places and write the percent symbol.

$.22 \quad = \quad 22.\%$

The average annual turnover rate is 22%.

About 13 million Americans were unemployed in 1933. This was about 25% of the nation's workers. This time was called "The Great Depression."

Exercise C Find each average annual turnover rate as a percent. Round percents to the nearest whole number.

	Total Employees	Turnover for 5 Years	Turnover Rate
1.	8,400	410, 416, 420, 450, 404	_____
2.	600	31, 39, 36, 34, 40	_____
3.	6,250	100, 113, 126, 154, 132	_____
4.	5,300	648, 710, 639, 601, 582	_____
5.	925	63, 68, 65, 61, 68	_____
6.	132	15, 21, 20, 19, 25	_____
7.	492	36, 40, 34, 35, 45	_____
8.	22,640	7,050; 6,792; 6,851; 6,472; 7,085	_____
9.	12,345	599, 642, 633, 634, 642	_____
10.	68	14, 13, 11, 11, 11	_____

Raise

Amount of pay
increase or percent
pay increase

Semiannually

Every 6 months

Many companies increase the pay of employees who do quality work. This increase in wages or salary is a **raise**. Raises motivate employees to work hard, and decrease the rate of employee turnover. A raise may be an amount or a percent of the employee's salary. Employers may review an employee's job performance at regular intervals, such as quarterly, **semiannually** (every 6 months), or annually. In general, the amount of the raise is based on the quality of the employee's job performance.

EXAMPLE   Petra's company uses the following job performance ratings to determine employees' raises.

Adequate   →   5% raise
Good   →   8% raise
Outstanding   →   10% raise

Petra's supervisor rates her job performance as good. Her hourly wage now is $8.00. What is the amount of her raise?

$8.00   Current wage
× .08   Percent raise as a decimal
$ .64   Raise

Petra's raise is $.64 per hour.

Exercise A   Find each raise. Use 5% for adequate, 8% for good, and 10% for outstanding.

Employee	Wage	Performance	Raise
1. Malik	$12.00 per hour	outstanding	_____
2. John	$10.00 per hour	good	_____
3. Meg	$2,000 per month	outstanding	_____
4. Liam	$40,000 per year	adequate	_____
5. Joan	$6.50 per hour	outstanding	_____
6. Terrance	$18.00 per hour	adequate	_____
7. Josephine	$18.00 per hour	outstanding	_____
8. Nat	$28,500 per year	good	_____
9. Ellen	$14,640 per year	adequate	_____
10. Phelps	$12.80 per hour	adequate	_____

Employees want to know the amount of their new wages, not just the amount of the raise.

EXAMPLE Kevin's salary is $2,200 per month. His performance is rated outstanding, so he is given a 10% raise. What will his new monthly salary be?

Method 1

Step 1   Multiply $2,200 by 10% to find Kevin's raise.

$2,200 × .1 = $220

Step 2   Add the raise to Kevin's salary now.

$2,200 + $220 = $2,420   New monthly salary

Method 2

Step 1   Add 100% for Kevin's salary and 10% for Kevin's raise.   100% + 10% = 110%

Step 2   Multiply $2,200 by 110%.

```
$  2,200   Kevin's salary now
×     1.1   Percent as a decimal
    220 0
   2200 0
$2,420.0   New monthly salary
```

Kevin's new monthly salary is $2,420.

Remember:
To change a percent to a decimal, move the decimal point to the left two places and remove the percent symbol.

Technology Connection

Spreadsheet and Graphing Technology

Human resource specialists use different types of technology to help them make decisions. They collect data from year to year, month to month, or day to day. They use the data to predict production needs, employee turnover rates, volume of sales, and more. Spreadsheet software helps them view this data in both tables and graphs. The tables and graphs are then used to make predictions, identify trends, and make informed decisions.

What type of information might human resource specialists study using graphing and spreadsheet technology? What might they want to predict? What trends might they look for? What decisions might this technology help them make? Use *The Occupational Outlook Handbook*, which is available in most libraries, to answer these questions, or find it at the Web site *http://stats.bls.gov/oco/ocos021.htm*. This resource gives a good overview of the issues handled by human resource personnel.

Exercise B Find each new wage with a 5% raise for adequate, 8% raise for good, and 10% raise for outstanding. Round annual wages to the nearest dollar.

Employee	Current Wage	Performance	New Wage
1. Emily	$32,000 per year	adequate	_____
2. Bruce	$24.50 per hour	good	_____
3. Candice	$800 per week	outstanding	_____
4. Ricardo	$64,800 per year	outstanding	_____
5. Cameron	$6,500 per month	good	_____
6. Dixie	$6.95 per hour	adequate	_____
7. Yoki	$4,870 per month	outstanding	_____
8. Carole	$45,700 per year	adequate	_____
9. Tami	$15.78 per hour	good	_____
10. Carmine	$9.75 per hour	outstanding	_____

PROBLEM SOLVING

Exercise C Use the table in Exercise B to solve. Round to the nearest cent.

1. How much more would Dixie's new hourly wage be if she had received a rating of outstanding?

2. How much more would Emily's annual salary be if she had received a rating of good?

3. If Cameron had received a rating of outstanding instead of good, what would her new monthly salary have been?

4. Which hourly employee received the greatest amount of wage increase?

5. How much more would Cameron's annual salary be for an outstanding rating than for a good rating?

Dependent

Person supported by a worker

Poverty level

Family income that is not enough to provide basic needs

The United States government issues annual guidelines for **poverty level** income. Income that is poverty level or below cannot pay for basic family needs. Basic needs may be food, clothing, shelter, or access to health care. Larger families with more **dependents** who are supported by the income need more money than smaller families with fewer dependents.

Gross pay is used to determine if the income is above or below poverty level. There are many federal and state food, shelter, and health programs for families below poverty level.

EXAMPLE   Emily has 3 dependent children. She works full-time for $8.15 per hour. Is her income above or below the poverty level?

Step 1   Find Emily's gross annual income.

40 hours a week $\times$ 52 weeks a year = 2,080 hours a year

2,080   Number of hours worked annually
$\times$ $8.15   Emily's hourly wage
$16,952   Emily's gross annual income

Step 2   Use the *2000 Federal Poverty Guidelines* on the next page to find the poverty level for a family of four.

The poverty level for a family of four is $17,050.

Step 3   Compare Emily's gross annual income to the poverty level for a family of four.

$16,952 < $17,050

Emily's gross annual income is below the poverty level.

2000 FEDERAL POVERTY GUIDELINES	
Number in Family	**Gross Annual Income**
1	$8,350
2	$11,250
3	$14,150
4	$17,050
5	$19,950
6	$22,850
7	$25,750
8	$28,650
Over 8, add for each child	$2,900

SOURCE: Oregon Center for Public Policy, 2000

Exercise A   Use the table above. Write *above* or *below* to compare each income to the poverty level.

Gross Pay	Number in Family	Above or Below Poverty Level?
1. $10.00 per hour	5	_____
2. $1,200 per month	4	_____
3. $12.00 per hour	6	_____
4. $14.00 per hour	7	_____
5. $1,500 per month	2	_____

Cost of living increase

Wage increase to help workers keep the same standard of living during inflation

Inflation

Increase in the price of consumer goods and services

Labor union

Organization of workers in the same industry

TRY THIS...

What is the minimum hourly wage a person supporting a family of 5 must earn in order to be above poverty level?

Inflation is the increase in the price of consumer goods and services. As prices rise, workers need to earn more money so they can maintain their standard of living. **Labor unions** are organizations of workers in the same industry. Representatives of labor unions work out agreements with employers for benefits and **cost of living increases**. A cost of living increase is a raise to help employees keep the same standard of living even when prices are increasing because of inflation.

	Joe belongs to a labor union. His annual gross pay is \$36,000. His union representatives negotiate a \$1,080 annual cost of living increase for workers in Joe's salary range. The rate of inflation is 2.4%. Is the percent cost of living increase greater or less than the inflation rate?
EXAMPLE	

Step 1 Divide Joe's cost of living increase by his annual salary to find the rate of increase as a decimal.

$$\begin{array}{r} .03 \\ 36{,}000\overline{)1{,}080.00} \\ \underline{-1\ 080\ 00} \end{array}$$

Step 2 Change the decimal to a percent.

.03 = 03.% = 3%

Step 3 Compare the percent cost of living increase to the rate of inflation.

3% > 2.4%

Joe's percent cost of living increase is greater than the rate of inflation.

Exercise B   Write *Yes* or *No* for whether the percent cost of living increase is greater than the rate of inflation. Round decimals to the nearest tenth of a percent.

SOURCE: Average Annual Earnings by Educational Attainment and Gender (for year-round, full-time workers, ages 18 and over)

	Annual Wage	Cost of Living Increase	Rate of Inflation	Greater Than Rate of Inflation?
1.	\$28,000	\$1,120	4.2%	_____
2.	\$12,000	\$600	3.4%	_____
3.	\$38,500	\$1,155	2.8%	_____
4.	\$45,275	\$2,220	4%	_____
5.	\$56,350	\$1,975	4%	_____

A college education costs both money and time. However, workers with more training or education usually have higher annual incomes. This means that the cost of education will almost always pay for itself in the long run.

AVERAGE ANNUAL EARNINGS BY EDUCATION		
Education Level	Men	Women
9th–12th grade (no diploma)	$25,283	$17,313
High school diploma	$32,521	$21,893
Some college, no degree	$38,491	$25,889
2-year college degree	$39,873	$28,403
4-year college degree	$52,354	$36,555
Master's degree	$70,859	$44,471
Doctoral degree	$86,436	$62,169
Professional degree	$112,873	$90,711

SOURCE: U.S. Bureau of the Census, as found in *The American Almanac of Jobs and Salaries, 2000*

EXAMPLES In the table above, what is the difference between the average annual earnings of a male high school graduate and a male 4-year college graduate?

$52,354   Earnings with 4-year college degree
−32,521   Earnings with high school diploma
$19,833   Difference in average annual earnings

Suppose it costs Jake $20,000 for a 4-year college degree. How many years after high school will his total earnings be greater than the total earnings of a high school graduate?

Years After High School	Total Earnings of Male with High School Diploma	Total Earnings of Male with 4-Year College Degree (minus $20,000 for cost of degree)
4	$130,084	$0
5	$130,084 + $32,521 = $162,605	$52,354 − $20,000 = $32,354
6	$162,605 + $32,521 = $195,126	$32,354 + $52,354 = $84,708
7	$195,126 + $32,521 = $227,647	$84,708 + $52,354 = $137,062
8	$227,647 + $32,521 = $260,168	$137,062 + $52,354 = $189,416
9	$260,168 + $32,521 = $292,689	$189,416 + $52,354 = $241,770
10	$292,689 + $32,521 = $325,210	$241,770 + $52,354 = $294,124
11	$325,210 + $32,521 = $357,731	$294,124 + $52,354 = $346,478
12	$357,731 + $32,521 = $390,252	$346,478 + $52,354 = $398,832

Jake's total earnings will be greater than those of a high school graduate 12 years after high school graduation, and 12 − 4 = 8 years after college graduation.

Exercise C Use the pattern in the average annual earnings table at the top of page 92 to solve.

1. Max spends $30,000 for a 4-year college degree. How many years after high school will Max's total earnings be greater than his total earnings if he had only a high school diploma?

2. Betsy spends $20,000 for a 4-year college degree. How many years after high school will Betsy's total earnings be greater than her total earnings if she had only a high school diploma?

3. Michael spends $40,000 for a 4-year college degree. His total earnings 16 years after college graduation will be how much greater than his total earnings if he had only a high school diploma?

4. Jenna and Samantha leave high school before finishing. At age 20, Jenna spends $2,000 and takes 1 year to complete her high school diploma. Samantha begins full-time work at age 20. Compare their total earnings at age 26. Whose total annual earnings are greater? how much greater?

5. Marta spends $40,000 and takes 6 years after high school to earn a Master's degree. How many years after high school will Marta's total earnings be greater than her total earnings if she had only earned a high school diploma?

Axis (Axes)
Line of reference on a graph

Bar graph
Graph that uses bars to compare amounts or sizes

Horizontal
Sideways

Vertical
Up and down

A good way to compare incomes is to show the data in a **bar graph**. A bar graph uses bars of different lengths to compare data. If the bars go up and down, the graph is a **vertical** bar graph. If the bars go sideways the graph is a **horizontal** bar graph. Each perpendicular reference line (on the left and bottom of a bar graph) is called an **axis**. Together these are called axes.

EXAMPLE   Make a bar graph to compare the average annual
          earnings of women. Use data from the table on
          the top of page 92.

Step 1   Decide whether to use vertical or horizontal bars.

Step 2   Choose a scale.

Step 3   Label the vertical and horizontal axes.

Step 4   Draw bars to represent the data.

Step 5   Give the graph a title.

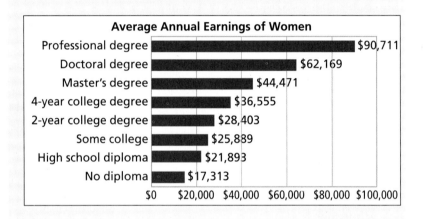

Average Annual Earnings of Women

Professional degree	$90,711
Doctoral degree	$62,169
Master's degree	$44,471
4-year college degree	$36,555
2-year college degree	$28,403
Some college	$25,889
High school diploma	$21,893
No diploma	$17,313

Exercise D   Make a bar graph to display the data below.

Occupation	Median Annual Income
1. Auto mechanic	$27,400
2. Legal secretary	$30,100
3. Chemical engineer	$64,800
4. Architect	$47,700
5. Drafter	$32,400
6. Teacher	$39,300
7. Human resource specialist	$49,010
8. Veterinarian	$51,000
9. Veterinary assistant	$16,200
10. News anchorperson	$65,500

SOURCE: Occupational Outlook Handbook 2000

Pay Raises at Abel & Baker

Alicia is the president of Abel & Baker Pet Supplies, Inc.

"What's our total annual payroll now?" she asked.

"It's just about three million dollars," came Hector's reply.

Hector is the head of the Human Resource Department. He and Alicia often meet over lunch to discuss company policy. On this day, Alicia was concerned that the company's payroll expense was growing too fast.

"I want 5% average pay raises for all employees next year; no more than that," came Alicia's order.

"OK, we'll limit payroll growth to 5%." Hector had gotten the message.

"You might as well give everyone a straight 5% raise, then. That's the easiest thing to do," Alicia offered.

"The easiest solution may not be the best way to go," Hector replied. "I have some very good people I really want to keep happy. Here's what I think. Instead of giving everyone the same raise, let's give the best workers 8%. We can still give the average workers 5%. And we can give just 2% to the workers who do the least."

"OK, Hector, it's your call. Let's go with your plan. It'll be up to your department, though, to decide who gets which raise."

For Discussion

1. How many employees do you think there are at Abel & Baker? Explain how you arrived at your estimate.
2. What are the benefits of Hector's plan? What are the possible difficulties? Discuss.
3. What will be the company's approximate total payroll next year?
4. As an employee, would you prefer that everyone get a 5% raise, or would you prefer Hector's plan? Why?

Write the letter of the answer that best completes each sentence.

1. A state's unemployment rate is a percent that compares the number of people who are unemployed to _____.

    a. the state's total population

    b. the number of employed people in the state

    c. the number of job openings in the state

    d. the number of people in the state who are capable of working

2. The term for a person who is supported by another person's income is _____.

    a. a dependent   c. part of the labor force

    b. a child   d. lazy

3. In 1995 Tony quit work to go to college. It cost him $35,000 and took 4 years to earn a 4-year college degree. He started working full-time right after college at $52,354 annual salary. Without figuring in any raises, the formula _____ can be used to estimate Tony's total earnings between 1995 and 2005.

    a. $(10 \times \$52,354) - \$35,000$

    b. $10 \times (\$52,354 - \$35,000)$

    c. $(6 \times \$52,354) - \$35,000$

    d. $6 \times (\$52,354 - \$35,000)$

Solve problems 4–9.

4. A manufacturing company has an annual production goal of 91,000 snowboards. If 1 worker can produce 10 snowboards per day, how many workers are needed to meet the production goal in 260 days?

5. In 2002 a company employed 2,525 people. During that year, a total of 101 employees left the company and were replaced. What was the turnover rate?

6. In 2000 a state's unemployment rate was 6.2%. In 2001 its unemployment rate was 4.8%. What was the change in the unemployment rate between 2000 and 2001?

7. Bob's wages are $2,200 a month. He receives an 8% raise for outstanding work. What is the amount of his raise?

8. Sue earns $12.00 per hour. She receives a 7% raise for good work. What is her new hourly wage?

9. Jack supports 4 dependents. His gross pay is $9.50 per hour working 2,080 hours a year. If the poverty level for a family of 5 is $19,950, is Jack's income above or below the poverty level?

Use the graph below for problem 10.

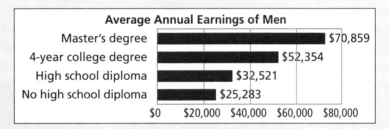

10. How much greater are a man's average annual earnings with a 4-year college degree than with a high school diploma?

Test-Taking Tip | When taking a math test, do the problems that are easy for you before tackling more difficult ones.

Chapter

5

Business Travel

Many employees have jobs that involve business travel. These trips cost money. Sometimes companies pay directly for employees' travel expenses. Often employees pay their own travel expenses, and employers pay them back. Examples of business-related travel expenses are airfare, hotels, rental cars, and meals. In order to be paid back, employees must keep accurate records of all the money they spend for business. Then employees must correctly report their expenses on company forms.

In this chapter, you will learn the math skills required to keep accurate records and calculate business-related expenses. You will also learn about comparing costs of airline tickets, lodgings, and meals.

Goals for Learning

▶ To calculate and compare costs of special airfares for different airlines

▶ To compare rates for luxury and economy lodging

▶ To compare hotel and meal costs in small and large cities

▶ To calculate total charges for a trip from a credit-card statement

▶ To fill out an expense form correctly

Airfare
Cost of a plane ticket

Round trip
A trip to a place and back, often over the same route

Most business travel begins with buying an airline ticket. **Airfare** is the cost of a plane ticket. Travelers can buy a ticket from one place to another, or they can buy a **round-trip** ticket. A round-trip ticket covers flying to one place, then back again. Many conditions affect the price of a ticket between the same cities. Understanding these conditions can help you find the lowest possible airfare.

Fareway Airlines One-Way Fare (Rates do not include a 5% tax.)					
CITY		REGULAR*		2-WEEK ADVANCE PURCHASE**	
From (To)	To (From)	Fri.–Mon.	Tues.–Thurs.	Fri.–Mon.	Tues.–Thurs.
San Jose	Chicago	$830	$740	$490	$440
San Jose	Los Angeles	$325	$280	$89	$89
Denver	Seattle	$590	$520	$340	$320
Cleveland	Houston	$525	$510	$250	$230
Santa Fe	St. Louis	$960	$900	$430	$400

* Tickets purchased less than 14 days before departure date
** Tickets purchased at least 14 days before departure date

EXAMPLE

Celia will leave on a business trip in 3 weeks. Today she buys a round-trip ticket from San Jose to Chicago. She will leave on Monday, June 30, and return on Thursday, July 2. What does her round-trip ticket plus tax cost on Fareway Airlines?

Step 1 Determine whether the ticket is advance purchase.

3 weeks > 2 weeks → Advance purchase

Step 2 Add to find the cost of an advance purchase round-trip ticket.

$490	San Jose to Chicago on a Monday
+440	Chicago to San Jose on a Thursday
$930	Round-trip airfare

Step 3 Find the tax.

$ 930	Round-trip airfare
× .05	Tax rate written as a decimal
$46.50	Tax on round-trip ticket

Step 4 Add the cost of the ticket and the tax.

$930.00	Round-trip airfare
+ 46.50	Tax
$976.50	Total cost of ticket and tax

Celia's round-trip ticket plus tax costs $976.50.

Exercise A Use the Fareway Airlines chart on page 100. Find the cost of each round-trip ticket plus tax.

	Cities	TRAVEL DATES		Advance Purchase?	Airfare
		Leave	Return		
1.	Santa Fe/St. Louis	Wed., June 3	Tues., June 9	Yes	_____
2.	San Jose/Los Angeles	Mon., Mar. 8	Sun., Mar. 14	No	_____
3.	San Jose/Los Angeles	Mon., Mar. 8	Sun., Mar. 14	Yes	_____
4.	Denver/Seattle	Tues., May 14	Sat., May 18	Yes	_____
5.	Denver/Seattle	Tues., May 14	Sat., May 18	No	_____

TRY THIS...

Find the lowest possible fare for a round-trip ticket between Cleveland and Houston. What conditions must be met to get this fare?

Business travelers usually compare fares for different airlines.

EXAMPLE Mark has business in Seattle. He will leave his home in Denver on Thursday, March 1, and return on March 5. If he buys his ticket 16 days before he leaves, which airline offers the lower airfare before tax, Fareway or On-Time?

Step 1 Find the day of the week that Mark returns.

Mar. 1	Mar. 2	Mar. 3	Mar. 4	Mar. 5
↓	↓	↓	↓	↓
Thurs.	Fri.	Sat.	Sun.	Mon.

Step 2 Find the airfare for Fareway on page 100.

Denver to Seattle $320   Thursday, advance purchase
Seattle to Denver   +340   Monday, advance purchase
                  $660   Fareway round-trip airfare

Step 3 Find the airfare for On-Time on page 102.

Denver to Seattle $310   Thursday, advance purchase
Seattle to Denver   +345   Monday, advance purchase
                  $655   On-Time round-trip airfare

Step 4 Compare airfares for both airlines.

$660 > $655

On-Time offers the lower airfare.

On-Time Airlines One-Way Fare (Rates do not include a 5% tax.)					
CITY		REGULAR*		2-WEEK ADVANCE PURCHASE**	
From (To)	To (From)	Fri.–Mon.	Tues.–Thurs.	Fri.–Mon.	Tues.–Thurs.
San Jose	Chicago	$850	$770	$510	$480
San Jose	Los Angeles	$335	$290	$119	$119
Denver	Seattle	$580	$510	$345	$310
Cleveland	Houston	$520	$500	$265	$240
Santa Fe	St. Louis	$920	$900	$480	$450

*Tickets purchased less than 14 days before departure date
**Tickets purchased at least 14 days before departure date

PROBLEM SOLVING

Exercise B   Use the airfares on page 100 and above to solve. Remember to include the tax.

1. Which airline offers the lower regular fares between Cleveland and Houston?

2. What is the difference in price between Fareway's lowest round-trip fare between Denver and Seattle and On-Time's lowest round-trip fare between Denver and Seattle?

3. Ron flies between San Jose and Chicago. He leaves on a Monday and returns the next day, with no advance purchase. Which airline offers the lower regular fare? How much lower?

4. Jan buys an advance-purchase round-trip ticket between St. Louis and Santa Fe. She returns on Friday, April 8. She could leave on either the previous Monday or Tuesday. How much could she save by leaving on Tuesday instead of on Monday, flying On-Time?

5. In problem 4, how much could Jan save if she leaves April 5 and returns April 12 instead of leaving Monday and returning Friday?

Double occupancy

Space for two people

Economy hotel

Thrifty lodging with fewer services and conveniences

Lodging

Place to stay while traveling

Luxury hotel

Expensive lodging with more services and conveniences

Single occupancy

Space for one person

Suite

Group of rooms occupied as a unit

Writing About Mathematics

Explain why you think a double room is not double the cost of a single room.

Part of overnight business travel is finding a place to stay or **lodging**. Some hotel rooms are for **single occupancy** or for one person. Some hotel rooms are for **double occupancy** or for two people. A **suite** is a group of rooms occupied as a unit. Suites are usually used by more than two people, or for business entertainment.

Lodging rates depend on the type of room and on the type of hotel. The more expensive **luxury hotels** offer services and conveniences that less expensive **economy hotels** may not offer. For example, luxury hotels may provide free conference rooms or free breakfasts. Luxury hotels may have room service, or a fax machine and Internet connection in each room.

The chart below compares the daily room rates and conveniences for four hotels.

Hotel	Daily Rates	Conference Room?	Room Service?	Exercise Room?	In-Room Fax/Internet?
ABC Hotel	Single: $59 Double: $79	No	No	No	No
Superior Inn	Single: $99 Double: $129 Suite: $219	No	Yes	No	Yes
Royal Inn	Single: $189 Double: $229 Suite: $349	Yes	Yes	No	Yes
Elite Hotel	Single: $290 Double: $320 Suite: $540	Yes	Yes	Yes	Yes

EXAMPLE   Virginia is planning a business trip for 4 salespeople. They need 2 double-occupancy rooms and a suite for 2 nights. They also need a conference room, in-room Internet, and room service. What is the least cost for lodgings that meet all Virginia's needs?

Step 1   Find the hotel with the needed services for the lowest rates. Use the chart on page 103.

Both Royal Inn and Elite Hotel meet the needs.
Royal Inn has lower rates than Elite Hotel.

Step 2   Find the daily rate for 2 double-occupancy rooms and a suite at Royal Inn.

$229	Double	$458	Rate for 2 doubles
× 2	Number of rooms	+349	Rate for suite
$458	2 doubles	$807	Total daily rate

Step 3   Multiply the daily rate by the number of days to find the total cost.

$ 807	Daily rate
× 2	Number of days
$1,614	Total cost

The least cost is $1,614 to stay 2 days at Royal Inn.

Exercise A   Use the chart on page 103 to complete. Choose the hotel that meets all the needs for the least cost.

Number of Days	Rooms Needed	Special Needs	Hotel Name	Daily Rate	Total Cost
1. 2	1 suite	None			
2. 2	4 suites	Exercise room and conference room			
3. 4	3 doubles, 1 single	In-room fax/ room service			
4. 3	4 doubles, 1 suite	Conference room			
5. 5	8 doubles, 3 singles	None			

AVERAGE HOTEL AND MEAL PRICES IN SELECTED CITIES			
City	Population	Average Hotel Rate	Average Meal Price
Grantsville	2,850	$69 single/$89 double	$6.95
Bakerton	430,940	$120 single/$140 double	$10.75
Schaefer	52,235	$100 single/$110 double	$9.50
Lafayette	990,032	$139 single/$159 double	$12.80
Lincoln	1,560,940	$189 single/$219 double	$14.35
Vly Summit	4,657	$85 single/$95 double	$8.90

EXAMPLE   How much more does an average double-occupancy room cost for
3 nights in Bakerton than in Vly Summit?

Step 1   Subtract to find the cost difference for 1 night.
   $140   Double-occupancy room in Bakerton
   − 95   Double-occupancy room in Vly Summit
   $ 45   Cost difference for 1 night

Step 2   Multiply the cost difference for 1 night by 3 nights.
   $ 45   Cost difference for 1 night
   × 3   Number of nights
   $135   Total cost difference

An average double-occupancy room for 3 nights costs $135 more in
Bakerton than in Vly Summit.

PROBLEM SOLVING

Exercise B   Use the chart above to solve.

1. How much more do 6 average meals cost in Lincoln than in Schaefer?

2. Ay Co. needs 8 double rooms and 1 meal each for 16 people. How much more is the daily cost in Bakerton than in Grantsville?

3. What is the average cost of 4 meals and a single room for 2 nights in Lafayette?

4. Ay Co. in problem 2 uses a hotel in Grantsville, and has meetings and meals in Bakerton. It rents a van for $300. How much money does it save by using a hotel in Grantsville and driving people to Bakerton?

Most business travelers **charge** or pay for travel expenses with a **credit card**. A credit card is used to charge expenses and pay for them at a later time. Credit cards also can be used to get **cash advances** from an **automated teller machine (ATM)**. A cash advance is money that must be repaid. ATMs are computer terminals that allow 24-hour access to bank accounts. Each month, a record or **statement** of credit-card charges is sent to the cardholder. If the balance is not paid promptly, an **interest** fee is charged on the unpaid balance. Statements can be used to track business expenses.

EXAMPLE   The statement on page 107 shows the expenses Dell charged to his credit card in one month. He used his credit card for both personal and business-related expenses. The business-related charges are starred. How much did Dell charge to his credit card for meals on his business trip?

Step 1   Find and estimate the business meal charges. Round to the nearest ten dollars. Then add.

The Eatery	$45.89 →	$50
Betty's Breakfast Nook	$8.50 →	$10
Joe's Café	$10.18 →	$10
The Supper Club	$18.94 →	$20
Pam's Pancake Hut	$10.77 →	+$10
		$100

Dell spent about $100 for meals on his business trip.

Step 2   Find the sum of the actual business meals.

The Eatery	$45.89
Betty's Breakfast Nook	8.50
Joe's Café	10.18
The Supper Club	18.94
Pam's Pancake Hut	+10.77
	$94.28

Dell charged $94.28 for business meals. The answer is close to the estimate, so it is reasonable.

Rounding money to the nearest ten dollars makes it easier to add the numbers mentally.

Dell Baxter
246 Samson Court
Andover, Kansas 67002

Account Number: 0000-0000-1111-0101
Statement Date: Nov. 15
Due Date: Nov. 30

Date	Company Name	Location	Amount
10/10	Fareway Airlines	Kansas City, KS	$425.78 ✳
10/15	Conrad's Dept. Store	Kansas City, KS	$89.99
10/18	Bill's Auto Repair	Overland Park, KS	$296.48
10/22	McKee's Steak House	Overland Park, KS	$128.59
10/29	The Eatery	Bakersville, OR	$45.89 ✳
10/29	Starlight Hotel	Bakersville, OR	$137.18 ✳
10/29	Bakersville Racquet Club	Bakersville, OR	$10.00
10/29	Hamway's Gift Store	Bakersville, OR	$95.82
10/29	Gas and Go	Bakersville, OR	$37.25 ✳
10/30	ATM cash advance	125 Lagoon Ave., Bakersville, OR	$102.50 ✳
10/30	Betty's Breakfast Nook	Clement, OR	$8.50 ✳
10/30	The Torchlight Inn	Clement, OR	$128.36 ✳
10/31	ATM cash advance	4th & Main, Salem, OR	$101.50 ✳
10/31	Bob's Gym	Salem, OR	$8.50
10/31	The Comfort Zone Hotel	Salem, OR	$159.15 ✳
10/31	Gas Mart	Salem, OR	$29.18 ✳
10/31	Joe's Café	Salem, OR	$10.18 ✳
10/31	The Supper Club	Pennsington, OR	$18.94 ✳
11/1	The Fuel Mart	Pennsington, OR	$32.85 ✳
11/1	Pam's Pancake Hut	Pennsington, OR	$10.77 ✳
11/1	ATM cash advance	Carver Mall, Bellevue, OR	$102.00 ✳
11/1	Portland Airport Shops	Portland, OR	$43.19
11/3	Avalon Car Rental	Cleveland, OH	$326.92

Each cash advance is for $100. The extra charge is an ATM fee. Only Dell's ATM fees are business expenses. Dell will keep other records for business expenses he pays for with cash.

Exercise A   Use Dell's credit-card statement on page 107 to solve.

1. How much are Dell's business charges for hotels?

2. What are Dell's business charges for gas?

3. Dell got three cash advances for $100 each. How much was his total charge for ATM fees?

4. Cash advances are not business expenses, but ATM fees are. What is the total of Dell's business expenses charged to his credit card?

5. About what percentage of the total business expenses on Dell's credit card was for food and hotels?

Technology Connection

Using Automated Teller Machines (ATMs)

ATMs make it possible for people to get cash anywhere in the world. Business travelers can use ATMs to deposit money, pay bills, and for other banking while they are away from home. ATMs can be found in public places such as airports, banks, stores, gas stations, restaurants, and hotels. Many people do all their banking at ATMs.

Take a survey. Ask adults if they use ATMs. Ask how often they use ATMs. Ask what their ATM charges are. Ask what banking they do on ATMs. Ask why they go to ATMs instead of to a bank. Ask if anyone has ever had a problem with an ATM. Organize your findings. Discuss the advantages and disadvantages of ATMs. Present the survey results to your class.

Receipt
Proof of purchase

Reimburse
Pay back

Companies usually **reimburse** or pay back employees for business expenses. Employees keep track of their own expenses. Credit-card statements show expenses that were charged. **Receipts** for business expenses show how money was spent. Employees record their expenses on a company reimbursement form. Then companies reimburse them.

EXAMPLE These are Elija's business expenses.

Date	Company	Purpose	Amount
3/6	Triple Crown Hotel	Hotel room	$449.85
3/6	Excel	Gas	$24.58
3/6	Hunan Garden	Meal and tip	$12.45
3/6	Ace Rental	Car rental	$289.60
3/6	On-Time Airline	Airfare	$689.19
3/7	Long distance carrier	Phone calls	$17.84
3/7	The Corner Café	Meal and tip	$10.00
3/7	Personal car expenses	Gas and mileage	$31.75
3/7	Elko Airport parking	Park car at airport	$28.00

Record Elija's business expenses on a reimbursement form. Write the information for each expense in the appropriate column. Add each row. Add each column. The sum of the *Total* row should be the same as the sum of the *Total* column. If it is not, find and correct the error.

Date	Company	Airfare	Lodging	Rental Car Expense	Meals and Tips	Misc.	Total
3/6	Triple Crown Hotel		$449.85				$449.85
3/6	Excel			$24.58			$24.58
3/6	Hunan Garden				$12.45		$12.45
3/6	Ace Rental			$289.60			$289.60
3/6	On-Time Airline	$689.19					$689.19
3/7	Long distance carrier					$17.84	$17.84
3/7	The Corner Café				$10.00		$10.00
3/7	Personal car expenses					$31.75	$31.75
3/7	Elko Airport parking					$28.00	$28.00
Total		$689.19	$449.85	$314.18	$22.45	$77.59	$1,553.26

The credit-card statement and receipts below show only business expenses from Sophia's recent business trip. The cash advance taken on 2/5 was for $200.

Sophia Patterson
131 Rodeo Lane
Dallas, Texas 75201

Account Number: 1010-1111-2222-0000
Statement Date: 2/17/03
Due Date: 3/1/03

Date	Company Name	Location	Amount
2/1	Gateway Airlines	Dallas, TX	$989.38
2/5	Lexington Hotel	San Francisco, CA	$289.45
2/5	The Nob Hill Café	San Francisco, CA	$18.68
2/5	ATM cash advance	2710 Market St., San Francisco, CA	$201.50
2/5	Best Car Rental	San Francisco, CA	$348.38
2/6	Jake's Grill	Santa Cruz, CA	$109.87
2/6	Steinway Hotel	Santa Cruz, CA	$196.80
2/7	Dallas Airport parking	Dallas, TX	$50.00
2/7	Joe's Gas Mart	San Francisco, CA	$32.82

Total Account Balance	Minimum Payment Due	Due Date
$2,236.88	$110.00	3/1/03

2/6
Gas and mileage to airport
$34.60
misc.

Bridge Toll

Date: 2/5
Amount: $2.50
----
rental car expense

UPTOWN GARAGE
Date: 2/6
Amount: $4.25
rental car expense

U-Park Garage
============
Date: 2/5
Amount: $8.50
rental car expense

2/5
pay phone
$3.75
misc.

Did You Know?

The United States leads the world in airline travel. Americans travel more than half a billion miles by air each year. The United Kingdom is next, traveling less than one fifth of that total.

Exercise A Complete the reimbursement form using the credit-card statement and cash receipts on page 110.

STERLING CORPORATION EMPLOYEE REIMBURSEMENT FORM

Expenses incurred by: *Sophia Patterson*   Date: *2/28/03*

Social Security #: *111-00-5555*

Company Number: *78943*

	Date	Company	Airfare	Lodging	Rental Car & Gas	Meals	Misc.	Total
1.	2/1	Gateway Airlines						
2.	2/5	Lexington Hotel						
3.	2/5	The Nob Hill Café						
4.	2/5	ATM cash advance						
5.	2/5	Best Car Rental						
6.	2/6	Jake's Grill						
7.	2/6	Steinway Hotel						
8.	2/7	Joe's Gas Mart						
9.	2/7	Dallas Airport parking						
10.	2/6	Uptown Garage						
11.	2/5	Bridge toll						
12.	2/6	Gas and mileage						
13.	2/5	Pay phone						
14.	2/5	U-Park Garage						
15.	Total							

Less Cash Advance: $200.00

15. Total Reimbursement: _____

Exercise B Use the travel reimbursement form on page 111 to solve.

1. Did Sophia spend more for airfare or for lodging?

2. What were Sophia's total expenses for meals and miscellaneous? (Hint: Remember not to count cash advances.)

3. How much more did airfare cost than lodging and meals?

4. About what percent of Sophia's business expenses was for lodging?

5. Would Sophia list a receipt for a $50 toy that she bought as a present for her grandchild? Explain.

TRY THIS...

Sophia pays only $110 of her $2,236.88 credit-card balance by the due date. She is charged 1.8% interest monthly on the unpaid balance. Find the amount of interest she is charged for one month. Round to the nearest cent.

The BMU Sales Meeting

Karl and Arlene are salespeople for Business Machines Universal, Inc. They sell copy machines. Every spring all the BMU salespeople attend a sales meeting to learn about new products.

"Arlene, have you made your travel plans for the sales meeting yet?" asked Karl.

"Not yet. What's the rush? The meeting is not until next month."

"You need to book your flight right away to get the super-saver fare," Karl advised.

"Those fares require a Saturday-night stay. I'm not staying over a Saturday night. I plan to come back that Thursday, right after the meeting."

"You forgot, Arlene. The sales meeting isn't Monday through Thursday this year. It's Friday through Monday. The company will save a lot of money on airfare and hotels."

"You're right, I did forget. That's really bad news," Arlene complained.

"What do you mean?" Karl asked. "We'll all benefit in the long run if the company saves money."

"But the sales meeting will ruin my weekend, just to save the company a little money. This company is really getting cheap!"

For Discussion

1. Who shows a more businesslike approach to the job, Karl or Arlene? Why?

2. A full-fare ticket costs $1,220. A super-saver airfare costs $267. Tell how much money the company saves by buying a super-saver ticket. Then estimate the company's total savings if 60 salespeople fly to the meeting.

3. The hotel charges $155 per night Monday through Thursday. It charges $85 per night Friday through Sunday. BMU will need about 80 rooms. Estimate BMU's total savings in hotel costs by moving the meeting to a weekend.

4. Why do you think the hotel charges less on weekends? Explain.

Use the tables below for problems 1–2. Remember to include the tax.

American Northern Airlines One-Way Fare (Rates do not include a 5% tax.)					
CITY		REGULAR		2-WEEK ADVANCE PURCHASE	
From (To)	To (From)	Fri.–Mon.	Tues.–Thurs.	Fri.–Mon.	Tues.–Thurs.
Boston	Milwaukee	$754	$702	$389	$349
Orlando	Portland	$978	$929	$572	$520

Getaway Airlines One-Way Fare (Rates do not include a 5% tax.)					
CITY		REGULAR		2-WEEK ADVANCE PURCHASE	
From (To)	To (From)	Fri.–Mon.	Tues.–Thurs.	Fri.–Mon.	Tues.–Thurs.
Boston	Milwaukee	$729	$685	$342	$318
Orlando	Portland	$935	$894	$541	$500

1. Suppose you want to fly from Orlando to Portland on Getaway Airlines. How much more does flying on a Monday cost than flying on a Tuesday?

2. Pat wants a round-trip ticket between Portland and Orlando, leaving Wednesday, April 12 and returning April 16. Which airline offers the lower regular fare? how much lower?

Use the lodging rates below for problem 3.

	*Economy Inn Lamberton, IL Pop.: 874,562	**Royal Gardens Grant City, IL Pop.: 8,549	**Luxury Hotel Petersburg, IL Pop.: 690,410
Single occupancy	$98	$119	$187
Double occupancy	$128	$149	$224
Suite	N/A	$280	$375

*Economy   **Luxury   N/A Not available

3. A single-occupancy room for 4 nights at a luxury hotel costs how much more in a large city than in a small city?

Use the credit-card statement and receipt for problems 4–10.

Jayson Elliot
1162 Lilly Drive
Oakland, CA 94605

Account Number: 1010-0000-0000-0101
Statement Date: Sept. 15
Due Date: Sept. 30

Date	Company Name	Location	Amount
9/4	Getaway Airlines	Boston, MA	$674.58*
9/4	Bandit Rental Cars	Milwaukee, WI	$178.93
9/4	John's Gas Mart	Milwaukee, WI	$24.81
9/4	Gulliver's Restaurant	Milwaukee, WI	$113.00

AIRPORT GARAGE
====================
Date: 9/4
Amount: $15.00

misc.

COMMONSHARE COMPANY EMPLOYEE REIMBURSEMENT FORM

Date	Company	Airfare	Hotel	Rental Car Expense	Meals and Tips	Misc.	Total
4. 9/4	Getaway Airlines						
5. 9/4	Bandit Rental Cars						
6. 9/4	John's Gas Mart						
7. 9/4	Gulliver's Restaurant						
8. 9/4	Airport garage						
9. Total							

10. Total Reimbursement:

Test-Taking Tip When reading a chart or table, use the edge of a sheet of paper to find the correct row or column. Put the edge below the row or beside the column.

Chapter

6

Corporate Banking

A successful business needs to make more money than it spends. However, a company's expenses occasionally are greater than its revenues. When this happens, the company may borrow money from a bank for a short period of time. The company pays interest on the money that it borrows. This interest is another expense for the company. Effectively managing the flow of money in and out is critical to the success of any business.

In this chapter, you will learn about corporate banking practices. You will also learn the math skills that companies use to manage their money.

Goals for Learning

▶ To compute simple and compound interest

▶ To determine lines of credit based on a company's value

▶ To calculate interest on credit for given periods of time

▶ To describe cash flow and understand why managing cash flow is important

▶ To calculate various types of product payment costs

Interest
Fee charged to a borrower for the use of money loaned

Principal
Amount of money loaned

Rate
Percent of interest charged for money loaned

Simple interest
Constant fee charged for the use of money loaned

Time
Period for which money is loaned

When a company borrows money from a bank, the bank collects **interest** from the company. Interest is the fee charged for the use of the money. **Simple interest** is an interest fee that does not change. It is always a percentage of the money loaned. The amount of money borrowed or loaned is called the **principal**.

The formula for calculating simple interest is $I = PRT$. I represents interest. P represents principal. R represents **rate**, which is the percent of interest charged. T represents the **time** for which the money is loaned.

EXAMPLES A company borrows $2,000 from a bank that charges 18% simple interest each year. How much interest is owed after 2 years?

Use the formula $I = PRT$ to find the interest.

$P = \$2,000 \quad R = 18\% \quad T = 2$ years
$I = \$2,000 \times 18\% \times 2$
$I = \$2,000 \times .18 \times 2$

$2,000	Principal
× .18	Rate
$ 360	Annual interest
× 2	Time in years
$ 720	Interest for 2 years

The company owes $720 in interest after 2 years.

What is the total amount the company has to pay back at the end of 2 years?

Add the interest after 2 years to the principal to find the total amount.

$2,000	Principal
+ 720	Interest
$2,720	Total amount

The company has to pay back $2,720 at the end of 2 years.

EXAMPLE   ABCD Inc. borrows $50,000 for 9 months at a simple interest rate of 15% a year. What is the total amount that ABCD Inc. pays the bank after 9 months?

Use the formula $I = PRT$.

Method 1   Use the annual interest rate.

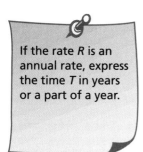

If the rate *R* is an annual rate, express the time *T* in years or a part of a year.

Step 1   Find the time as a decimal part of a year.
Divide 9 months by 12 months.

$$\begin{array}{r} .75 \\ \hline 12\overline{)9.00} \end{array}$$

Step 2   Find the interest.

$I = \$50,000 \times 15\% \times .75$

$I = \$50,000 \times .15 \times .75 = \$5,625$

Step 3   Add to find the total amount owed.

$50,000   Principal
+ 5,625   Interest
$55,625   Total amount owed

Method 2   Use the monthly interest rate.

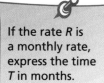

If the rate *R* is a monthly rate, express the time *T* in months.

Step 1   Find the rate *R* as a monthly rate.
Divide the yearly rate 15% by 12 months.

$$\begin{array}{r} 1.25\% \\ \hline 12\overline{)15.00\%} \end{array}$$ Monthly rate

Yearly rate

Step 2   Find the interest after 9 months.

$I = \$50,000 \times 1.25\% \times 9$

$I = \$50,000 \times .0125 \times 9 = \$5,625$

Step 3   Add to find the total amount owed.

$50,000   Principal
+ 5,625   Interest
$55,625   Total amount owed

ABCD Inc. has to pay the bank $55,625 after 9 months.

Exercise A Find the interest and amount owed at the end of each time period using the annual interest rate.

Principal	Annual Rate	Time	Interest	Amount Owed
1. $1,000	5%	1 year	_____	_____
2. $1,000	6%	3 years	_____	_____
3. $3,800	8%	1 year	_____	_____
4. $3,800	4%	3 years	_____	_____
5. $12,000	5%	4 years	_____	_____
6. $10,000	18%	$1\frac{1}{2}$ years	_____	_____
7. $25,000	15%	2 years, 3 months	_____	_____
8. $32,500	22%	6 months	_____	_____
9. $120,000	10%	9 months	_____	_____
10. $15,000	6%	15 months	_____	_____

Exercise B Find the interest and amount owed at the end of each time period using the monthly interest rate.

Principal	Annual Rate	Time	Interest	Amount Owed
1. $32,400	12%	7 months	_____	_____
2. $57,000	24%	3 months	_____	_____
3. $15,000	15%	4 months	_____	_____
4. $84,500	15%	1 year, 4 months	_____	_____
5. $856,800	18%	2 years, 1 month	_____	_____

Compound interest

Interest paid on the principal plus any interest added to date

Often banks charge **compound interest** on money that they lend. The borrower pays compound interest on the principal plus any interest added over a given period of time.

EXAMPLE | JoyCo borrows $10,000 at an annual rate of 12% compounded monthly. How much money does JoyCo owe after 2 months?

Step 1 Since the interest is compounded monthly, change the annual interest rate to a monthly interest rate. Be sure to use 1 month as the time period.

$I = PRT$

$I = \$10,000 \times \frac{12\%}{12} \times 1$

$I = \$10,000 \times \frac{.12}{12} \times 1$

$I = \$10,000 \times .01 \times 1$

	$10,000	Principal
×	.01	Monthly rate
$	100	Monthly interest
×	1	Time in months
$	100	Interest

Change annual rate to monthly rate because interest is compounded monthly. The time is 1 month because interest is compounded monthly.

Step 2 Add the interest to the principal to find the amount owed after 1 month.

	$10,000	Principal
+	100	Interest for first month
	$10,100	Amount owed after 1 month

Step 3 Compute the interest on the amount owed after 1 month.

$I = PRT$

$I = \$10,100 \times .01 \times 1$

	$10,100	Amount owed
×	.01	Monthly rate
$	101	Monthly interest
×	1	Time in months
$	101	Interest

Writing About Mathematics

Use the example on this page. Explain how to find the amount owed after 2 months using the annual interest rate compounded monthly.

Step 4 Add the interest to the amount owed after 1 month to find the amount owed after 2 months.

	$10,100	Amount owed after 1 month
+	101	Interest for second month
	$10,201	Amount owed after 2 months

After 2 months JoyCo owes $10,201.

Sometimes interest is compounded semiannually, or every 6 months.

EXAMPLE TG Inc. borrows $5,000 at an annual interest rate of 8% compounded semiannually. Find the amount TG Inc. owes at the end of one year.

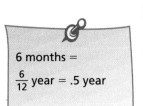

6 months = $\frac{6}{12}$ year = .5 year

Step 1   Find the interest for the first 6 months.

$I = PRT$

$I = \$5,000 \times 8\% \times \frac{6}{12}$

$I = \$5,000 \times .08 \times .5$

$5,000	Principal
× .08	Annual rate
$ 400	Annual interest
× .5	Time in years
$ 200	Interest

Step 2   Add the interest to the principal to find the amount owed after 6 months.

$5,000	Principal
+ 200	Interest for first 6 months
$5,200	Amount owed after 6 months

Step 3   Find the interest for the second 6 months.

Use the amount owed after the first 6 months.

$I = PRT$

$I = \$5,200 \times .08 \times .5$

$5,200	Amount owed
× .08	Annual rate
$ 416	Annual interest
× .5	Time in years
$ 208	Interest

Step 4   Add the interest to the amount owed after the first 6 months.

$5,200	Amount owed after 6 months
+ 208	Interest for second 6 months
$5,408	Amount owed after 1 year

At the end of 1 year, TG Inc. owes $5,408.

Exercise A Find the amount owed after 3 months when interest is compounded monthly. Round money to the nearest dollar.

Principal	Annual Interest Rate	Monthly Interest Rate	Amount Owed
1. $1,000	12%	_____	_____
2. $8,000	24%	_____	_____
3. $15,500	18%	_____	_____
4. $24,000	15%	_____	_____
5. $20,000	9%	_____	_____

Exercise B Find the amount owed after 1 year when interest is compounded semiannually. Round money to the nearest dollar.

Principal	Annual Interest Rate	Semiannual Interest Rate	Amount Owed
1. $84,000	10%	_____	_____
2. $122,000	12%	_____	_____
3. $524,700	18%	_____	_____
4. $10,000	15%	_____	_____
5. $690,000	12.5%	_____	_____

Technology Connection

Finding Compound Interest Using a Calculator

In the world of business, interest is often compounded daily for many years. Banks and businesses use spreadsheets to keep track of loans at compound interest. You can use a calculator with an x^y key.

To find the amount owed (*A*) on principal (*P*) at an interest rate (*R*) compounded daily, use this formula: $A = P(1 + R)^n$
R represents the rate of interest for the compounding period, and *n* represents the compounding period.

For example, a company borrows $500 at 6.5% annual interest compounded daily. Find the amount owed after 5 years using the formula $A = P(1 + R)^n$.

Since interest is compounded daily, multiply 5 years by 365 days per year to make *n* the compounding period. Divide the annual interest rate 6.5% by 365 to make *R* a daily interest rate.

$P = \$500$ $R = \frac{6.5\%}{365}$ $n = 5 \times 365 = 1{,}825$ $A = 500(1 + \frac{.065}{365})^{1{,}825}$

Use the following keystroke sequence on a calculator that has an x^y key.
.065 ÷ 365 = + 1 = x^y 1,825 = × 500 =   The display reads: 691.9953.
The company owes $692 after borrowing $500 for 5 years.

Interest may also be compounded quarterly, or every 3 months.

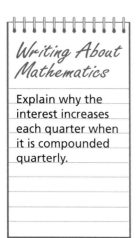

EXAMPLE A company borrows $10,000 at 12% annual interest compounded quarterly. Find the amount owed at the end of 1 year.

There are 4 quarters in a year. The interest rate for 1 quarter is 12% ÷ 4 = 3%.

First Quarter   *I = PRT*
I = $10,000 × 3% × 1 quarter
I = $10,000 × .03 × 1
I = $300
Amount owed = $10,000 + $300 = $10,300

Second Quarter   *I = PRT*
I = $10,300 × .03 × 1
I = $309
Amount owed = $10,300 + $309 = $10,609

Third Quarter   *I = PRT*
I = $10,609 × .03 × 1
I = $318.27
Amount owed = $10,609 + $318.27 = $10,927.27

Fourth Quarter   *I = PRT*
I = $10,927.27 × .03 × 1
I = $327.82
Amount owed = $10,927.27 + $327.82 = $11,255.09

The amount owed at the end of 1 year is $11,255.09.

Exercise C   Find each amount owed at the end of 1 year when interest is compounded quarterly. Round money to the nearest dollar.

	Principal	Annual Rate	Amount Owed
1.	$1,000	12%	_____
2.	$3,000	16%	_____
3.	$12,500	24%	_____
4.	$50,800	12%	_____
5.	$20,000	16.8%	_____

Asset

Item of value owned by a company

Line of credit

Arrangement with a bank allowing a company the right to borrow up to a specific amount of money

Receivable

Money owed to a company for goods and services sold on credit

Many businesses arrange with a bank the right to borrow money. Businesses can then borrow what they need, when they need it, and up to a specific amount. This is called a **line of credit**.

The bank allows a company to borrow an amount of money based on the value of the company's **assets**. A company asset is anything owned by the company. If the company does not repay the loan, the bank has the right to take the company's assets. Then the bank can sell the assets to repay the loan. A company's assets include its **receivables**, which is money still owed it for goods or services already delivered.

EXAMPLE

A company has the assets shown below. Its line of credit is 70% of the total value of its assets. How much money can the company borrow using its line of credit?

Asset	Value
Inventory	$98,000
Receivables	$57,430
Real estate	$483,980
Equipment	$10,800
Cash/savings	$24,873

Step 1 Add to find the total value of the assets.

$ 98,000	Inventory
57,430	Receivables
483,980	Real estate
10,800	Equipment
+ 24,873	Cash/savings
$675,083	Total assets

Step 2 Find 70% of the total assets.

$ 675,083	Total assets
× .7	70% written as a decimal
$472,558.10	Line of credit

Round to the nearest dollar. $472,558.10 ≈ $472,558

The company can borrow up to $472,558 using its line of credit.

Exercise A

Use 70% of total assets to find each line of credit. Round money to the nearest dollar.

	ASSETS					Total Assets	Line of Credit
	Inv.	Rec.	Real Estate	Equip.	Cash/ Sav.		
1.	$800,000	$290,000	$1,450,000	$354,000	$125,000	_____	_____
2.	$120,000	$480,000	$45,000	$12,830	$39,290	_____	_____
3.	$73,800	$134,000	$73,380	$8,428	$12,843	_____	_____
4.	$592,438	$537,923	$387,390	$23,842	$93,403	_____	_____
5.	$187,438	$64,892	$873,989	$38,882	$43,254	_____	_____

Exercise B

Find the line of credit using each company's percentage of assets. Round money to the nearest dollar.

	ASSETS					Percentage of Assets	Line of Credit
	Inv.	Rec.	Real Estate	Equip.	Cash/ Sav.		
1.	$23,138	$38,438	$0	$2,871	$93,629	75%	_____
2.	$79,103	$60,393	$369,205	$87,509	$44,397	65%	_____
3.	$230,931	$848,300	$765,378	$24,107	$223,798	68%	_____
4.	$680,013	$312,189	$735,800	$3,099	$87,309	73%	_____
5.	$1,200,000	$800,000	$3,400,000	$80,000	$720,000	71%	_____

A line of credit is a source of short-term borrowed money. The money can be paid back as soon as the company wants to. Paying back money before the loan comes due saves interest expense. In other loans, money must be borrowed for a specific length of time, such as 6 months.

Humor on the Job

How is a finance company like a good movie?

I give up. How?

It keeps your interest.

EXAMPLE	A company has a $200,000 line of credit. It borrows $20,000 at 12% simple interest for 3 months. How much money does it owe at the end of 3 months?

Step 1

Method 1   Use the annual interest rate.

Write 3 months as part of a year.

$$I = \$20,000 \times 12\% \times \frac{3}{12} \rightarrow I = \$20,000 \times .12 \times .25$$

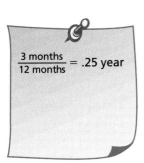

$$\frac{3 \text{ months}}{12 \text{ months}} = .25 \text{ year}$$

	$20,000	Principal
×	.12	Annual interest rate
	$ 2,400	Annual interest
×	.25	Time in years
	$ 600	Total interest

Method 2   Use the monthly interest rate.

Divide 12% by 12 to find the monthly interest rate.

$$I = \$20,000 \times \frac{12\%}{12} \times 3 \rightarrow I = \$20,000 \times .01 \times 3$$

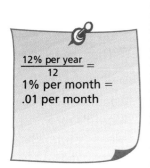

$$\frac{12\% \text{ per year}}{12} =$$
1% per month =
.01 per month

	$20,000	Principal
×	.01	Monthly interest rate
	$ 200	Monthly interest
×	3	Time in months
	$ 600	Total interest

Step 2   Add the interest to the principal.

	$20,000	Principal
+	600	Interest
	$20,600	Total amount owed

The company owes $20,600 at the end of 3 months.

Exercise C   Find the interest and amount owed for each simple interest rate. Round to the nearest dollar.

	Principal	Annual Rate	Time	Interest	Amount Owed
1.	$50,000	12%	1 month	_____	_____
2.	$40,000	8%	6 months	_____	_____
3.	$200,000	15%	4 months	_____	_____
4.	$100,000	10%	9 months	_____	_____
5.	$400,000	24%	5 months	_____	_____

EXAMPLE A company borrows $40,000 using its line of credit. It pays 18% annual interest compounded monthly. How much does the company owe after 2 months?

Step 1 Find the monthly interest rate. Then find the interest for the first month.

Remember

$$\frac{\text{annual interest rate}}{} =$$

monthly interest rate

$I = PRT$

$I = \$40,000 \times \frac{18\%}{12} \times 1$

$I = \$40,000 \times \frac{.18}{12} \times 1$

$I = \$40,000 \times .015 \times 1$

$40,000	Principal
× .015	Monthly rate
$ 600	Monthly interest
× 1	Time in months
$ 600	Interest

Step 2 Add the interest to the principal to find the amount owed after 1 month.

$40,000	Principal
+ 600	Interest after 1 month
$40,600	Amount owed after 1 month

Step 3 Find the interest for the second month.

$I = PRT$

$I = \$40,600 \times .015 \times 1$

$40,600	Amount owed
× .015	Monthly rate
$ 609	Monthly interest
× 1	Time in months
$ 609	Interest

Step 4 Add the interest to the amount owed after 1 month to find the amount owed after 2 months.

$40,600	Amount owed after 1 month
+ 609	Interest
$41,209	Amount owed after 2 months

The company owes $41,209 after 2 months.

Exercise D Find the amount owed after 2 months when interest is compounded monthly. Round money to the nearest dollar.

	Principal	Annual Rate	Amount Owed
1.	$50,000	12%	_____
2.	$50,000	24%	_____
3.	$180,000	15%	_____
4.	$245,600	18%	_____
5.	$600,000	9%	_____

Cash flow

Amount of money that a company receives and pays out in a specific time period

Cash flow statement

Form used to track cash flow over a period of time

Negative cash flow

The cash flow during a period when expenses are greater than revenue

Layoff

Firing employees, often temporarily

Payroll

Total wages paid to employees

Positive cash flow

The cash flow during a period when revenue is greater than expenses

Cash flow is the amount of money that a company receives and pays out over a specific time period. If a company's revenues are greater than its expenses during the same time period, it has a **positive cash flow**. If its expenses are greater than its income during the same time period, it has a **negative cash flow**.

Companies try to control expenses. Expenses such as rent, interest, and taxes are difficult to control. Expenses such as office supplies and business travel are easier to control. **Payroll**, which is the total wages paid to employees, may seem easy to control by **layoffs**. However, union contracts may protect workers from being laid off.

A **cash flow statement** is used to track cash flow over a period of time.

The diagram below shows how cash flows into a company from sales and other income such as investment income. It also shows how cash flows out of a company when expenses are paid.

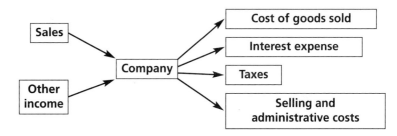

A cash flow statement is shown below. It shows the cash flow in January, and estimates the revenues and expenses for February through July. What is the cash flow for January?

PROJECTED MONTHLY CASH FLOW							
	Jan.	Feb.	Mar.	Apr.	May	June	July
INCOME							
Cash Sales	$5,720	$13,864	$14,072	$7,435	$4,557	$8,650	$12,790
Receivables	$1,500	$2,000	$8,065	$3,172	$960	$1,067	$60,954
Other Income	$837	$719	$1,115	$145	$0	$0	$45
Total Revenue	$8,057						$73,789
EXPENSES							
Inventory	$1,943	$870	$2,964	$4,632	$3,979	$1,719	$612
Payroll	$10,654	$11,064	$10,950	$12,640	$14,675	$13,706	$12,084
Maintenance/Repairs	$527	$0	$214	$912	$2,350	$630	$0
Rent	$1,200	$1,200	$1,200	$1,200	$1,200	$1,200	$1,200
Marketing and Sales	$318	$547	$816	$2,075	$1,840	$1,812	$138
Interest	$333	$333	$333	$333	$333	$333	$333
Total Expenses	$14,975						$14,367
Cash Flow	($6,918)						

Step 1 Find the total revenue for January.
$5,720 + $1,500 + $837 = $8,057

Step 2 Find the total expenses for January.
$1,943 + $10,654 + $527 + $1,200 + $318 + $333 = $14,975

Step 3 Subtract the greater number from the lesser number.

$14,975   Total expenses
− 8,057   Total revenue
$ 6,918   Cash flow

Step 4 Determine whether the cash flow is negative or positive. Compare total revenue to total expenses. $14,975 > $8,057
Expenses are greater than revenues, so the cash flow is negative.

Step 5 Write the cash flow in parentheses on the statement to show that it is negative.

> **Did You Know?**
>
> Bookkeepers and accountants used to write negative cash flows in red ink. Now *in the red* means *in debt*, and negative cash flows are written in parentheses.

The month of January shows a negative cash flow of $6,918.

Exercise A   Use the cash flow statement on page 130 to complete the table below.

Month	Total Revenue	Total Expenses	Difference	Cash Flow
1. February				
2. March				
3. April				
4. May				
5. June				

A company must make a profit in order to stay in business. However, negative cash flows for short periods of time may be necessary when a company is growing. When a company needs more cash, it can use its line of credit.

Remember

Profit =
Revenue − Expenses

$\dfrac{3 \text{ months}}{12 \text{ months}} = .25$ year

EXAMPLE   Look at the cash flow statement on page 130. Suppose the company has a $60,000 line of credit. It will need money to pay expenses for April, May, and June. If the company pays 12% simple annual interest, how much interest will it pay to borrow the money it needs?

Step 1   Add the negative cash flows to find how much money the company needs to borrow.

($11,040)   April
($18,860)   May
+($9,683)   June
($39,583) $39,583 ≈ $40,000

The company needs to borrow $40,000.

Step 2   Find the time period for the loan.

April + May + June = 3 months

Step 3   Find the simple interest for 3 months.

$I = PRT$ $I = \$40,000 \times 12\% \times \dfrac{3}{12}$

$I = \$40,000 \times .12 \times .25 = \$1,200$

It will cost the company $1,200 to borrow $40,000 to meet its expenses in April, May, and June.

Exercise B Find the missing information for August in the cash flow statement below. Use the statement to solve problems 1–4.

PROJECTED MONTHLY CASH FLOW				
	Aug.	Sept.	Oct.	Nov.
INCOME				
Cash Sales	$12,650	$16,970	$70,845	$150,937
Receivables	$4,806	$2,810	$4,732	$10,960
Other Income	$1,374	$1,864	$0	$8,754
Total Revenue		$21,644	$75,577	$170,651
EXPENSES				
Inventory	$4,547	$6,741	$80,652	$5,935
Payroll	$7,650	$7,210	$9,540	$11,670
Maintenance/Repairs	$700	$500	$500	$500
Rent	$4,000	$4,000	$4,000	$4,000
Marketing and Sales	$2,500	$2,500	$4,700	$6,320
Debt Repayment	$1,520	$1,520	$1,520	$1,520
Total Expenses		$22,471	$100,912	$29,945
Cash Flow		($827)	($25,335)	$140,706

1. What is the projected monthly revenue for August? the total projected expenses for August?

2. What is the projected cash flow for August?

3. To the nearest ten thousand dollars, how much money does this company need to borrow to meet its expenses through October?

4. The company borrows the amount of money in problem 3 for 3 months at 12% annual interest compounded monthly. How much money does the company owe at the end of 3 months?

Product payment cost

Cost associated with processing cash, checks, or credit transactions

Product payment costs are expenses associated with processing cash, checks, and credit transactions. For example, the salaries of employees who calculate payroll and process paychecks are product payment costs. When a customer pays with a credit card, the company pays a fee to the credit card company. This fee is also a product payment cost. Companies keep track of product payment costs and include these expenses in their cash flow projections and budgets. Here are some examples of product payment costs:

- Check Processing Fees
- Dishonored Check Fees
- Personnel Costs to Process Checks
- Cash Transactions
- Counterfeit Monies
- Cost of Credit Transactions

EXAMPLE   A company's payroll is $49,973.22. The cost to process paychecks is about 4% of the total payroll. About how much does it cost the company to process paychecks?

Step 1   Round the payroll to the nearest $100.

$49,973.22 ≈ $50,000

Step 2   Find 4% of the payroll.

$50,000	Payroll
× .04	Percent as a decimal
$ 2,000	Cost to process paychecks

It costs the company about $2,000 to process paychecks.

Exercise A   Solve.

1. One month a company has credit card sales of $158,970. The company pays a 1.8% monthly fee on all credit transactions. How much does the company spend for credit card fees?

2. A company spends 3% of its total sales annually for dishonored checks and collection fees. If the projected annual sales are $438,500, how much money is budgeted for dishonored checks and collection fees?

3. A company pays a checking account fee of $18.00 a month plus $.08 for each check it issues. If it issues 1,800 checks in a year, how much does it spend for checking account fees that year?

4. A company spends 1% of its total annual sales to process cash sales. It spends 2.4% of its total annual sales to process checks. If its total annual sales are $873,430, how much more does it cost to process checks than to handle cash sales?

5. Product payment costs are 8.5% of a company's total annual expenses. Its total annual expenses are $155,800. Receiving counterfeit money accounts for 1% of the company's product payment costs. How much does receiving counterfeit money cost the company?

Although product payments are only a small business expense, companies keep track of them so they do not become too great.

EXAMPLE A company estimates a cost of about $22,000 a year to process payments made by check. One year its total annual expenses are $549,783. About what percent of its total annual expenses are for processing checks?

Step 1 Round the total annual expenses to the nearest $1,000.

$549,783 \approx $550,000

Step 2 Write the ratio of the cost to the rounded total expenses.

$\dfrac{\$22,000}{\$550,000}$ Check processing costs
Total annual expenses

Simplify the ratio.

$22,000 \div \dfrac{1,000}{550,000} \div 1,000 = \dfrac{22}{550}$

Step 3 Divide to write the ratio as a decimal. Then write the decimal as a percent.

$\overset{.04}{550\overline{)22.00}}$ $.04 = 4\%$

Step 4 Estimate to check your answer.

The check processing cost is about $20,000.
Total annual expenses are about $500,000.

The ratio of the cost to total expenses is about $\dfrac{\$20,000}{\$500,000}$.

Simplify the ratio.

$\dfrac{\$20,000}{\$500,000} = \dfrac{2}{50} = \dfrac{1}{25}$

Divide to write the ratio as a decimal.

$\overset{.04}{25\overline{)1.00}}$ $.04 = 4\%$

The company spends about 4% of its total annual expenses for processing checks.

Annual Expenses (Total = $300,000)

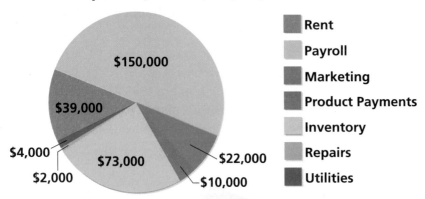

- Rent
- Payroll
- Marketing
- Product Payments
- Inventory
- Repairs
- Utilities

$150,000
$39,000
$4,000
$2,000
$73,000
$22,000
$10,000

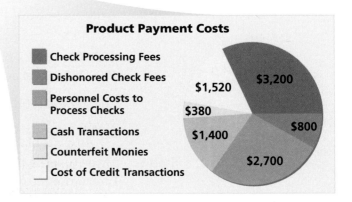

Product Payment Costs

- Check Processing Fees
- Dishonored Check Fees
- Personnel Costs to Process Checks
- Cash Transactions
- Counterfeit Monies
- Cost of Credit Transactions

$1,520
$3,200
$380
$800
$1,400
$2,700

PROBLEM SOLVING

Exercise B   Use the circle graphs above to solve. Round to the nearest hundredth of a percent.

1. About what percent of total annual expenses is for dishonored checks?

2. About what percent of total annual expenses is for processing credit transactions?

3. What percent of payroll is the expense of personnel costs to process paychecks?

4. About what percent of total annual expenses is for product payment costs?

5. Which product payment cost is 14% of the total product payment costs?

Cash Flow: The Key to Business Success

Rosie and Joel run a software development company. They make and sell software for use by accountants and other business people. They started the company three years ago. They have invested nearly all of their own money in the company. Now the venture is about to pay off.

"Joel, we've turned a profit! The business is now officially a success!" Rosie screamed.

Rosie is creative. She is in charge of software development, and she has a right to be proud.

"But we're still short of cash," Joel cautioned. Joel takes care of all the financial matters.

Rosie wondered how that could be true. She picked up a big stack of orders that had arrived that week. "Look at these orders, Joel. And they're still pouring in! Why, these orders alone will mean a big profit for us this year."

Big orders are good news. But orders aren't cash. Joel knows that the business needs cash now. Software development is expensive, and there are big bills to pay.

"First, we'll need to fill those orders. That takes time and money. And customers don't always pay right away, you know. Several months may pass before we get the cash," Joel explained. "Meanwhile, we have bills to pay."

"What can we do?" Rosie asked.

"As I see it, we have two choices. We can borrow cash for a few months. But that's an extra expense, and interest rates are high. We could pay our bills later, when we get the cash. But that would really annoy our creditors."

The two headed out to talk about it over an inexpensive dinner.

For Discussion

1. What are the two choices that Rosie and Joel are considering?
2. What is the main advantage of borrowing money now? What is the main disadvantage? Discuss.
3. What is the main risk in paying the bills late?

Write the letter of the best answer to each question.

1. _____ can be used to find the simple interest on $5,000 borrowed at 12% annual interest for 4 years.

   a. $I = \$5,000 \times 12 \times 4$ **c.** $I = \$5,000 \times .01 \times 4$

   b. $I = \$5,000 \times .12 \times 4$

2. A company pays _____ in interest if it borrows $2,000 for 4 years at 7% annual simple interest.

   a. $5,600   **b.** $560   **c.** $420   **d.** $140.28

3. _____ can be used to find the interest for 1 month if a company borrows $1,000 at 12% annual interest.

   a. $I = \$1,000 \times .12 \times 1$ **c.** $I = \$1,000 \times .01 \times 1$

   b. $I = \$1,000 \times .01 \times 12$

4. A company owes _____ after $2\frac{1}{2}$ years if it borrows $4,000 at an annual simple interest rate of 10%.

   a. $1,000   **b.** $2,500   **c.** $4,500   **d.** $5,000

Solve problems 5–9.

5. A company borrows $8,000 at an annual interest rate of 18%. If the interest is compounded semiannually, how much does the company owe after 1 year?

6. A company's assets are valued at $500,000. If its line of credit is 75% of its assets, what is the most money that it can borrow?

7. A company's assets are valued at $150,000. Its line of credit is 60% of its assets. The company borrows the greatest possible amount of money for 3 months at 15% annual simple interest. How much does it pay in interest?

8. A company borrows $3,000 at an annual interest rate of 18% compounded monthly. This is how Joe found the amount the company owes after 1 month:
   ($3,000 × .18 × 1) + $3,000 = $3,540
   What did Joe do wrong? What is the actual amount owed after 1 month?

9. A company uses its line of credit to borrow $10,000. The bank charges 20% annual interest compounded semiannually. How much money is owed at the end of 2 years?

Use the cash flow statement below for problems 10–13.

PROJECTED MONTHLY CASH FLOW				
	May	June	July	August
INCOME				
Cash Sales	$3,800	$2,200	$1,000	$6,000
Receivables	$450	$450	$450	$8,450
Other Income	$200	$550	$0	$1,200
Total Revenue	$4,450	$3,200	$1,450	$15,650
EXPENSES				
Inventory	$800	$2,300	$3,800	$2,800
Payroll	$2,800	$2,370	$2,700	$3,100
Rent	$600	$600	$600	$600
Marketing and Sales	$100	$150	$600	$500
Total Expenses	$4,300	$5,420	$7,700	$7,000
Cash Flow	$150		($6,250)	$8,650

10. What is the cash flow for the month of June?

Test-Taking Tip

11. For which months is a positive cash flow projected?

12. For which months is a negative cash flow projected?

In problems where you use a formula to find the answer, write the formula before starting to calculate. For example, write $I = PRT$ before you multiply the numbers to find the interest.

13. What is the combined cash flow for May through August?

Solve problems 14–15.

14. It costs a company about 2% of its annual payroll to process paychecks. If the annual payroll is $500,000, about how much does the company spend to process paychecks?

15. A department store spends $8,100 for the month of July in fees for processing credit card purchases. If the credit card purchases for July are $270,000, what percentage of this total are fees for processing credit card purchases?

Operating Expenses

Operating expenses are administrative costs of running a business. All businesses have operating expenses. They may be for employee salaries, renting space to do business, or transportation. Companies and industries spend different amounts and percents for operating expenses. Knowing how to calculate operating expenses is an important part of managing a company's finances.

In this chapter, you will learn about different types of operating expenses. You will also practice the math skills that companies use to calculate and analyze their operating expenses.

Goals for Learning

▶ To determine the percent of a company's income required for salaries

▶ To determine the different costs of benefits for small, medium, and large companies

▶ To determine office space needed based on the number of employees

▶ To calculate the costs of computers and software programs for one department of a company

▶ To calculate transportation costs

▶ To determine the fraction of total operating expenses spent for transportation

Operating expense

Administrative cost not directly related to manufacturing or marketing a product

Operating expenses are the administrative costs of running a business. They include costs such as rent, utilities, and advertising. One of a company's greatest operating expenses is employee salaries. The expense for salaries is often given as a percent of the company's income.

EXAMPLE | A company's annual income is $1,000,000. It spends $400,000 annually on employee salaries. What percent of the company's income is required for employee salaries?

Step 1 | Write a ratio comparing the part of the annual income spent on salaries to the whole annual income.

$$\frac{part}{whole} = \frac{Employee\ salaries}{Annual\ income} = \frac{\$400,000}{\$1,000,000}$$

Step 2 | Simplify the fraction, then write it as a decimal.

$$\frac{400,000 \div 100,000}{1,000,000 \div 100,000} = \frac{4}{10}$$

$$\begin{array}{r} .4 \\ 10\overline{)4.0} \\ \underline{4\ 0} \end{array}$$

Step 3 | Write the decimal as a percent.

.40 = 40.% = 40%

Paying employee salaries takes 40% of the company's income.

Remember

A percent symbol has 2 zeros. To change a decimal to a percent, move the decimal point to the right 2 places and write the percent symbol.

EXAMPLE   Company A spends $\frac{3}{16}$ of its annual income on employee salaries. Company B spends $\frac{1}{6}$ of its annual income on employee salaries. Which company spends a greater fraction of its annual income on salaries? How much greater?

Step 1   Find the LCD of $\frac{3}{16}$ and $\frac{1}{6}$. List the multiples of each denominator.

16, 32, **48**, 64, . . .

6, 12, 18, 24, 30, 36, 42, **48**, . . .

Step 2   Write $\frac{3}{16}$ and $\frac{1}{6}$ as equivalent fractions with 48 as the denominator.

$$\frac{3}{16} = \frac{3 \times 3}{16 \times 3} = \frac{9}{48}$$

$$\frac{1}{6} = \frac{1 \times 8}{6 \times 8} = \frac{8}{48}$$

Step 3   Compare the fractions.

$9 > 8$, so $\frac{9}{48} > \frac{8}{48}$ and $\frac{3}{16} > \frac{1}{6}$.

Step 4   Subtract the fractions.

$$\frac{9}{48} - \frac{8}{48} = \frac{1}{48}$$

Company A spends $\frac{1}{48}$ more of its annual income on employee salaries than Company B does.

TRY THIS...

A company's annual income is $1,000,000. It spends $320,000 annually on employee salaries. The company wants to spend 30% of its income on salaries. How much less should it spend on employee salaries?

Exercise A   Find the percent of income required for employee salaries.

Total Income	Employee Salaries	Ratio	Percent
1. $100,000	$35,000	__ _____	_____
2. $400,000	$100,000	_____	_____
3. $870,000	$330,600	_____	_____
4. $500,000	$162,500	_____	_____
5. $3,800,000	$1,014,600	_____	_____

Unemployment insurance

Insurance coverage that pays money to employees who are laid off

Workers' compensation

Insurance coverage that pays money to employees who cannot work because of job-related injuries

Employee benefits are also operating expenses. Some benefits are required by law. These benefits are federal and state **unemployment insurance**, social security, and **workers' compensation**. Unemployment insurance pays monthly income to employees who are laid off. Workers' compensation pays monthly income to employees who cannot work because they were injured on the job. Companies may or may not provide benefits such as paid vacations, sick leave, health and life insurance, and pension plans.

The bar graph below compares the average costs of different employee benefits for small, medium, and large companies. The bars show the average cost of the benefit for each hour an employee works.

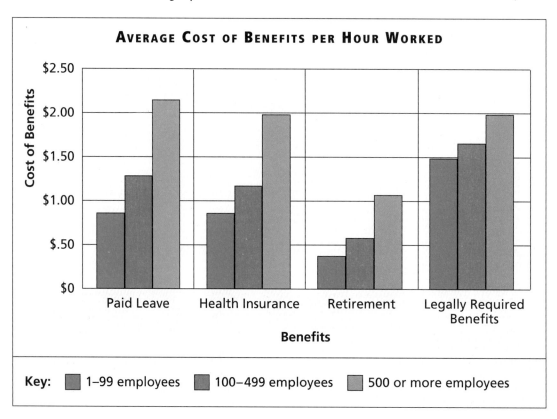

EXAMPLE A small company has 5 employees. The employees work a total of 10,000 hours annually. How much does the company spend for the benefits shown on the bar graph on page 144?

Step 1   Add to find the total amount spent for employee benefits per hour worked.

$\begin{array}{rl}
\$\ \ .90 & \text{Paid leave} \\
.90 & \text{Health insurance} \\
.40 & \text{Retirement} \\
+1.50 & \text{Legally required benefits} \\
\hline
\$\ 3.70 & \text{Cost of benefits per hour worked}
\end{array}$

Step 2   Multiply by the total number of hours worked.

$\begin{array}{rl}
10,000 & \text{Total hours worked} \\
\times\ \$3.70 & \text{Cost of benefits per hour worked} \\
\hline
\$37,000 & \text{Total cost of employee benefits}
\end{array}$

A small company whose employees work 10,000 hours annually spends $37,000 for employee benefits.

PROBLEM SOLVING

Exercise B   Use the bar graph on page 144 to solve.

1. How much does a large company with 500 or more employees spend per hour worked for employee benefits?

2. A small company has 81 employees. How much less does it spend per hour worked for paid leave than a large company?

3. A company has 320 employees who work a total of 400,000 hours annually. How much does it spend for health insurance?

4. A medium-sized company has 250 employees. How much more does it spend per hour worked for voluntarily provided benefits than for legally required benefits?

5. A company has 762 employees who work a total of 1.5 million hours annually. How much does it spend for retirement and health insurance?

Square foot (ft.²)

A measure of the area of a square with 1-foot sides

A company may rent, lease, or own its building. The cost of office space is an operating expense. In order to control costs, a company determines how much office space it needs. The amount of office space needed depends on the number of employees using the space. Employees earning more money usually have larger offices.

Office space is measured in square units. A **square foot (ft.²)** is the area of a square with 1-foot sides.

EXAMPLE   A marketing firm makes a table of the office space it needs. How many square feet of office space does it need?

	Senior Managers	Directors	Managers	Staff	Lunchroom	Supply Room
Area per person (ft.²)	500	300	200	85	20	10
Number of people	3	9	20	250		

Step 1   Add to find the total number of employees.

        3 Senior managers
        9 Directors
       20 Managers
     +250 Staff
      282 Number of employees

Step 2   Find the total number of square feet needed.

Senior managers	500×3	=	1,500
Directors	300×9	=	2,700
Managers	200×20	=	4,000
Staff	85×250	=	21,250
Lunchroom	282×20	=	5,640
Supply room	282×10	=	+2,820
Total square feet needed			37,910

The company needs 37,910 square feet of office space.

Exercise A   Find the area of office space in square feet that each company needs.

SENIOR MANAGERS		DIRECTORS		MANAGERS		STAFF				
Area	No.	Area	No.	Area	No.	Area	No.	Lunchroom (area per employee)	Other Common Areas (area per employee)	Total Square Feet Needed
1. 750	1	600	1	240	3	120	9	55	25	_____
2. 600	1	420	1	180	10	60	38	15	20	_____
3. 300	2	400	4	125	8	25	45	8	15	_____
4. 520	3	375	10	95	12	75	60	22	32	_____
5. 475	3	210	15	100	40	45	285	20	10	_____

Technology Connection

Using a Calculator for Financial Analysis

The table below lists a company's operating expenses. Companies find each expense as a percent of the total operating expenses. They compare expense percents from year to year. A big change in a percent makes a company examine the expense more closely. Companies also compare their percents to the percents of other companies in the same industry. Spending a higher percent than the industry average for any expense warns a company to check its expense.

Complete the table using a calculator. Find each expense as a percent of total expenses. First add the expenses to find the total expenses. Store this number in the memory by pressing M+ . Press AC to clear the display. Then divide each expense by the total expenses stored in memory. Use the MR (memory recall) key and this keystroke sequence:
[expense amount] ÷ MR = % .
Round to the nearest whole percent.

Expense	Amount	Percent of Total Expenses
Salaries	$414,578	
Benefits	$134,809	
Building facility	$289,873	
Insurance	$89,734	
Advertising/marketing	$54,392	
Transportation	$58,325	
Equipment	$29,112	
Total expenses		

Buying office equipment is another operating expense. Most businesses buy computers, printers, and software. The cost of office equipment is related to the number of office employees.

EXAMPLE A company buys new computers for each of its 8 human resource specialists. Each computer costs $1,895. It also buys 6 software programs for $129 each. How much do the computers and software cost?

Step 1 Estimate the total cost.

Round the dollar amounts.

$1,895 ≈ $2,000 $129 ≈ $100

Multiply the cost by the number needed.

$ 2,000 Estimated cost per computer $100 Estimated cost of software
×   8 Number of computers needed   × 6 Number of programs needed
$16,000 Estimated cost of computers $600 Estimated cost of software

Add to find the total estimated cost.

$16,000 + $600 = about $16,600

Step 2 Find the total cost of the computers.

$ 1,895 Cost of 1 computer
×   8 Number of computers needed
$15,160 Total cost of computers

Step 3 Find the total cost of the software.

$129 Cost of 1 software program
× 6 Number of software programs needed
$774 Total cost of software

Step 4 Add to find the total cost.

$15,160 Cost of computers
+   774 Cost of software
$15,934 Total cost

The total cost of the equipment is $15,934. The answer is close to the estimate of $16,600, so it is reasonable.

Exercise B   Use the information below to solve.

CALL COMPUTER	CALL COMPUTER	BRAINWAVE COMPUTERS	MICROTECH COMPUTER
• Model 1100 • 440 mHz processor • 12″ screen • 56K modem w/ printer • Price: **$1,495**	• Model 1400 • 660 mHz processor • 14″ screen • 56K modem w/ printer • Price: **$2,249**	• Models 154, 184, 194 • 56K fax/modem • 660 mHz processor w/ printer • Price: **$2,120**	• Model 97zx • 56K fax/modem • 880 mHz processor • Price: **$2,095** w/ printer: **$2,435**

Software	Price per Package	Price per Package of 10
Firefly	$89	$640
Office Mate	$169	$1,390
Quick Flash	$279*	$2,390**
Zenith Power Plus	$189	$1,590
Cameo Deluxe	$425	$3,950

*$40 rebate for owners of earlier versions   **$400 rebate for owners of earlier versions

1. A company buys 3 Brainwave computers, 8 copies of Cameo Deluxe, and 15 copies of Zenith Power Plus. What is the best price for this equipment?

2. How much more do 5 Call Model 1400 computers cost than 5 Call Model 1100 computers?

3. A company needs 8 copies of Firefly. Which costs less, buying 8 copies or buying a package of 10? how much less?

4. An accounting department has 32 employees. It needs 1 Microtech computer for each employee and 1 new printer for every 4 computers. It also needs 1 copy of Office Mate. How much does this equipment cost?

5. A company buys 12 Brainwave computers and 8 Call Model 1400 computers. It also buys 16 copies of Quick Flash. All 16 copies replace earlier versions of Quick Flash. What is the best price for the computers and software?

Did You Know?

An office building is being constructed. Each floor is square, 100 feet by 100 feet. It will stand five stories tall. Surprisingly, all the office space in the building would fit easily into the area of one football field.

Depreciation

Distribution of the cost of an asset over its useful life

Many companies provide cars for employees whose jobs require frequent car travel. Employees who have company cars may use them for personal use as well. Most companies pay for the maintenance and insurance of company cars. They also reimburse employees for gas bought on business trips. Companies divide the cost of their cars by the number of years the cars will be used. This cost is an annual **depreciation** expense for the company.

EXAMPLE A company's sales force uses 12 company cars. The table below shows the monthly costs of maintaining and operating these cars. Find the company's total monthly transportation expense.

Average Monthly Mileage	Gas Cost (per mile)	Maintenance/ Repair (per mile)	Insurance Cost (per car)	Depreciation Cost (per mile)
10,000	$.05	$.28	$279	$.35

Method 1

Step 1 Find the cost for each expense category.

Gas $.05 × 10,000 = $500
Maintenance/repair $.28 × 10,000 = $2,800
Insurance $279 × 12 = $3,348
Depreciation $.35 × 10,000 = $3,500

Each mile that a car is driven reduces the value of the car. You can think of depreciation as the steady loss in value of an asset.

Step 2 Add to find the monthly transportation expense.

$ 500   Gas
2,800   Maintenance/repair
3,348   Insurance
+ 3,500   Depreciation
$10,148   Monthly transportation expense

Method 2

Step 1   Add the per-mile costs. $.05 Gas
                                      .28 Maintenance/repair
                                    +.35 Depreciation
                                    $.68 Transportation cost per mile

Step 2   Multiply to find the total cost for 10,000 miles and the insurance for 12 cars.

10,000 Miles driven $ 279 Insurance cost per car
×$ .68 Cost per mile   ×   12 Number of cars
$6,800 Total mileage cost $3,348 Total insurance cost

Step 3   Add to find the monthly transportation expense.

$ 6,800 Total mileage cost
+ 3,348 Total insurance cost
$10,148 Monthly transportation expense

The company's monthly transportation expense is $10,148.

Exercise A   Find each monthly transportation expense. Use one method to solve.
Use the other method to check your work.

Number of Cars	Average Monthly Mileage	Gas (per mile)	Maintenance/ Repair (per mile)	Insurance (per car)	Depreciation (per mile)	Monthly Transportation Expense
1. 60	30,000	$.05	$.30	$157	$.38	_____
2. 32	12,000	$.08	$.18	$228	$.31	_____
3. 15	11,800	$.12	$.28	$309	$.45	_____
4. 120	144,000	$.04	$.20	$129	$.25	_____
5. 870	522,000	$.06	$.22	$98	$.51	_____

TRY THIS...

The company in which problem of Exercise A has the greatest
monthly transportation expense per car?

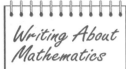
Transportation costs can be written as a fraction of the total operating expenses. This fraction can be used to estimate future transportation costs. It also can be used to compare transportation costs among companies.

EXAMPLE A company spends $\frac{3}{16}$ of its annual operating expenses on transportation. One year the company budgets $438,640 for operating expenses. How much money is in the budget for transportation?

Find $\frac{3}{16}$ of $438,640. *Of* means *multiply*.

$$\frac{3}{16} \times \frac{438,640}{1} = \frac{3 \times 438,640}{16 \times 1} = \frac{1,315,920}{16}$$

$$16\overline{)1,315,920} \quad \frac{82,245}{}$$

The company budgets $82,245 for transportation.

Exercise B Find each company's transportation costs.

Company	Fraction of Operating Expenses for Transportation	Operating Expenses Budget	Transportation Budget
1. Becker Insurance	$\frac{1}{10}$	$400,000	_____
2. Taylor Florist	$\frac{1}{5}$	$750,000	_____
3. Merry Cleaners	$\frac{3}{10}$	$150,000	_____
4. Medical Delivery Co.	$\frac{2}{5}$	$45,750	_____
5. Tale Realty	$\frac{3}{8}$	$1,200,000	_____

TRY THIS...

Order the companies in problems 1–5 from the least to greatest fraction of operating expense for transportation. Then order the companies from the least to greatest amount budgeted for transportation.

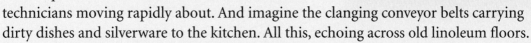

Improving FasTrak's Lunchroom

FasTrak, Inc. assembles computers. The company owns a medium-sized plant with about 90 employees per shift. The workers, mostly technicians, are well educated and well paid.

FasTrak enjoys a good reputation in the community. It is considered an attractive place to work. The benefits and working conditions are quite good.

There is just one problem—the noise in the 1,350-square-foot lunchroom! Picture dozens of technicians moving rapidly about. And imagine the clanging conveyor belts carrying dirty dishes and silverware to the kitchen. All this, echoing across old linoleum floors.

"We have to quiet things down in here," complained Art, the plant manager. "Let's install carpeting in the lunchroom."

"You're right, Art," came the president's reply. "I've put it off long enough. We can afford it now. A quieter lunchroom will benefit everyone."

"Not only quieter, but also safer. But it's expensive. It'll run about $40 per square yard installed."

The president started calculating out loud. "Let's see, 1,350 square feet . . . divided by 3 . . . times 40 dollars . . ."

Art interrupted, "No boss, don't divide by 3. It's expensive, but not that expensive. There are 9 square feet in a square yard."

The president was embarrassed. "That's why you're the plant manager. Let's go get some lunch."

For Discussion

1. What common arithmetic error did the president make?

2. Find the total cost of installing carpeting in the lunchroom. Explain how you arrived at the figure.

3. Explain how to find the number of square feet in 1 square yard.

Write the letter of the best answer to each question.

1. A company spends $320,000 on employee salaries. If its total income is $800,000, what percentage of its income is required for employee salaries?

   a. 32%   **b.** 40%   **c.** 50%   **d.** 80%

2. A company spends $1.50 per hour worked for paid leave. Its employees work 420,000 hours annually. How much does the company spend for paid leave?

   a. $150,000   **b.** $220,000   **c.** $420,000   **d.** $630,000

3. A company leases an average of 75 square feet of office space for each employee. If there are 22 employees, how many square feet of office space does the company lease?

   a. 1,650 ft.^{2} **b.** 1,600 ft.^{2} **c.** 970 ft.^{2} **d.** 97 ft.^{2}

Use the bar graph for problems 4–5.

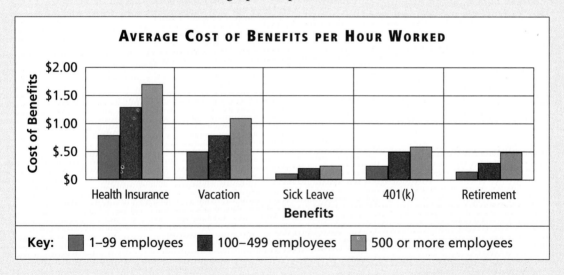

4. How much does an average company with 350 employees spend per hour worked on vacation and sick leave?

5. How much less does an average small company spend per hour worked on retirement than on 401(k) benefits?

Use the table below for problems 6–7.

OFFICE SPACE FOR THE BEECHER COMPANY						
	Senior Managers	Directors	Managers	Staff	Lunchroom	Supply Room
Area per person (ft.²)	450	275	240	90	40	15
Number of people	2	4	17	120		

6. How many square feet are for the lunchroom and supply room?

7. How many square feet of office space does The Beecher Company have?

Solve problems 8–10.

8. A company buys the following office equipment:
- 18 computers for $1,389 each
- 6 printers for $345 each
- 18 software programs for $289 each or 10 for $2,459

What is the best price for this equipment?

9. A company spends $\frac{2}{7}$ of its operating expenses on transportation. If the total operating expenses are $1,820,000, how much is spent on transportation?

10. Company A spends $\frac{2}{5}$ of its operating expenses on transportation. Company B spends $\frac{3}{7}$ of its operating expenses on transportation. Which company spends a greater fraction of its operating expenses on transportation?

Test-Taking Tip If you know two ways to solve a problem, solve it using one method, and check your answer using the other method.

Chapter
8

Business Management

Businesses want to manage the costs of production, marketing, selling, and inventory efficiently. They use charts and graphs to show changes over time and to compare data. Businesses analyze data often.

In this chapter, you will calculate business costs and use charts and graphs to analyze business data. You will also find percents of increase or decrease.

Goals for Learning

▶ To read, interpret, compare, and create graphs showing production costs

▶ To determine the costs of marketing and selling a product

▶ To calculate the value and turnover rate of inventory

▶ To calculate profit and loss

▶ To read and interpret charts showing profit and loss

Cost of production

Expense of manufacturing a product

Fixed cost

Cost that remains the same however many units are produced

Output

Number of units produced

Variable cost

Cost that changes with the number of units produced

Cost of production is the expense of manufacturing a product. Production costs can be **fixed costs** or **variable costs**. Fixed costs are the same however many units are produced. Rent on a plant that manufactures bricks is a fixed cost. The rent is the same whether 1 brick or 300,000 bricks are produced. Variable costs, such as materials for production, change with the **output**, or number of units produced. A line graph can be used to show the relationship between costs and output.

EXAMPLES | The line graph on page 159 shows three relationships. One line shows the relationship between output and fixed costs. Another line shows the relationship between output and variable costs. The third line shows the relationship between output and total costs. What is the fixed cost to produce 200 units? 2,000 units?

Step 1   Find 200 on the "Output" axis.

Step 2   Move directly up to the *Fixed Costs* line.

Step 3   Look directly to the left for the value on the "Production Cost" axis. The production cost on the fixed costs graph is $1,000 for an output of 200.

Fixed costs are $1,000 to produce 200 units.

Repeat Steps 1–3 to find the fixed costs of producing 2,000 units. The production cost on the fixed costs graph is $1,000 for an output of 2,000. Fixed costs are $1,000 to produce 2,000 units.

What is the total cost of producing 400 units?

Step 1   Find 400 on the "Output" axis.

Step 2   Move directly up to the *Total Costs* line.

Step 3   Look directly to the left for the value on the "Production Cost" axis. The production cost on the total costs graph is $1,400 for an output of 400.

Total costs are $1,400 to produce 400 units.

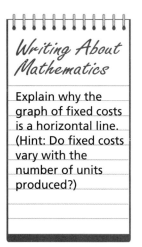

Writing About Mathematics

Explain why the graph of fixed costs is a horizontal line. (Hint: Do fixed costs vary with the number of units produced?)

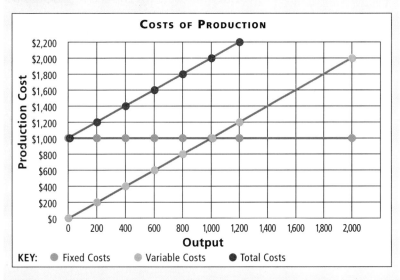

COSTS OF PRODUCTION

Production Cost (y-axis): $0, $200, $400, $600, $800, $1,000, $1,200, $1,400, $1,600, $1,800, $2,000, $2,200

Output (x-axis): 0, 200, 400, 600, 800, 1,000, 1,200, 1,400, 1,600, 1,800, 2,000

KEY: ● Fixed Costs ● Variable Costs ● Total Costs

PROBLEM SOLVING

Exercise A   Use the graph above for problems 1–5.

1. What is the variable cost to produce 2,000 units?

2. What is the variable cost to produce 200 units? the total cost to produce 200 units?

3. How much more is the total cost to produce 1,200 units than the total cost to produce 600 units?

4. How much more is the variable cost to produce 1,200 units than the variable cost to produce 600 units?

5. What is the total cost to produce 2,000 units? Use the graph of fixed costs and variable costs.

TRY THIS...

Suppose the variable cost is $2 per unit and the fixed cost is $1,000. What is the total cost to produce 2,500 units?

You can use a **double bar graph** to compare fixed and variable production costs for different times of the year. A double bar graph compares two sets of data using two bars.

EXAMPLE   Make a vertical double bar graph to show J & P's fixed and variable costs for January through June.

J & P TENNIS SHOE MANUFACTURING PRODUCTION COSTS, 1/02–6/02						
Costs	January	February	March	April	May	June
Fixed costs	$10,000	$10,000	$10,000	$10,000	$10,000	$10,000
Variable costs	$15,000	$20,000	$25,000	$30,000	$40,000	$50,000

Step 1   Choose a scale.

The dollar amounts in the table range from $10,000 to $50,000. Mark off the vertical axis in $5,000 units from $0 to $50,000.

Step 2   Label the vertical and horizontal axes.

The horizontal axis shows the month of production. Label it "Month." The vertical axis shows costs of production. Label it "Production Cost."

Step 3   Draw bars to represent the data.

There are two production costs each month. Draw a bar for fixed costs in one color, such as blue. Draw a bar for variable costs in another color, such as red.

Step 4   Give the graph a title. Use the company name and the dates in the title.

Title the graph "J & P Production Costs, January 2002–June 2002."

Step 5   Make a key that shows what the different colors represent.

The key tells that the blue bar represents fixed costs and the red bar represents variable costs.

The graph on the top of page 161 is an example of how the graph might look.

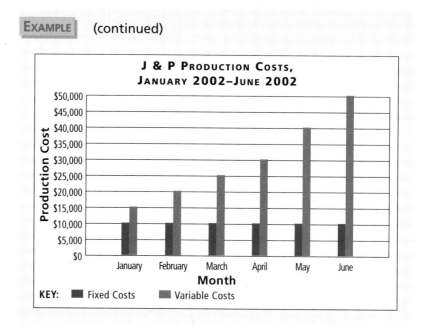

J & P Production Costs, January 2002–June 2002

Exercise B   Make a horizontal double bar graph to show Royal Court's fixed and variable production costs for September through February.

ROYAL COURT TENNIS RACQUET MANUFACTURING PRODUCTION COSTS, 9/02–2/03						
Costs	Sept.	Oct.	Nov.	Dec.	Jan.	Feb.
Fixed	$5,000	$5,000	$5,000	$5,000	$5,000	$5,000
Variable	$40,000	$25,000	$20,000	$20,000	$35,000	$30,000

Marketing

All business activity that gets goods and services from the producer to the consumer

The money a company spends to sell its products is called the cost of sales, or **marketing** cost. Marketing is all business activity that gets goods and services from the producer to the consumer. Some examples of marketing costs are advertising, catalogs, product packaging, and trade shows and exhibits. The kinds of marketing costs vary from business to business.

EXAMPLES The table below shows the marketing expenses and sales for the Fun and Sun Travel Company. What is the total marketing cost for the first quarter of 2002?

FUN AND SUN TRAVEL COMPANY MARKETING EXPENSES, 2002				
Marketing Expense	First Quarter	Second Quarter	Third Quarter	Fourth Quarter
Advertising	$52,000	$33,000	$87,000	$62,000
Literature	$7,000	$5,000	$10,000	$10,000
Web sites	$3,000	$11,800	$5,500	$8,700
Promotions	$1,000	$0	$3,000	$1,000
Service	$4,000	$5,000	$5,000	$6,000
Other	$3,000	$3,000	$3,000	$3,000
Total marketing expenses	?????	$57,800	$113,500	$90,700
Total sales	$1,400,000	$1,200,000	$1,800,000	$1,500,000

(continued)

Add to find the total marketing expenses.

$52,000	Advertising
7,000	Literature
3,000	Web sites
1,000	Promotions
4,000	Service
+ 3,000	Other
$70,000	Total marketing expenses

The Fun and Sun Travel Company spends $70,000 on marketing costs in the first quarter of 2002.

Total marketing expenses are what percentage of total sales for the first quarter of 2002?

Step 1 Find the ratio of marketing expenses to total sales for the first quarter. Simplify the ratio.

$$\frac{\$70,000}{\$1,400,000} \quad \text{Total marketing expenses} \atop \text{Total sales} \quad \rightarrow \quad \frac{7}{140}$$

> Divide numerator and denominator by 10,000 by moving each decimal point 4 places to the left.

Step 2 Write the fraction as a decimal.

$$\begin{array}{r} .05 \\ 140\overline{)7.00} \\ -7\,00 \end{array}$$

Step 3 Write the decimal as a percent.

$$.05 = 05.\% = 5\%$$

The Fun and Sun Travel Company spends 5% of its sales on marketing expenses in the first quarter of 2002.

Humor on the Job

Gil started his own company. He manufactures sails for sailboats, and is very successful. A reporter asked him for the secret of his success. He replied, "Keeping down the cost of sails."

Exercise A   Complete the table. Then use the table for problems 9–10. Round to the nearest whole percent.

CITY VIEW 3/01/02–6/30/02				
Marketing Expense	March	April	May	June
Local TV	$0	$2,546	$0	$2,546
Magazines	$528	$528	$528	$528
Local newspapers	$290	$290	$290	$290
Local radio	$585	$585	$585	$585
City View special events	$1,275	$0	$1,415	$0
Customer happiness representative	$1,750	$1,750	$1,750	$1,750
Total marketing expenses	1.	2.	3.	4.
Total Sales	$17,712	$29,995	$26,870	$37,993
Percentage of Sales for Marketing	5.	6.	7.	8.

9. In which month did City View spend the greatest percentage of sales for marketing expenses?

10. In which month was the ratio of total marketing expenses to total sales the least?

Technology Connection

Marketing Plans on the Internet

You can find sample marketing plans for different types of businesses at the Web site *http://www.bplans.com/marketingplans/*. Find "Sample Marketing Plans" near the top center of the page. Select a company. Then click "go." On the company's page, under "Plan Outline," click "4.0 Financials." You can read financial plans for your sample company. Review the plans. Then answer these questions:

1. What are the categories of financial information?

2. What types of charts and graphs are shown?

3. What is the marketing budget of the company you selected?

4. Choose one of the bar graphs. What information is in the graph?

Exercise B Complete the table. Then use the table for problems 19–20. Round to the nearest tenth of a percent.

BACHMAN FINANCIAL CONSULTING, INC. THIRD QUARTER, 2002				
Marketing Expense	July	August	September	Totals
TV advertising	$580,000	$580,000	$580,000	**1.**
Radio advertising	$246,000	$246,000	$246,000	**2.**
Newspaper advertising	$105,200	$105,200	$105,200	**3.**
Graphics and printing	$84,730	$41,630	$15,790	**4.**
Public relations	$28,700	$0	$12,730	**5.**
Travel	$3,940	$4,115	$0	**6.**
Web sites	$5,060	$5,060	$5,060	**7.**
Seminars	$10,750	$0	$0	**8.**
Telemarketing	$63,640	$67,920	$72,590	**9.**
Market research	$8,195	$5,230	$7,440	**10.**
Total marketing expenses	**11.**	**12.**	**13.**	**14.**
Total Sales	$12,800,000	$9,200,000	$11,600,000	$33,600,000
Percentage of Sales for Marketing	**15.**	**16.**	**17.**	**18.**

19. Which was the greatest marketing expense in the third quarter? the least?

20. What was the average monthly marketing expense?

Average cost method

A method of calculating the value of an inventory using the average cost of all items in the inventory

Inventory valuation

The process of determining the value of an inventory

Inventory is an important business asset. The process of determining the value of an inventory is called **inventory valuation**. There are several different methods of inventory valuation. All require keeping accurate records. The **average cost method** uses the average cost of all similar items to determine the value of the inventory.

EXAMPLE   The table below shows the number and cost of bicycles purchased by a sporting goods store during May. At the end of May, 25 bikes are in stock. What is the value of the inventory on May 31?

Date	Inventory	Unit Cost	Total Cost
Beginning inventory	12	$180	$2,160
May 10 purchase	28	$162	$4,536
May 19 purchase	20	$198	$3,960
Totals	60		$10,656

Step 1   Find the average cost of the 60 bikes.

$$\text{Average cost} = \frac{\$10,656}{60} \quad \begin{array}{l}\text{Total cost}\\ \text{Number of bikes}\end{array}$$

$177.6 = $177.60

$$\begin{array}{r} \$177.6 \qquad \$177.60 \\ 60\overline{)\$10656.0} \\ -\ 60 \\ \overline{465} \\ -420 \\ \overline{456} \\ -420 \\ \overline{36\ 0} \\ -36\ 0 \\ \hline \end{array}$$

Step 2   Multiply the average cost by the number of bikes in inventory.

$$\begin{array}{r} \$\ 177.60 \quad \text{Average cost} \\ \times\quad\ 25 \quad \text{Bikes in inventory on May 31} \\ \hline \$4,440.00 \quad \text{Value of inventory} \end{array}$$

The value of the inventory on May 31 is $4,440.

Exercise A Complete the table below to find the average value of the inventory. Round to the nearest cent.

Date	Inventory	Unit Cost	Total Value
Beginning inventory	150	$49	$7,350
November 9 purchase	275	$35	**1.**
November 18 purchase	240	$40	**2.**
November 29 purchase	180	$45	**3.**
Totals	845		**4.**

Average Cost of Inventory: **5.** _____

Exercise B Complete the table. Find the average cost. Find the value of the inventory at the end of the month, when 72 items are in stock. Round to the nearest cent.

Date	Inventory	Unit Cost	Total Value
Beginning inventory	190	$55	**1.**
March 15 purchase	45	$95	**2.**
March 22 purchase	20	$100	**3.**
Totals	255		$16,725

Average Cost of Inventory: **4.** _____

Value of Inventory: **5.** _____

Inventory turnover

Number of times inventory is replaced during a given period of time

An important part of managing a business is choosing the amount of inventory. If inventory is too low, there may not be enough goods to satisfy customer demand. However, money invested in inventory takes cash that would otherwise be available for other things.

Businesses want to keep inventories low enough to avoid unnecessary costs, such as costs for storage of outdated goods. **Inventory turnover** is the number of times a business replaces its inventory during a given period of time.

Cost of goods sold

Cost of manufacturing or buying the product that is sold

The **cost of goods sold** is the cost of manufacturing or buying the product that is sold. The inventory turnover is the ratio of the cost of goods sold to the value of the inventory.

$$\text{Inventory turnover} = \frac{\text{Cost of goods sold}}{\text{Value of inventory}}$$

EXAMPLE Last year the cost of goods sold by a clothing store was $856,400. The value of the inventory at the beginning of the year was $185,000. At the end of the year it was $243,800. What is the annual inventory turnover?

Step 1 Find the average inventory value.

$$\frac{\$185,000 + \$243,800}{2} = \frac{\$428,800}{2} = \$214,400$$

Step 2 Divide the cost of goods sold by the average value of the inventory. Round to the nearest whole number.

$$\frac{\$856,400}{\$214,400} \approx 4$$

An inventory turnover of 4 means that inventory is replaced every 12 ÷ 4 or 3 months.

Exercise C Find the average inventory value.

	Beginning Inventory	Ending Inventory	Average Inventory
1.	$8,200	$6,650	_____
2.	$13,450	$22,310	_____
3.	$43,190	$54,200	_____
4.	$383,304	$873,538	_____
5.	$42,539	$30,896	_____

Exercise D Find the inventory turnover. Round to the nearest tenth.

	Average Inventory	Cost of Goods Sold	Inventory Turnover
1.	$87,240	$305,340	_____
2.	$264,210	$2,007,996	_____
3.	$14,950	$86,170	_____
4.	$597,315	$1,533,556	_____
5.	$14,780,000	$52,835,000	_____

PROBLEM SOLVING

Exercise E Solve. Round answers to the nearest tenth.

1. The cost of goods sold at Golf Galaxy was $913,100 in 2002. On January 1 the inventory was $123,700. On December 31 the inventory was $107,800. What was the inventory turnover?

2. The inventory for Cleo's Salon was $2,540 on February 1. On February 28 the inventory was $1,450. The cost of goods sold was $5,327. What was the inventory turnover?

3. The Towle Corporation wants to know the change in annual inventory turnover. Has its inventory turnover increased or decreased? by how much?

	Last Year	This Year
Cost of goods sold	$374,400	$456,980
January 1 inventory	$78,430	$143,300
December 31 inventory	$97,390	$84,580

4. Buck's Furniture wants to know the change in annual inventory turnover. Has its annual inventory turnover increased or decreased? by how much?

	Last Year	This Year
Cost of goods sold	$2,897,400	$2,184,350
January 1 inventory	$346,900	$372,870
December 31 inventory	$462,700	$426,380

Accounting period

Period of time covered by an income statement

Gross profit

Difference between net sales and cost of goods sold

Income statement

Statement of income and expenses showing a profit or loss during a given period of time

Net income

Difference between gross profit and operating expenses

Net sales

Difference between sales revenue and amount for returned and defective merchandise

A company's profit or loss for a given period of time is calculated using an **income statement**. An income statement shows the income and expenses during a given period of time. The **accounting period** is the time covered by the income statement. All businesses prepare income statements at least annually. A quarterly accounting period covers $\frac{1}{4}$ of a year, or 3 months.

Sales revenue is the most important source of income. **Net sales** is the total sales revenue less the amount for returns and allowance for defective goods. **Gross profit** is net sales less the cost of goods sold. **Net income** before income tax is gross profit less total operating expenses. Net income after income tax is the profit or loss.

You can remember these basic equations for income statements:
Net sales = Revenue from sales − Sales returns and allowances
Gross profit = Net sales − Cost of goods sold
Net income = Gross profit − Operating expenses

EXAMPLE The quarterly income statement for the Wexford Company is shown on page 171. Find the net sales, gross profit, and net income before income tax.

Step 1 To find net sales, subtract the returns and allowances from sales.

$542,960 − $21,380 = $521,580

Net sales are $521,580.

Step 2 To find gross profit, subtract cost of goods sold from net sales.

$521,580 − $262,460 = $259,120

Gross profit is $259,120.

Step 3 To find net income before taxes, subtract total operating expenses from gross profit.

$259,120 − $119,505 = $139,615

Net income before taxes is $139,615.

(continued)

Wexford Company, Inc.
Fourth Quarter Income Statement, 2003

Revenue from sales:	
Sales	$542,960
Less sales returns and allowances	21,380
Net sales	?????
Cost of goods sold:	
Merchandise inventory 10/1	$128,490
Plus purchases	385,640
Merchandise available for sale	$514,130
Less merchandise inventory 12/31	251,670
Cost of goods sold	$262,460
Gross profit	??????
Operating expenses:	
Cost of sales	$ 68,754
General expenses	34,871
Interest expense	15,880
Total operating expenses	$119,505
Net income before income tax	?????

Exercise A   Complete the income statement.

R & F MANUFACTURING, INC.		
INCOME STATEMENT FOR 1/1/02–3/31/02		

Revenue from sales:

Sales		$67,430
Less sales returns and allowances		1,300
Net sales	**1.**	_____

Cost of goods sold:

Merchandise inventory 1/1		$24,590
Plus purchases		38,640
Merchandise available for sale	**2.**	_____
Less merchandise inventory 3/31		20,540
Cost of goods sold	**3.**	_____
Gross profit	**4.**	_____

Operating expenses:

Cost of sales		$13,468
General expenses		2,970
Interest expense		954
Total operating expenses		$17,392
Net income before income tax	**5.**	_____

TRY THIS...

If net sales increase by 10% next year, what will be next year's gross profit?

Base year

The earlier year, in calculating percent change

Horizontal analysis

Comparison of the same income statement categories for different accounting periods

Businesses compare their income statements for different accounting periods to find changes in profits or losses. A **horizontal analysis** compares the same income statement categories for different accounting periods. Businesses find the percent change in revenue, expense, profit, or loss using the increase or decrease in that category.

EXAMPLES   The fourth quarter net sales for the Wexford Company were $521,580 in 2003. The fourth quarter net sales were $473,210 in 2002. What was the change in net sales from 2002 to 2003?

Subtract to find the difference between the net sales for the two years.

$ 521,580   Net sales in 2003
−473,210   Net sales in 2002
$ 48,370   Difference in net sales

$521,580 > $473,210, so sales increased.

Net sales increased $48,370 from 2002 to 2003.

What was the percent increase in net sales from 2002 to 2003?

Step 1   Divide the increase in net sales by the net sales for the **base year**. The base year is always the earlier year. Round to three decimal places.

$$\frac{\$48,370}{\$473,210} \approx .102$$

Step 2   Write the decimal as a percent.

.102 = 10.2%

Net sales increased 10.2% between 2002 and 2003.

Exercise A Complete the horizontal analysis. Find each change and percent change from 2001 to 2002. Round to the nearest whole percent.

THE MONTANA COMPANY ANNUAL INCOME STATEMENTS FOR 2001 AND 2002				
	2001	2002	Change	Percent Change
Revenue from sales:				
Sales	$795,000	$1,275,000	1. _____	60%
Less sales returns and allowances	10,800	12,600	2. _____	3. _____
Net sales	$784,200	$1,262,400	4. _____	5. _____
Cost of goods sold:				
Inventory 1/1	$98,600	$128,000	6. _____	7. _____
Purchases	364,200	398,500	8. _____	9. _____
Goods available for sale	$462,800	$526,500	10. _____	11. _____
Less inventory 12/31	184,320	218,300	12. _____	13. _____
Cost of goods sold	$278,480	$308,200	14. _____	15. _____
Gross profit	$505,720	$954,200	16. _____	17. _____
Operating expenses:				
Cost of sales	$293,184	$338,018	18. _____	19. _____
General expenses	92,442	88,442	20. _____	21. _____
Interest expense	10,620	10,620	$0	$0
Total operating expenses	$396,246	$437,080	22. _____	23. _____
Net income before income tax	$109,474	$517,120	24. _____	25. _____

PROBLEM SOLVING

Exercise C Use the income statement above to solve.

1. Which category was less in 2002 than in 2001?

2. Of all the categories that increased, which had the least percent increase?

3. Which category increased by the greatest amount of money?

4. Which category increased by the greatest percent?

By the Book

Books R Us Company publishes self-help books. It is putting the finishing touches on what should be a best-seller.

"Are we ready for the printer?" asks Julia, the president.

"We are," responds Bill, the senior editor. "How many books will we print, Julia?"

"That's a good question. Let's see what the unit costs are." They look at the table that the production department has given Julia. It reads as follows:

Number of Books Printed	Unit Cost
5,000	$7.60
10,000	$6.80
20,000	$6.40

"Let's go ahead and print 20,000 books, Julia. That's the lowest unit cost. We'll save a lot of money in the long run."

"There are other things to think of besides the lowest unit cost, Bill. This is a complicated decision."

Bill knows they don't want to print more books than they can sell. But he knows they will eventually sell at least 20,000 books.

"I'm certain that we will sell all 20,000 books," Bill replies.

"There's much more to it than that, Bill. What if it takes five years to sell the books? We'll have all that inventory cost tied up in these books." Bill hadn't thought of that.

"And what if you discover some important errors in the book, just after they are printed?" Julia continues. "No, I'd rather reprint once or twice a year, even if we end up paying a higher unit price."

For Discussion

1. Compare the total cost of printing 20,000 books now to the total cost of 4 printings of 5,000 books each.
2. Use the patterns in the table to estimate the unit cost for a printing of 30,000 books.
3. What are the risks of printing too few books?
4. What are the risks of printing too many books?

Write the letter of the best answer to each question.

1. _____ remain(s) the same no matter how many units are produced.

    a. Fixed costs   **c.** Total costs

    b. Variable costs   **d.** Output

2. _____ is the number of times inventory is replaced in a given time period.

    a. Output   **c.** Average inventory

    b. Beginning inventory   **d.** Inventory turnover

3. Net income before income tax is calculated by subtracting operating expenses from _____.

    a. cost of goods sold   **c.** sales

    b. net sales   **d.** gross profit

Use the graph for problems 4–6.

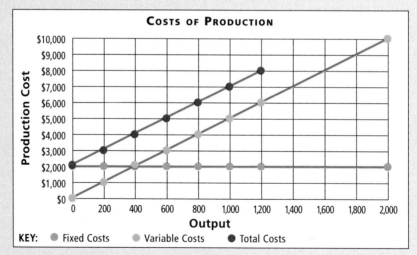

4. What is the fixed cost to produce 800 units? the variable cost?

5. How much more is the fixed cost to produce 1,000 units than the fixed cost to produce 200 units? the variable cost?

6. What is the total cost to produce 2,000 units?

Complete the table for problems 7–11. Find the average cost. Find the value of the inventory at the end of the month, when 65 items are in stock. Round to the nearest cent.

Date	Inventory	Unit Cost	Total Value
Beginning inventory	75	$120	$9,000
February 10 purchase	115	$100	**7.**
February 22 purchase	70	$120	**8.**
Totals	260		**9.**

Average Cost of Inventory: **10.** _____

Value of Inventory: **11.** _____

Solve problems 12–15.

12. In 2002 a company's sales revenue was $575,000 and its marketing expenses were $126,500. Marketing expenses are what percentage of total sales?

13. A company's cost of goods sold was $7,640 in 2002. Its inventory on January 1, 2002, was $1,250. Its inventory on December 31, 2002, was $2,900. What was the inventory turnover? Round to the nearest tenth.

14. A company's annual income statement shows net sales of $1,460,825. The cost of goods sold is $495,269. The operating expenses are $294,523. What is the net income before income tax?

15. In 2001 a company's net sales were $35,800. In 2002 its net sales were $44,320. What is the percent change in net sales from 2001 to 2002? Round to the nearest whole percent.

Test-Taking Tip | Estimate your answer first. Then complete the problem. To see if your answer is reasonable, compare it with your estimate.

Chapter
9

Casualty Insurance

Sometimes business operations are interrupted by disasters such as accidents, fires, or thefts. Casualty insurance pays money to replace property that has been damaged, stolen, or destroyed. Casualty insurance may also pay the expense of lawsuits and medical care for people injured in car accidents. Without casualty insurance, such disasters would bankrupt many businesses.

In this chapter, you will learn about different types of casualty insurance. You will also use the math skills needed to compute the premiums for different types of casualty insurance.

Goals for Learning

▶ To identify types of insurance that businesses need and the relative costs of each type

▶ To define five types of auto insurance (liability, collision, medical, property, and comprehensive) and compute auto insurance premiums

▶ To compute premiums for fire/theft insurance

▶ To define a policy rider and find a fractional percent of a number

▶ To calculate the difference between the benefit and cash value of a straight life policy from a table

▶ To calculate the amount paid during the term of an endowment policy

Casualty insurance

Insurance coverage that pays for injuries to others and for the repair or replacement of damaged or destroyed property

Liability insurance

Insurance coverage that pays money to anyone injured or to anyone whose property is damaged by the insured

12 months = 1 year

Each year many companies without casualty insurance go out of business because of fires, accidents, lawsuits, and thefts. **Casualty insurance** pays for injuries to others and for the repair or replacement of property damaged or destroyed in a disaster. One type of casualty insurance is **liability insurance**. It pays money for injuries to others or for damage to another person's property. Other types of casualty insurance are fire insurance, theft insurance, automobile insurance, and Workers' Compensation insurance. The cost of the insurance is the premium. A higher premium pays for more insurance coverage.

EXAMPLE   Each month Daytola Enterprises pays for these casualty insurance policies: fire/theft insurance, $2,450; liability insurance, $1,480; automobile insurance, $965.30; and Workers' Compensation insurance, $2,456.85. What is the total annual premium for casualty insurance?

Step 1   Find the total monthly premium.

$2,450.00   Fire/theft insurance
1,480.00   Liability insurance
965.30   Automobile insurance
+2,456.85   Workers' Compensation insurance
$7,352.15   Total monthly premium

Step 2   Multiply to find the annual premium.

$ 7,352.15   Monthly premium
× 12   Number of months
$88,225.80   Total annual premium

The total annual premium for casualty insurance is $88,225.80.

Insurance companies charge different prices for the same amount of insurance coverage. Businesses find the cost of insurance from several companies before deciding which insurance company to use.

Exercise A Each company's coverage is the same. Find the total monthly and annual premiums for each insurance company.

	Fire/Theft	General Liability	Auto	Workers' Compensation	Total Monthly Premium	Total Annual Premium
1. Mutual of Temecula	$3,581.75	$2,031.56	$341.50	$2,185.71	_____	_____
2. Casualty of Denmark	$2,156.23	$2,845.71	$528.32	$2,185.71	_____	_____
3. Premium Insurance Company	$2,008.75	$1,986.35	$447.50	$2,185.71	_____	_____
4. Arrow Insurance Group	$3,194.00	$2,056.80	$478.25	$2,185.71	_____	_____
5. Baker Insurance Company	$1,859.45	$1,563.20	$498.75	$2,185.71	_____	_____

TRY THIS...

List the companies in problems 1–5 in order of the lowest to the highest annual premium.

Technology Connection

Defining Insurance Terms

You can use the Internet to find the meaning of terms describing types of insurance. Go to the Web site *http://www.ucalgary.ca/MG/inrm/glossary*. Click on the first letter of an insurance term. For example, go to the letter *C* to find the definition of *casualty insurance*.

The cost of liability insurance for a retail business is often based on the area of the building. The table below shows higher premiums for greater amounts of space.

Area	Annual Premium
Less than 1,000 square feet	$500
1,000 square feet to 1,999 square feet	$750
2,000 square feet to 2,999 square feet	$1,000
3,000 square feet to 3,999 square feet	$1,250
4,000 square feet to 4,999 square feet	$1,500
5,000 square feet to 5,999 square feet	$1,750

Writing About Mathematics

Look at the table to the right. Suppose the pattern relating the premium to the area stays the same. Explain how to find the cost for 12,850 square feet.

EXAMPLE Tony's Toys rents space that measures 50 feet by 69 feet. How much is its annual liability insurance premium?

Step 1 Find the area of the store. Use the formula $A = lw$.
$l = 69$ feet $w = 50$ feet
$A = 69$ feet $\times$ 50 feet $= 3,450$ square feet

$3,000 < 3,450 < 4,000$ means that 3,450 is greater than 3,000 and less than 4,000.

Step 2 Find the annual premium for 3,450 square feet.
$3,000 < 3,450 < 4,000$

Tony's Toys' annual liability insurance premium is $1,250.

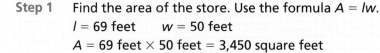

PROBLEM SOLVING

Exercise B Use the table above and the formula $A = lw$ to solve.

1. Hunter Hobby has 4,861 square feet of floor space. How much is its annual liability insurance premium?

2. Easterly Earthenware has 2,150 square feet of floor space and plans to add on 1,400 square feet. How much will its annual liability insurance premium be after the addition?

3. Karen's Cuisine has floor space measuring 70 feet by 70 feet. How much is its annual liability insurance premium?

4. Cards Central has floor space measuring 25 feet by 45 feet. How much is its annual liability insurance premium?

Bodily injury
Physical injury to a person

Collision
Damage to the insured's car caused by a car accident

Comprehensive
Damage to the insured's car not caused by a collision

Medical
Treatment of injuries to the driver and passengers of the insured's car

Property damage
Damage to someone else's property

Auto insurance may include coverage for **bodily injury, property damage, comprehensive, collision**, and **medical** expenses. Bodily injury coverage pays for injuries caused by the insured's car. Property damage coverage pays for property damaged by the insured's car. Collision coverage pays for accident damage to the insured's car. Comprehensive coverage pays for all other damage to the insured's car. Medical coverage pays for injuries to the driver and passengers of the insured's car.

EXAMPLE   Parts-R-Us owns 15 trucks. Its annual auto insurance premium for 1 truck includes these premiums: bodily injury, $128; property damage, $119; comprehensive, $250; collision, $340; and medical, $85. What is its total annual premium with a 4% discount for airbags?

Step 1   Find the total premium for 1 truck.

$128 + $119 + $250 + $340 + $85 = $922

Step 2   Multiply the premium by the number of trucks.

$922 × 15 = $13,830   Total premium for 15 trucks

Step 3   Multiply by 4% to find the discount.

$13,830 × 4% = $13,830 × .04 = $553.20

Step 4   Subtract the discount.

$13,830.00 − $553.20 = $13,276.80

Parts-R-Us pays an annual premium of $13,276.80.

PROBLEM SOLVING

Exercise C   The premiums are annual. Solve.

1. A delivery service has 20 trucks. The premiums for 1 truck are: bodily injury, $115; property damage, $84; comprehensive, $120; collision, $250; and medical, $46. What is the total premium for 20 trucks?

2. A store has 6 trucks. The premiums for 1 truck are: bodily injury, $116; property damage, $132; comprehensive, $216; collision, $245; and medical, $52. What is the total premium with a 10% discount?

One insurance policy usually provides coverage for both fire and theft. Fire/theft insurance pays to replace or repair a building, inventory, machines, or other things of value that are burned or stolen.

A company should have enough coverage to pay for replacing its building and contents. A greater amount of coverage costs more than a smaller amount of coverage.

> **EXAMPLE** A furniture manufacturer buys fire/theft insurance. The annual cost is $12.25 per $10,000 of coverage. The company needs $500,000 in coverage. What is the annual premium?
>
> **Step 1** Write a proportion.
>
> $$\frac{\text{Cost of coverage}}{\text{Amount of coverage}} \quad \frac{12.25}{10,000} = \frac{\blacksquare}{500,000}$$
>
> **Step 2** Find the missing term in this proportion.
>
> Find the cross products.
>
> $$\frac{12.25}{10,000} = \frac{\blacksquare}{500,000} \qquad \begin{array}{l} 12.25 \times 500,000 = 10,000 \times \blacksquare \\ 6,125,000 = 10,000\,\blacksquare \end{array}$$
>
> Divide both sides by 10,000. $\quad 10,000\overline{)6,125,000.0}$ with quotient 612.5
>
> The annual premium for fire/theft insurance is $612.50.

To divide 6,125,000 by 10,000, move the decimal point in 6,125,000 to the left four places (one place for each zero in 10,000).

6,125,000.

Exercise A Find the annual premium for each amount of coverage.

Coverage	Cost per $10,000 of Coverage	Annual Premium
1. $1,000,000	$23.15	_____
2. $500,000	$19.07	_____
3. $900,000	$45.61	_____
4. $1,500,000	$16.75	_____
5. $5,500,000	$28.17	_____

It is against the law to drive without auto insurance. Bodily injury and property damage coverage are required. Comprehensive, collision, and medical coverage are usually optional. Coverage for bodily injury is stated in terms of the limits per person and per accident. Bodily injury coverage of 15/30 means the insurance company pays up to $15,000 per person but no more than $30,000 per accident. Property damage is per accident. Property damage coverage of 10 means the insurance company pays up to $10,000 for property damaged in an accident. Medical coverage is per person.

A deductible reduces the premium without reducing the amount of coverage. The deductible amount must be paid before the insurance company pays a claim. The greater the deductible, the lower the premium.

EXAMPLE C. Catchers owns 15 vehicles. Its coverage is 25/50 for bodily injury, 15 for property damage, and $3,000 for medical. It has a $250 deductible for comprehensive and collision. What is the company's premium for all 15 vehicles?

Step 1 Find each coverage in the table on page 186. Add the premiums.

$124	Bodily injury
83	Property damage
215	Comprehensive
415	Collision
+ 46	Medical
$883	Total premium for 1 vehicle

Step 2 Multiply the premium for 1 vehicle by the number of vehicles.

$ 883	Premium for 1 vehicle
× 15	Number of vehicles
$13,245	Total premium for 15 vehicles

C. Catchers' premium is $13,245.

Another way to solve the problem is to find the premiums for 15 vehicles first.

The table below shows the premiums for four levels of coverage.

Bodily Injury	15/30	25/50	50/100	100/300
Premium	$82	$124	$167	$198
Property Damage	10	15	50	100
Premium	$61	$83	$129	$173
Comprehensive Deductible	$100	$250	$500	$1,000
Premium	$382	$215	$175	$125
Collision Deductible	$100	$250	$500	$1,000
Premium	$462	$415	$337	$218
Medical	$1,000	$2,000	$3,000	$4,000
Premium	$23	$35	$46	$68

Exercise B   Find the total annual premium using the table above.

Number of Vehicles	Bodily Injury	Property Damage	Comprehensive Deductible	Collision Deductible	Medical	Total Premium
1. 8	15/30	10	$100	$100	$2,000	_____
2. 10	50/100	50	$250	$250	$1,000	_____
3. 12	25/50	15	$1,000	$1,000	$3,000	_____
4. 5	25/50	15	$250	$250	$4,000	_____
5. 20	15/30	10	$250	$250	$4,000	_____

Rider

A change to the original policy

A policy can have a **rider** that changes the original policy. If a new feature is added, the cost of the rider is usually a percentage of the premium.

| EXAMPLE | A company's annual auto insurance premium is $22,560. The company adds a rider covering substitute transportation. The additional cost is $\frac{1}{2}$% of the premium. What is the annual cost of the rider? |

Step 1   Change the fractional percent to a decimal.

$$\frac{1}{2} = 1 \div 2 = .5 \quad \rightarrow \quad \frac{1}{2}\% = .5\% = .005$$

Step 2   Multiply the premium by the percent.

$$\begin{array}{ll} \$22,560 & \text{Annual premium} \\ \times \quad .005 & \tfrac{1}{2}\% \text{ written as a decimal} \\ \hline \$112.80 & \text{Cost of the rider} \end{array}$$

The rider costs $112.80 annually.

PROBLEM SOLVING

Exercise C   Each auto insurance premium is for 1 year. Solve.

1. Jumpers pays a premium of $9,340. It adds a rider covering towing for $\frac{1}{2}$% of the premium. What does the rider cost?

2. World pays a premium of $13,580. It adds a rider covering towing for $\frac{3}{4}$% of the premium. What does the rider cost?

3. Harry's pays a premium of $4,296. It adds a rider covering towing for $\frac{5}{8}$% of the premium. What does the rider cost?

4. G.G. Inc. pays a premium of $3,200. It adds a rider covering towing for $\frac{3}{4}$% of the premium. What is the total premium for auto insurance?

5. K.O.T. pays a premium of $16,200. It adds a rider covering towing for $\frac{3}{8}$% of the premium. What is the total premium for auto insurance?

Cash value

Money available to
an owner who ends a
whole life insurance
policy

Liability

Financial
responsibility

Whole life

Life insurance that
has a cash value

Whole life insurance combines protection with investment. The **cash value** is the money available to an owner who ends the policy. It is the investment part of the premiums paid. The cash value increases with each premium, but it is always less than the total premiums paid. The insurance company's **liability** is its financial responsibility to pay either the death payment or the cash value. As the cash value increases, the cost of the death payment decreases for the insurance company. Thus the insured pays a greater share of the death benefit with each premium. So the actual cost of the insurance increases for the insured.

EXAMPLE   Joe buys a whole life policy at age 25. What is his actual cost per $1,000 coverage at age 35? His death payment at age 35 is $100,000. The cash value at age 35 is $2,850. His annual premium is $1,200.

Step 1   Find the cost of the death payment for the insurance company.

Subtract the cash value at age 35 from the death payment.

$100,000   Death payment
− 2,850   Cash value at age 35
$ 97,150   Cost for insurance company

Step 2   Find the insurance company's cost per $1,000 of coverage.

$97,150 ÷ 1,000 = $97.15

Step 3   To find Joe's actual cost per $1,000 of coverage, divide the annual premium by the insurance company's cost per $1,000 of coverage.

$$\begin{array}{r} \$12.352 \\ \$97.15)\overline{\$1,200.00000} \end{array}$$ Round to the nearest cent.

$12.352 ≈ $12.35

Joe's actual cost per $1,000 coverage at age 35 is about $12.35.

Move the decimal point to the right two places in the divisor and the dividend. Put the decimal point in the quotient directly above the decimal point in the dividend. Notice that you will need to add more zeros as you divide.

Exercise A Find the insurance company's cost for the death payment and Joe's actual cost per $1,000 coverage for each given age. Round to the nearest cent.

Age	Annual Premium	Death Payment	Cash Value	Cost to Insurance Co.	Actual Cost per $1,000 Coverage
1. 40	$1,200	$100,000	$8,940	_____	_____
2. 45	$1,200	$100,000	$15,980	_____	_____
3. 50	$1,200	$100,000	$35,620	_____	_____
4. 55	$1,200	$100,000	$48,730	_____	_____
5. 60	$1,200	$100,000	$62,350	_____	_____

Endowment policy

Life insurance policy that has a guaranteed cash value at the end of its term

Term

Period of time that insurance coverage is in effect

Some investors use a life insurance **endowment policy** as an investment. An endowment policy pays the insured a guaranteed cash value at the end of its **term**. The term of a policy is the period of time that the coverage is in effect. Premiums and cash values for endowment policies are greater than for the same amount of straight life coverage.

EXAMPLE Mrs. Johnson buys an endowment policy with a death benefit of $5,000. The monthly premium is $7.62. The term is 25 years. At the end of 25 years, the endowment policy will pay her $13,140. How much does she pay over the term of the policy?

Step 1 **Estimate** the total premiums.

$7.62 ≈ $8   12 ≈ 10
$8 × 10 × 25 = **about $2,000**

Step 2 Multiply $7.62 by 12 months to find the annual premium.

$ 7.62   Monthly premium
×   12   Months in 1 year
$91.44   Annual premium

Step 3 Multiply the annual premium by the number of years.

$ 91.44   Annual premium
×   25   Number of years
$2,286.00   Total premiums

Mrs. Johnson pays a total of $2,286 over the term of the policy.

TRY THIS...

Solve this problem by finding the total monthly premiums first.

Exercise B   Find the total premiums paid over the term of each endowment policy.

	Policy Term (years)	Monthly Premiums	Death Payment	Cash Value at Term	Total Premiums
1.	20	$26.89	$100,000	$19,249	_____
2.	18	$124.09	$150,000	$43,636	_____
3.	20	$27.13	$200,000	$17,072	_____
4.	25	$64.83	$250,000	$41,309	_____
5.	25	$87.50	$150,000	$59,638	_____

Humor on the Job

Overheard after a minor car accident:

"Looks like you're liable for these damages."

"Yeah. Looks like I'm liable to be in big trouble when I get home, too."

Little Shop of Flowers

"Business has been slow lately," Elvira thought. "We have to cut costs somewhere." Elvira owns the Say It With Flowers flower shop. She was thinking out loud, and Bob overheard her.

"I know where you can cut costs, but I didn't know things were so bad," said Bob.

"Oh, hi Bob. Don't pay any attention to me. The business has its ups and downs, that's all. We're doing all right. It's just that I'm always looking for ways to cut costs."

Bob knows the business well. He keeps the books, makes repairs, and makes deliveries. There are two delivery vans, four full-time employees, and some part-time help as well. It's quite a big operation.

"Bob, where do you think we can cut costs? You said you had an idea."

"I sure do. Get rid of the collision insurance on the vans. That would save a couple of thousand dollars every year."

"Oh, I wouldn't think of going without insurance. One accident could ruin my business!"

"I know you have to have insurance, especially liability insurance. But collision coverage is different. Even if I totaled one of the vans, we would collect only a few thousand dollars."

"Those vans are eight years old," Bob continued. "Collision made sense when they were newer. But I think that dropping collision coverage now is a risk worth taking." "Besides," he added, "I've never had an accident, have I?"

For Discussion

1. Suppose the shop's collision coverage costs $1,065 per year per van. Find the total cost of collision coverage for the 2 vans over 5 years.

2. Why did Bob refer to dropping collision insurance as "a risk"? Explain.

3. Why does collision insurance make more sense for newer vans?

4. Do you think dropping collision insurance is a good idea? Why?

Use this liability insurance table for problems 1–2.

Area	Annual Premium
Less than 1,000 square feet	$600
1,000 square feet to 1,999 square feet	$750
2,000 square feet to 2,999 square feet	$900
3,000 square feet to 3,999 square feet	$1,050

1. Vicki's Victorian Delight has floor space measuring 41 feet by 50 feet. How much is its annual premium for liability insurance?

2. The Tool Center has floor space measuring 43 by 93 feet. How much is its annual premium for liability insurance?

Solve problems 3–8.

3. Fresh Food pays these monthly insurance premiums: fire/theft, $803.21; liability, $961.45; auto, $81.37; and Workers' Compensation, $1,963.56. What is the total annual premium for casualty insurance?

4. Herbert's Repairs has 10 trucks. The annual premiums for 1 truck are: bodily injury, $72; property damage, $51; comprehensive, $91; collision, $116; and medical, $17. What is the total annual premium for 10 trucks?

5. Service to You has 57 trucks. Its annual auto insurance premium is $36,574. What is its annual premium with a 5% discount?

6. Fratina Manufacturers buys a $1,000,000 fire/theft insurance policy. The annual premium is $23.56 per $10,000 of coverage. What is the total annual premium for fire/theft insurance?

7. An endowment policy has a death benefit of $50,000. At the end of the 25-year term, the policy pays $17,472. The monthly premium is $15.71. How much are the premiums over the term of the policy?

8. Easy Close pays an annual auto insurance premium of $6,472. The company adds a rider covering towing for $\frac{1}{2}$% of the premium. What does the insurance with the rider cost?

The table for problem 9 shows the premiums for four levels of auto insurance coverage.

Bodily Injury	15/30	25/50	50/100	100/300
Premium	$127	$146	$185	$234
Property Damage	10	15	50	100
Premium	$108	$135	$151	$196
Comprehensive Deductible	$100	$250	$500	$1,000
Premium	$309	$264	$218	$75
Collision Deductible	$100	$250	$500	$1,000
Premium	$415	$357	$268	$120
Medical	$1,000	$2,000	$3,000	$4,000
Premium	$38	$52	$74	$92

9. Carry Cartoons owns 6 vehicles. It has 25/50 coverage for bodily injury, 15 for property damage, and $2,000 for medical. It has a $500 deductible for comprehensive and collision. What is the company's annual premium?

The table for problem 10 is for a $100,000 straight life policy bought at age 25.

Age	Annual Premium	Death Payment	Cash Value	Cost to Insurance Co.	Actual Cost per $1,000 Coverage
25	$1,900	$100,000	$0	$100,000	$19.00
30	$1,900	$100,000	$3,852	$96,148	
35	$1,900	$100,000	$8,964		

10. What is the insured's actual cost per $1,000 coverage at age 35? Round to the nearest cent.

| Test-Taking Tip | Read the titles and labels on tables carefully. They will help you understand how the numbers in the table relate to each other.

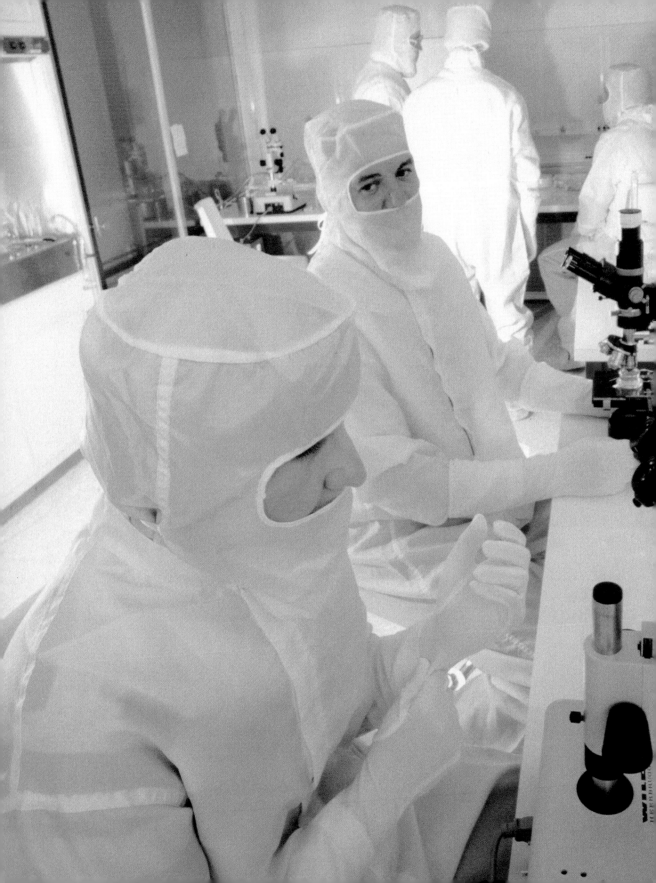

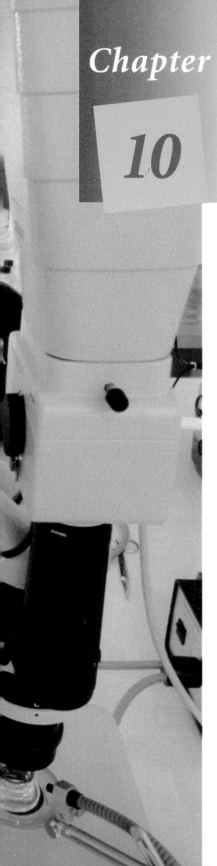

Chapter 10

Government Regulations

Businesses must comply with many local, state, federal, and even international regulations. The regulations may require licenses, tariffs, and taxes. Government regulations may require companies to make building changes for safety and environmental reasons. The Environmental Protection Agency (EPA) makes regulations to control pollution. The Occupational Safety and Health Administration (OSHA) regulations apply to employee safety. A company must know the regulations before starting and while operating a business. All regulations have an impact on the profits of a business.

In this chapter, you will learn about some of the costs of government regulations. You will calculate some of the costs of reducing pollution in the workplace. You will learn about making the workplace accessible to people with a disability. You will compute the costs of licenses and tariffs. You will use the same math skills that businesses use to calculate these costs.

Goals for Learning

▶ To determine costs to a company of installing pollution-control equipment

▶ To determine costs to a company of making an entrance accessible for people with a disability

▶ To identify which licenses a company needs to participate in interstate commerce and other costs

▶ To describe international business agreements and costs related to global business operations

Pollutant

Unhealthy or unnatural material introduced into the environment

Companies use furnaces in manufacturing and also to produce electricity. A furnace uses fuel that produces **pollutants**. Pollutants are unhealthy or unnatural materials introduced into the environment. Environmental regulations call for pollution-control equipment on smoke stacks. This equipment removes pollutants before exhaust is released into the air. For example, coal-fired boilers produce sulfur dioxide (SO_2) gas in the exhaust fumes. Environmental regulations require that companies remove this gas or reduce its amount before releasing exhaust into the air. Companies do this by installing different types of equipment.

EXAMPLE | An electric company uses a coal-fired boiler. It installs a wet flue gas desulfurization (FGD) system to reduce pollution. The system has to be installed on each of its 4 smokestacks. Each FGD system costs $75,923 plus $16,530 for installation. What is the total cost?

Step 1 Estimate the total cost.

$75,923 \approx $80,000 $16,530 \approx $20,000
$80,000 + $20,000 = $100,000
$100,000 \times 4 = $400,000

The total cost is about $400,000.

Step 2 Find the total cost of one system.

$75,923   Cost of 1 FGD
+16,530   Installation fee
$92,453   Total cost of 1 FGD system

Step 3 Multiply to find the total cost of 4 systems.

$ 92,453   Total cost of 1 FGD system
×   4   Number of FGD systems
$369,812   Total cost of 4 FGD systems

The electric company pays $369,812 for the 4 FGD systems.

Did You Know?

An FGD system is capable of removing 95% of SO_2 from exhaust. The system produces commercial-grade gypsum, which is used in the manufacturing of wallboard.

The table below shows the cost of buying and installing nine types of FGD systems.

FGD Type	Cost	Installation Fee
I	$58,340	$11,231
II	$26,919	$6,230
III	$47,815	$7,910
IV	$75,923	$16,530
V	$64,621	$8,453
VI	$112,328	$28,451
VII	$41,002	$15,290
VIII	$19,138	$786
IX	$21,649	$1,803

TRY THIS...

Find the cost plus installation for each FGD type. List the costs in order from least to greatest.

PROBLEM SOLVING

Exercise A   Use the table above to solve.

1. The Erratic Electricity Company has 5 smokestacks that require a Type I FGD system. What is the total cost to buy and install the 5 systems?

2. An electric company installs 3 Type III FGD systems and 2 Type IX FGD systems. What is the total cost to buy and install the 5 systems?

3. A manufacturer may install either 4 Type III FGD systems or 4 Type VII FGD systems. Which type of system costs less with installation? How much less?

4. Nelson Manufacturing spent $199,240 buying and installing 10 FGD systems at several plants. Which system did they install?

Environmental regulations also cover air pollution in the workplace. Companies must install air-purifying systems that clean the air inside their buildings. A system that cleans the inside air has 3 parts: a collection unit, a filter, and a fan. Most systems remove 99.9% of pollutants from inside air.

EXAMPLE | A manufacturer installs an air-purifying system. The collection unit costs $2,986.03, the filter costs $4,813.37, and the fan costs $5,107. The company installs this system in 8 manufacturing plants. What is the total cost of 8 systems?

Step 1 | Find the total cost of 1 system.

> $ 2,986.03 Cost of collection unit
>   4,813.37 Cost of filter
> + 5,107.00 Cost of fan
> $12,906.40 Total cost of 1 system

Line up decimal points before adding. Write a decimal point to the right of a whole number. 5,107 = 5,107.

Step 2 | Multiply by the number of systems needed.

> $ 12,906.40 Total cost of 1 system
> ×   8 Number of systems
> $103,251.20 Total cost of 8 systems

Eight air-purifying systems cost $103,251.20.

Exercise B Find the total cost of the air-purifying systems.

Company	Number of Systems	Collection Unit	Filter	Fan	Total Cost
1. Welden Welders	3	$3,408.10	$2,560.13	$6,871.92	_____
2. Arc Point	8	$2,750.08	$3,872.25	$4,509.00	_____
3. Plastics Pieces	5	$3,005.00	$7,508.27	$5,156.82	_____
4. Sunburst	18	$2,183.62	$6,468.10	$6,254.20	_____
5. Castaways	9	$2,863.49	$2,987.68	$4,238.15	_____

Businesses measure the pollutants left in the air. In this way, they know if their air-purifying systems are working.

EXAMPLE An air-purifying system removes 99.9% of air pollutants from a building. Suppose the air in a building collects 2 cubic yards of pollutants in a month. How many cubic yards of pollutants does the air-purifying system leave in the air that month?

Step 1   Change the percent to a decimal.

99.9% = .999   Move the decimal point two places to the left and remove the percent symbol.

Step 2   Multiply the volume of pollutants by .999.

2 × .999 = 1.998   Volume removed

Step 3   Subtract the volume removed from the original volume.

2 − 1.998 = .002   Volume left

The air-purifying system leaves .002 cubic yards of pollutants in the air.

TRY THIS...

Another way to solve this problem is to subtract 99.9% from 100% first, and then multiply by 2.

PROBLEM SOLVING

Exercise C   Solve.

1. Arc Point produces 1.0 cubic yard of air pollutants monthly. Its air-purifying system leaves .1% of pollutants in the air. How many cubic yards of pollutants are left in the air?

2. Kryak produces 1.0 cubic yard of air pollutants each month. Its air purifier removes 99.9% of the pollutants. How many cubic yards of air pollutants does the system remove each month?

3. Pin Point produces 1.5 cubic yards of air pollutants each month. Its air purifier removes 99.8% of air pollutants. How many cubic yards of pollutants are left in the air each month?

4. Metal Mart produces .75 cubic yard of air pollutants each month. Its air purifier collects only 89.5% of air pollutants. How many cubic yards of pollutants are left in the air each month?

Slope

Fraction describing the steepness of a line, in which the numerator is the vertical change and the denominator is the horizontal change

Volume

Measure in cubic units of space inside a container

The Americans with Disabilities Act (ADA) requires businesses to give qualified people with disabilities an equal opportunity to work. Buildings must be accessible to people in wheelchairs. Wheelchair ramps may be needed. Ramps are built so the **slope**, which is the steepness of the ramp, is not too great.

EXAMPLE   A business builds a solid concrete ramp that is 20 feet long, 4 feet wide, and 6 inches high. Concrete costs $65 per cubic yard. How much does the concrete for the ramp cost?

Step 1   Find the **volume** of the ramp, which is the amount of space inside the ramp. Use the formula $V = \frac{lwh}{2}$.

$l = 20$ feet $w = 4$ feet $h = 6$ inches
$V = (20 \text{ ft.} \times 4 \text{ ft.} \times .5 \text{ ft.}) \div 2 = 20$ cu. ft.

Step 2   Write and solve a proportion to change cubic feet to cubic yards.

$\frac{\text{Cubic feet}}{\text{Cubic yards}}$ $\frac{27}{1} \diagdown \frac{20}{\blacksquare}$

Find the cross products.
$\frac{27}{1} = \frac{20}{\blacksquare}$ $27 \times \blacksquare = 20 \times 1$ $27 \blacksquare = 20$

Divide both sides by 27. $\begin{array}{r} .7 \approx 1 \\ 27\overline{)20.0} \end{array}$

Step 3   Multiply the cost per cubic yard by the number of cubic yards.

$65 per cubic yard $\times$ 1 cubic yard = $65

The concrete for the ramp costs $65.

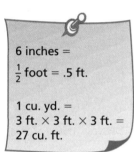

6 inches =
$\frac{1}{2}$ foot = .5 ft.

1 cu. yd. =
3 ft. $\times$ 3 ft. $\times$ 3 ft. =
27 cu. ft.

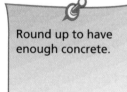

Round up to have enough concrete.

Exercise A   Find the cost of each ramp. Remember to round up to the next cubic yard.

Length	Width	Height	Cost of Concrete	Total Cost
1. 42 ft.	4 ft.	1 ft.	$65 per cu. yd.	_____
2. 36 ft.	3 ft.	1.5 ft.	$65 per cu. yd.	_____
3. 58 ft.	4 ft.	1 ft.	$75 per cu. yd.	_____
4. 62 ft.	3.5 ft.	1.5 ft.	$75 per cu. yd.	_____
5. 84.5 ft.	4 ft.	6 in.	$68.50 per cu. yd.	_____

The cost of concrete is not the only expense of building a ramp. A ramp must also have handrails along both sides for safety. Some handrails must have upper and lower rails.

EXAMPLE A company installs handrails for a ramp that is 32 feet long. The handrails use ten 6-foot posts, ten post caps, and 128 feet of railing. A welder spends 6.5 hours making the handrails. The welder earns $35.72 per hour. Posts cost $4.58 per foot, post caps cost $.75 each, and railing costs $3.17 per foot. What is the total cost of the handrails?

Step 1   Find the cost of materials.

Posts:
10 × 6 ft. × $4.58 per ft. = $274.80
Post caps:
10 × $.75 each = $7.50
Railing:
128 ft. × $3.17 per ft. = $405.76

Step 2   Find the wages of the welder.

6.5 hr. × $35.72 per hr. = $232.18

Step 3   Add the cost of the materials and the wages.

$274.80
    7.50
  405.76
+232.18
$920.24

The total cost of the handrails is $920.24.

Exercise B   Find the total cost of the handrails. Posts cost $4.58 per foot. Post caps cost $.75 each. Railing costs $3.17 per foot. The welder earns $35.72 per hour.

Posts Needed	Number of Post Caps	Amount of of Railing	Number of Welder's Hours	Total Cost of Handrails
1. Twelve 6-ft. posts	12	80 ft.	8	_____
2. Twenty 5-ft. posts	20	144 ft.	12.5	_____
3. Ten 4-ft. posts	10	64 ft.	6	_____
4. Eighteen 6-ft. posts	18	128 ft.	11	_____
5. Forty 6-ft. posts	40	608 ft.	45.5	_____

Doors may need to be changed or adjusted so wheelchairs can fit through them.

EXAMPLE

A business installs 2 automatic doors with crash bars. They are each 7 feet 5 inches tall and $47\frac{1}{2}$ inches wide. The doors cost $75.78 per square foot. How much do both doors cost?

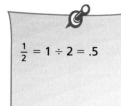

$\frac{1}{2} = 1 \div 2 = .5$

Step 1 Change each measurement to inches.

7 ft. = 7 × 12 in. = 84 in.
7 ft. 5 in. = 84 in. + 5 in. = 89 in.
$47\frac{1}{2}$ in. = 47.5 in.

Step 2 Find the area of 1 door. Use the formula $A = lw$.

l = 89 in. w = 47.5 in.
A = 89 in. × 47.5 in. = 4,227.5 sq. in.

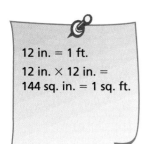

12 in. = 1 ft.
12 in. × 12 in. = 144 sq. in. = 1 sq. ft.

Step 3 Since the cost is given per square foot, find the area in square feet. Divide square inches by 144 to find square feet. Round up to the next whole square foot.

$$\frac{29.3}{144)4,227.5} \approx 30 \text{ sq. ft.}$$

Step 4 Multiply the area of 1 door by the cost per square foot to find the cost per door.
30 sq. ft. × $75.78 per sq. ft. = $2,273.40

Step 5 Multiply the cost per door by the number of doors.
$2,273.40 × 2 = $4,546.80

The 2 doors cost $4,546.80.

Technology Connection

Changing Units

You can use the Internet to change square inches to square feet. Go the Web site *http://www.convertit.com/Go/Convertit/Measurement/Converter.ASP.* Enter *4,227.5 in^2* in the "Convert From" box and *ft^2* in the "Convert To" box. Click on "Convert It!." The answer is *4227.5 inch^2 = 29.3576388888889 foot^2.* The answer rounds to 29.36 square feet.

You can use a calculator to change square inches to square feet. Divide 4,227.5 square inches by 144 square inches.

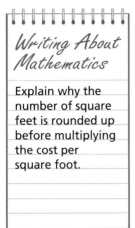

Exercise C Find the total cost of each type and size of door. For the problems with costs listed per square foot, round up to the next whole square foot before finding the total cost.

	Type of Door	Height	Width	Cost	Total Cost
1.	Easy Slider 5250	7 ft. 2 in.	$45\frac{1}{2}$ in.	$.89 per sq. in.	_____
2.	Easy Slider 5250	7 ft. 5 in.	41 in.	$.89 per sq. in.	_____
3.	Easy Slider 7350	7 ft. 10 in.	$42\frac{3}{4}$ in.	$1.15 per sq. in.	_____
4.	Easy Slider 7350	7 ft. 3 in.	46 in.	$1.15 per sq. in.	_____
5.	Easy Slider 8750	7 ft. 1 in.	35 in.	$1.35 per sq. in.	_____
6.	Easy Slider 8750	7 ft. 11 in.	37 in.	$1.35 per sq. in.	_____
7.	Top Glide I	7 ft. 3 in.	43 in.	$65.73 per sq. ft.	_____
8.	Top Glide I	7 ft. 7 in.	$42\frac{1}{2}$ in.	$65.73 per sq. ft.	_____
9.	Top Glide II	7 ft. 9 in.	$46\frac{3}{4}$ in.	$82.09 per sq. ft.	_____
10.	Top Glide III	7 ft. 8 in.	$45\frac{5}{8}$ in.	$96.34 per sq. ft.	_____

International Fuel Tax Agreement (IFTA)

Organization of most U.S. states and Canadian provinces that is responsible for distributing fuel taxes fairly

Interstate commerce

Business conducted across state lines

Miles per gallon (mpg)

Number of miles that can be driven on 1 gallon of fuel

Interstate commerce is business across state borders. Conducting business in several states may require special licenses and fees. A trucking company that carries goods across the United States pays fuel taxes to each state it drives through. Each state has its own fuel tax rate. The amount of tax depends on the number of gallons of fuel used in the state. Many states and Canadian provinces belong to the **International Fuel Tax Agreement (IFTA)**. A trucker or company from a state that belongs to the IFTA pays fuel taxes directly to the IFTA. The IFTA then distributes the taxes fairly to the states or provinces driven through.

EXAMPLE   A trucker drove 25,000 miles in Arizona and 38,000 miles in California. Arizona charges $.26 per gallon and California charges $.25 per gallon in fuel taxes. The truck gets 4.5 **miles per gallon (mpg)**. This is the number of miles the truck can go on 1 gallon of fuel. What is the fuel tax for both states?

Step 1   Find the number of gallons used in each state. Round to the nearest whole gallon. Write and solve a proportion.

Arizona $\frac{25,000 \text{ mi.}}{\blacksquare \text{ gal.}} = \frac{4.5 \text{ mi.}}{1 \text{ gal.}}$ $4.5 \blacksquare = 25,000$

quotient
$$\frac{5,555.5}{4.5)\overline{25,000.0}} \approx 5,556 \text{ gallons}$$
divisor   dividend

California
$$\frac{8,444.4}{4.5)\overline{38,000.0}} \approx 8,444 \text{ gallons}$$

Step 2   Multiply the number of gallons by the tax rate.
Arizona: $5,556 \times \$.26 = \$1,444.56$
California: $8,444 \times \$.25 = \$2,111$

Step 3   Find the total fuel taxes.
$\$1,444.56 + \$2,111 = \$3,555.56$.

The fuel tax for both states is $3,555.56.

Dividing by a Decimal
1) Move the decimal in the divisor to the right of the number.
2) Move the decimal in the dividend the same number of places to the right.
3) Place the decimal in the quotient above the decimal in the dividend.
4) Divide.

The table below shows the fuel tax rate for selected states.

State	Cost per Gallon	State	Cost per Gallon	State	Cost per Gallon
Arizona	$.26	New Hampshire	$.18	Tennessee	$.17
California	$.25	New Mexico	$.18	Texas	$.20
Idaho	$.25	New York	$.2945	Vermont	$.26
Maine	$.23	North Dakota	$.21	Virginia	$.16
Missouri	$.17	Ohio	$.22	Washington	$.23
Montana	$.2775	Oklahoma	$.13	West Virginia	$.2535
Nebraska	$.239	South Dakota	$.22	Wyoming	$.13

Data obtained from Web site *http://.iftach.org/taxmatrix/printrates.asp?QY=4Q2000&F=2* using the 4th quarter data

PROBLEM SOLVING

Exercise A   Use the table above to solve. Round to the nearest whole gallon before finding the tax.

1. Melvin's trucking company drove 12,470 miles in Virginia, 8,056 miles in West Virginia, and 9,452 miles in Ohio in one month. His trucks get 5 mpg. How much is the fuel tax?

2. Ms. Diaz's truck gets 6 mpg. In three months, this is where she drove: Washington, 1,350 mi.; Idaho, 512 mi.; Montana, 2,782 mi.; North Dakota, 1,734 mi.; and South Dakota, 864 mi. What is her fuel tax?

3. A trucking company makes regular runs between New York City and Bangor, Maine. Each run is 430 miles in New York, 120 miles in Vermont, 150 miles in New Hampshire, and 224 miles in Maine. Each truck gets 5.5 mpg. How much fuel tax is owed for each run?

4. Haul-Em has a fleet of 9 trucks. Each truck gets 4.5 mpg. Each truck makes the same monthly run through these states: Tennessee, 428 mi.; Missouri, 729 mi.; Nebraska, 1,156 mi.; Wyoming, 862 mi.; Idaho, 361 mi.; and Washington, 1,346 mi. How much is the fuel tax for all 9 trucks for one year?

Apportioned plate

License plate that allows a vehicle to operate in several states

Businesses must license their trucks in states where they are regularly driven. A license for several states is called an **apportioned plate**. A business computes the percentage of miles a truck is driven in each state. The business then pays the correct percentage of the normal license fee to each state. A business applies for an apportioned plate in the state where the business is located. Some states may still require an additional fee or license. Yearly fees are based on the mileage driven the previous year.

EXAMPLES   Ms. Kelsey drove 46,134 miles in 1999. Of the total miles, she drove 9,688 miles in North Carolina. The annual fee for her apportioned plate in 2000 is $4,836. What percent of the fee does North Carolina receive?

Step 1   Write the ratio as a decimal.

$$\frac{9,688 \text{ mi.}}{46,134 \text{ mi.}} \quad \begin{array}{l} \text{North Carolina mileage} \\ \text{Total mileage} \end{array}$$

$$\begin{array}{r} .209 \\ 46,134\overline{)9,688.000} \end{array}$$

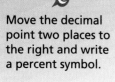

Move the decimal point two places to the right and write a percent symbol.

Step 2   Write the decimal as a percent. Round to the nearest whole percent.

$.209 = 20.9\% \approx 21\%$

North Carolina receives 21% of the license fee.

How much money does North Carolina receive?

Step 1   Write the percent as a decimal.

$21\% = .21$

Move the decimal point two places to the left and remove the percent symbol.

Step 2   Multiply the fee by the percent.

$$\begin{array}{r} \$ \quad 4,836 \\ \times \quad\quad .21 \\ \hline \$1,015.56 \end{array}$$

North Carolina receives $1,015.56 of the apportioned plate fee.

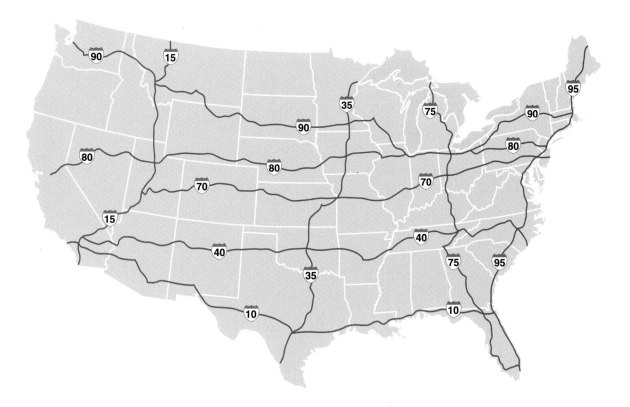

Exercise B Find each state's mileage percent and fee. Round to the nearest cent.

State	Total Annual Mileage	Annual State Mileage	State Mileage Percent	Apportioned Plate Fee	Fee Paid to State
1. Kentucky	82,561	24,768	_____	$6,342.00	_____
2. Alabama	65,920	16,480	_____	$3,782.50	_____
3. South Carolina	75,140	30,056	_____	$4,264.23	_____
4. California	61,590	21,556	_____	$3,904.38	_____
5. Kansas	94,170	7,533	_____	$5,420.65	_____
6. Iowa	128,304	19,245	_____	$6,004.90	_____
7. New Jersey	74,162	5,137	_____	$5,235.17	_____
8. Illinois	106,473	48,951	_____	$5,852.75	_____
9. New Mexico	134,281	68,234	_____	$6,953.28	_____
10. Rhode Island	92,308	1,236	_____	$6,247.11	_____

International business is conducted across national borders. A business operating in another country pays fees to both countries. A **tariff** is a tax on goods entering from another country. Tariffs are usually highest for goods that are also manufactured in the country they are shipped to. Tariffs encourage people to buy goods made in their own country by making foreign products more expensive. Each country has different tariffs for different goods. A tariff is usually a percentage of the **CIF**. The CIF is the sum of the **C**ost of goods and **I**nsurance and **F**reight for the goods.

EXAMPLE   A company ships 50,000 toys to Chile. The average cost of each toy is $9.72. The insurance costs $3,465.19. The freight costs $5,360.24. What is the CIF for the shipment?

Step 1   Multiply to find the total cost of the toys.

50,000 × $9.72 = $486,000

Step 2   Add to find the CIF.

$486,000.00   Cost of toys
    3,465.19   Insurance
+   5,360.24   Freight
$494,825.43   CIF

The CIF for the toys is $494,825.43.

TRY THIS...

Suppose the CIF for 62,000 medical kits is $7,999,607.40. If the insurance and freight remain the same as listed in problem 5 below, what is the average cost per medical kit?

Exercise A   Find the CIF for each shipment.

Item	Number of Items	Average Cost per Item	Insurance	Freight	CIF
1. Infant clothes	250,000	$3.75	$2,191.34	$3,468.70	_____
2. Baseball bats	75,000	$7.42	$3,171.48	$6,472.93	_____
3. Radios	45,000	$13.48	$4,965.27	$8,560.09	_____
4. Computers	25,000	$348.50	$10,560.12	$15,347.38	_____
5. Medical kits	62,000	$118.62	$8,431.74	$7,435.62	_____

Export

Sell to another country

Import

Buy from another country

Governments make trade agreements, such as the North American Free Trade Agreement (NAFTA). Governing bodies such as the United States Congress then accept or reject the trade agreements. Trade agreements usually include tariffs between countries. A business hopes for lower tariffs on goods it **exports**. Exporting goods is selling goods to another country. **Importing** goods is buying goods from another country.

TRY THIS...

Suppose the tariff is $5,386 for a CIF of $26,930. What is the tariff as a percentage of CIF?

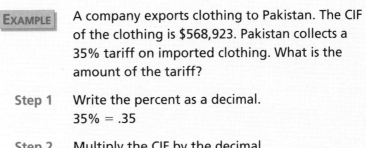

EXAMPLE A company exports clothing to Pakistan. The CIF of the clothing is $568,923. Pakistan collects a 35% tariff on imported clothing. What is the amount of the tariff?

Step 1 Write the percent as a decimal.
$35\% = .35$

Step 2 Multiply the CIF by the decimal.

$$
\begin{array}{r}
\$\ \ 568,923 \quad \text{CIF} \\
\times \underline{\qquad .35} \quad \text{Tariff as a decimal} \\
\$199,123.05 \quad \text{Tariff}
\end{array}
$$

The company has to pay a tariff of $199,123.05.

Exercise B Compute the tariff for each CIF and percent. Round to the nearest cent.

CIF	Tariff Percent	Tariff
1. $236,341	22%	_____
2. $439,468	18%	_____
3. $626,802	7%	_____
4. $192,564	11%	_____
5. $75,658	9%	_____
6. $196,358.25	25%	_____
7. $846,597.15	30%	_____
8. $1,568,672.28	45%	_____
9. $3,793,106.34	26%	_____
10. $5,809,687.05	19%	_____

Companies pass on the costs of foreign taxes, tariffs, and even international phone calls to their customers. This increases the price of goods sold in foreign countries.

EXAMPLE   A French company sells a pair of gloves in France for $11.35. After paying United States taxes and tariffs, it sells the gloves in the United States for $23.71. What is the percent increase in price?

Method 1

Step 1   Subtract the original price from the new price.
$23.71 − $11.35 = $12.36   Price increase

Step 2   Divide the price increase by the original price.
Divide until you have three decimal places.

$$
\begin{array}{r}
1.088 \\
11.35\,)\overline{12.36\,000}
\end{array}
\qquad 12.36 \div 11.35 \approx 1.088
$$

Step 3   Write the decimal as a percent. Round to the nearest whole percent.
1.088 = 108.8% ≈ 109%   Percent increase

Method 2

Step 1   Divide the new price by the original price.
Divide until you have three decimal places.
23.71 ÷ 11.35 ≈ 2.088

Step 2   Write the decimal as a percent. Round to the nearest whole percent.
2.088 = 208.8% ≈ 209%   Percent of new price to old price

Step 3   Subtract 100% to find the percent Increase.
209% − 100% = 109%

Taxes and tariffs increase the price of the gloves 109%.

PROBLEM SOLVING

Exercise C   Solve. Round answers to the nearest whole percent.

1. A company sells a football in its own country for $6.07. After foreign taxes and tariffs, the price is $18.34. What is the percent increase?

2. A company sells a blouse in its own country for $9.51. After foreign taxes and tariffs, the price is $13.68. What is the percent increase?

3. A company sells a sack of rice in its own country for $5.19. After foreign taxes and tariffs, the price increases 158%. What is the new price?

4. A company sells 10,000 CDs in its country for $21.90 each. Taxes and tariffs increase the price 85%. What is the new price of 10,000 CDs?

The Pipes Are Calling

"Asbestos? We've got to get rid of it—no question about it!" stated John. He was convinced he was right. But he didn't have all the facts.

John is the new president of Playtime USA, a manufacturer of toys and electronic games. The company has been in operation for a long time. John has been the president for just a year. He knows that asbestos is a harmful material that can cause health problems.

"But the air in the building has been checked over and over. It's clean," replied Alex, who is in charge of maintenance. Alex has been with Playtime USA for many years. He remembers when Playtime manufactured only small pinball machines.

"John, I've had experts look into it," Alex continued. "The asbestos is wrapped around pipes in the basement. There's no way anyone can breathe it. In fact, removing it could cause more harm than good. It could release asbestos fibers into the air. We decided long ago just to leave it alone. Plus, it would cost a fortune to remove it properly."

"Some of the workers think it's a problem," replied John. "And if they think it's a problem, then it is a problem. I don't want to lose even one good person because of this."

"Then maybe we can educate them. John, I really don't want to remove it. We'll have to shut down for a week if we decide the asbestos has to go. Is it worth it?"

"You bring up some good points, Alex. Let's get some more information and keep discussing this. But sooner or later, I think it will have to be done. How expensive did you say it is?"

"I didn't. But five years ago, the cost was about $30,000."

For Discussion

1. The cost for the removal job today is 25% higher than it was five years ago. Find the approximate cost of removal today.

2. What are Alex's main arguments against removing the asbestos that is wrapped around the basement pipes?

3. What are John's main concerns?

4. What do you think they should do? Explain.

Write the letter of the best answer to each question.

1. Zap Electric needs 3 FGD systems. Each system costs $28,451 plus $3,185 to install. What is the total cost of buying and installing the 3 systems?
   a. $31,636   b. $31,188   c. $62,272   d. $94,908

2. Grind Manufacturers installs 5 air-purifying systems. Each system has a collection unit, filter, and fan. The collection unit costs $2,187.32. The filter costs $4,919.80. The fan costs $7,248.55. What is the total cost of buying and installing the 5 systems?
   a. $86,134.02   b. $71,778.35   c. $43,067.01   d. $14,355.67

Use the mileage table for problem 3.

Truck Number	Miles Driven in Illinois	Miles Driven in Iowa	Miles Driven in Michigan	Miles Driven in Wisconsin	Miles Driven in Indiana
158	4,591	7,108	3,802	2,557	1,373

3. What percent of truck #158's total miles were driven in Michigan? Round to the nearest whole percent.

Solve problems 4–15.

4. The Model 2385 Clean Air system removes 99.7% of pollutants from the air. Suppose the manufacturing process produces 2.0 cubic feet of pollutants. How many cubic feet of air pollutants are not removed by the air purifier?

5. A store needs a wheelchair ramp 41 feet long, 4 feet wide, and 1 foot high. The ramp will be solid concrete. How many cubic feet of concrete are used in the ramp? Use the formula $V = \frac{lwh}{2}$.

6. A ramp uses 324 cubic feet of concrete. How many cubic yards of concrete are in the ramp? (HINT: 27 cu. ft. = 1 cu. yd.)

7. Hernandez & Sons installs handrails on both sides of a wheelchair ramp. The handrails use eight 6-foot posts, eight post caps, and 48 feet of railing. Posts cost $3.79 per foot. Post caps cost $.91 each. Railing costs $2.85 per foot. How much do the materials for the handrails cost?

8. An office building needs a new automatic door. The height of the door is 7 feet 2 inches, and the width is $41\frac{1}{2}$ inches. What is the total area of the door in square inches?

9. A truck can go 5 miles on 1 gallon of fuel. It is driven 78,000 miles. How many gallons of fuel does it use?

10. A company's truck drove 24,560 miles in Tennessee. The truck averages 5.5 miles per gallon. Tennessee charges $.17 per gallon for fuel tax. How much does the company owe Tennessee for fuel tax?

11. Dash Trucking Company drove a total of 458,322 miles. They drove 48,261 of the miles in Georgia. What percent of the total miles were driven in Georgia? Round to the nearest whole percent.

12. Crawley Industries ships 4,200 electronic components to Brazil. Each component costs $2.17. The insurance for shipping costs $1,103.25. The freight costs $2,315.62. What is the total cost, including shipping and freight?

13. A company imports steel from the United States. The CIF for the steel is $195,306.71. The tariff is 48% of the CIF. What is the total amount of CIF and tariff? Round to the nearest cent.

14. Making Industries sells a picture in its own country for $7.50. After foreign taxes and tariffs, the price of the picture in other countries is $23.81. What is the percent increase in price? Round to the nearest whole percent.

15. A vase costs an importer $10.50 before taxes and tariffs. After taxes and tariffs, the vase costs 152% of its original cost. What is the cost of the vase after taxes and tariffs? Round to the nearest cent.

Test-Taking Tip	Before substituting values in a formula, write what each variable represents. For example, before writing $V = (3 \times 2 \times 1.5) \div 2$ in the volume formula $V = \frac{lwh}{2}$, write $l = 3$ ft., $w = 2$ ft., $h = 1.5$ ft.

Risks for Business Owners

Businesses are affected by many events that cannot be predicted. Companies may have to raise their prices because inflation raises their costs. Business owners buy insurance to protect their businesses from some of the risks. They buy catastrophic insurance to protect themselves from losing crops and other assets. They buy malpractice insurance to protect themselves from losses resulting from lawsuits. All these costs increase the prices of their products and services. Unless business owners increase their prices to cover increased costs, their profits will decrease, and their businesses may go bankrupt.

In this chapter, you will learn about one measure of inflation. You will learn about catastrophic insurance and malpractice insurance. You will use math skills to compute the price increases necessary to cover these expenses.

Goals for Learning

▶ To compute price increases and new prices based upon inflation

▶ To calculate the Consumer Price Index

▶ To calculate costs of catastrophic loss

▶ To understand how the cost of malpractice insurance increases industry costs

Overhead

Expenses that are not costs of production or sales, such as rent, utilities, and insurance

To keep the same profits, business owners raise prices when expenses increase. Some expenses are administrative costs, such as rent, utilities, and insurance. These are called **overhead**.

> Move the decimal point two places to the left and remove the percent symbol.

> The product has the same number of decimal places as the sum of the decimal places in each factor.

EXAMPLE Sheila owns a small dry cleaning business. She charges $2.25 to clean a pair of pants. This year the electric company raised her rates by 25%. Her rent was raised by 5%, and cleaning supplies cost 3% more than last year. She decides to raise her prices by 25%. What will Sheila charge for cleaning a pair of pants?

Step 1 Write the percent as a decimal.

25.% = .25

Step 2 Multiply the price by the decimal increase to find the price increase.

2 decimal places + 2 decimal places = 4 decimal places
↓ ↓ ↓
$2.25 × .25 = $.5625

Round to the nearest cent. $.5625 ≈ $.56

Step 3 Add the price increase to the original price.

$2.25   Original price
+ .56   Price increase
$2.81   New price

Sheila will charge $2.81 for cleaning a pair of pants.

Exercise A Find the new price of each item. Round to the nearest cent.

Item	Original Price	Percent Increase	New Price
1. Desk	$189.00	15%	_____
2. Calculator	$25.95	20%	_____
3. In-line skates	$245.00	7%	_____
4. Soda	$.85	8%	_____
5. Shoes	$58.95	6%	_____

The general cost of goods and services increases with inflation. Business owners may raise their prices by the same percent as the inflation rate to keep from losing profits.

EXAMPLE Robert owns a bike shop. He sells a bike for $235.78. The yearly inflation rate is 3.6%. What is the new price of the bike after the price is increased by the percent of inflation?

Step 1   Write the percent as a decimal.   3.6% = .036

Step 2   Multiply to find the increase in price.

$ 235.78	Original price	← 2 decimal places
× .036	Decimal increase	← 3 decimal places
$8.48808	Price increase	← 5 decimal places

Round to the nearest cent. $8.48808 ≈ $8.49

Step 3   Add the price increase to the original price.

$235.78 + $8.49 = $244.27

The new price of the bike is $244.27.

PROBLEM SOLVING

Exercise B   Each business owner raises prices the same percent as the inflation rate. Round to the nearest cent.

1. A bed-and-bath store sells baskets for $34.85 each. The inflation rate is 2.1%. How much does the store raise the price of each basket?

2. Lisa owns a repair shop. She charges $45 per hour for labor. The inflation rate is 1.3%. How much does she raise the price for labor?

3. A store sells a dress for $85.91. The inflation rate is 3.4%. What is the price of the dress when it is adjusted for inflation?

4. Marvin charges $125 per hour for labor. The monthly inflation rate is .5%. He raises his hourly labor rate the same percent as the yearly inflation rate. What is his new labor rate?

The **Consumer Price Index (CPI)** is a measure of the change in price of certain goods and services. The prices of many goods and services around the United States are listed. The average prices are compared with the average prices of the same items from an earlier month or year. The earlier time is the base period.

The CPI for the same goods may be different for different areas. A lower CPI for housing in one area means that housing prices increased more in other areas. Within the same month, one area may have an increase in the CPI for housing and a decrease in the CPI for food.

EXAMPLE   In 1980 a loaf of bread cost $.85 in Town A and $.95 in Town B. In 2000 a loaf of bread cost $1.23 in Town A and $1.33 in Town B. What is the CPI for each town?

Step 1   Because 1980 is the base period, the CPI in 1980 for each town is 100.

	BASE PERIOD		CURRENT PERIOD	
Town	Average Price	Index	Average Price	Index
Town A	$.85	100	$1.23	???
Town B	$.95	100	$1.33	???

Step 2   Divide the current price by the base price for each town. Round to the nearest hundredth.

$$1.447 \approx 1.45$$

Town A $.85\overline{)1.23\,000}$

$$1.4$$

Town B $.95\overline{)1.33\,0}$

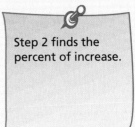

Step 2 finds the percent of increase.

Step 3   Multiply by the base period index to find the current period index.

Town A $1.45 \times 100 = 145$

Town B $1.4 \times 100 = 140$

The CPI for Town A is 145. The CPI for Town B is 140. A $.10 price increase in Town A causes a greater change in CPI than a $.10 price increase in Town B.

Exercise C Find the CPI for the same item in each city. Round to the nearest unit.

	BASE PERIOD		CURRENT PERIOD	
City	Average Price	Index	Average Price	Index
1. A	$1.50	100	$1.80	_____
2. B	$5.60	100	$5.88	_____
3. C	$8.30	100	$9.55	_____
4. D	$.62	100	$.81	_____
5. E	$.93	100	$1.26	_____
6. F	$23.45	100	$39.20	_____
7. G	$61.29	100	$75.28	_____
8. H	$9.18	100	$10.00	_____
9. I	$132.60	100	$145.80	_____
10. J	$205.60	100	$211.00	_____

Technology Connection

Value of Money

You can use the Internet to find the value today of $1.00 in 1950.
Go the Web site *http://woodrow.mpls.frb.fed.us/economy/ calc /
cpihome.html.*

Enter *1950* in the first box after "if in." The second box already has
"1.00" in it. Enter *2000* in the third box after "in." Click "Calculate."
The answer is *$7.15.* This means that you needed $7.15 in the year
2000 to buy goods that cost $1.00 in 1950. Repeat for other values
and years.

A business can go bankrupt if it is not insured against **catastrophic losses**. These are major losses caused by a natural disaster such as an earthquake, flood, tornado, hurricane, or blizzard. Business owners can protect themselves by buying catastrophic insurance to cover possible disasters.

Farmers buy catastrophic insurance to protect their incomes from loss of crops caused by natural disasters. This insurance guarantees payment of 50% of the average crop **yield**. The yield is the amount of crops produced per acre. Insurance companies use an average of 4 years.

Writing About Mathematics

A dozen eggs cost about $.30 in 1965 and about $1.80 in 2000. Was the value of money in 2000 greater or less? How can you determine this?

EXAMPLE   Mr. Johnson has catastrophic insurance. His insurance guarantees payment for 50% of the average crop yield. The last 4 years he has had yields of 84 bushels, 82 bushels, 90 bushels, and 98 bushels. For how many bushels per acre does his insurance guarantee payment?

Step 1   Find the average number of bushels.

$$84 + 82 + 90 + 98 = 354 \quad \text{Sum of the 4 yields}$$
$$354 \div 4 = 88.5 \quad\quad\quad\quad \text{Average yield}$$

Step 2   Write the percent of crops covered as a decimal.

$$50.\% = .50$$

Step 3   Find the number of bushels per acre covered by the policy.

$$
\begin{array}{ll}
88.5 & \text{Average number of bushels} \\
\times \;\; .5 & \text{Percentage of bushels covered as a decimal} \\
\hline
44.25 & \text{Number of bushels covered by policy}
\end{array}
$$

Mr. Johnson's catastrophic insurance guarantees payment for 44.25 bushels per acre.

Exercise A   An insurance company guarantees payment for 50% of the average yield. Find each average yield and the guaranteed payment number of bushels per acre.

Bushels per Acre for 4 Years	Average Yield per Acre	Guaranteed Payment Number of Bushels per Acre
1. 92 bushels, 100 bushels, 110 bushels, 98 bushels	_____	_____
2. 100 bushels, 120 bushels, 140 bushels, 120 bushels	_____	_____
3. 62 bushels, 58 bushels, 50 bushels, 74 bushels	_____	_____
4. 60 bushels, 65 bushels, 70 bushels, 80 bushels	_____	_____
5. 120 bushels, 110 bushels, 110 bushels, 130 bushels	_____	_____
6. 94 bushels, 96 bushels, 95 bushels, 93 bushels	_____	_____
7. 138 bushels, 109 bushels, 115 bushels, 127 bushels	_____	_____
8. 104 bushels, 86 bushels, 78 bushels, 95 bushels	_____	_____
9. 100 bushels, 116 bushels, 92 bushels, 125 bushels	_____	_____
10. 102 bushels, 80 bushels, 76 bushels, 72 bushels	_____	_____

TRY THIS...

Suppose the insurance company guarantees payment for 60% of the average yield. Find the number of guaranteed payment bushels per acre.

Catastrophic insurance guarantees payment for a certain crop yield. The payment is a percentage of the current market value of the crop.

EXAMPLE   Catastrophic insurance guarantees a farmer payment for 80 bushels per acre at 60% of the market price. Because of a hailstorm, the farmer harvests only 20 bushels per acre. The current market price is $3.00 per bushel. How much money per acre does the insurance pay for the loss? How much does the insurance pay for a 4,000-acre farm?

Step 1   Find the covered number of bushels.

   80 Guaranteed payment number of bushels per acre
−20 Number of bushels harvested per acre
   60 Bushels per acre paid for by insurance

Step 2   Find the price the insurance company pays per bushel.

Write the percent as a decimal.   60% = .60 = .6

$3.00 Market price
× .6 Percent of price as a decimal
$1.80 Insurance payment per bushel

Step 3   Find the insurance payment per acre.

$ 1.80 Insurance payment per bushel
×   60 Number of bushels per acre insurance pays for
$108.00 Insurance payment per acre

The catastrophic insurance pays $108 per acre for the loss.

Step 4   Find the insurance payment for the farm.

$ 108 Insurance payment per acre
× 4,000 Number of acres
$432,000 Total insurance payment for the farm

The catastrophic insurance pays $432,000 for the loss of crops on a 4,000-acre farm.

Exercise B   Complete the table. Catastrophic insurance pays 60% of the market price. Find the catastrophic insurance payment per bushel and per acre. Then find the total insurance payment for each size farm.

Number of Farm Acres	Guaranteed Payment Number of Bushels per Acre	Bushels per Acre Produced	Market Price per Bushel	Insurance Payment per Bushel	Insurance Payment per Acre	Total Insurance Payment
1. 3,000	50	20	$2.50	_____	_____	_____
2. 4,000	60	10	$3.50	_____	_____	_____
3. 2,000	70	40	$1.50	_____	_____	_____
4. 5,000	90	80	$2.80	_____	_____	_____
5. 5,600	100	42	$3.10	_____	_____	_____
6. 7,300	84	26	$2.70	_____	_____	_____
7. 4,500	78	19	$1.60	_____	_____	_____
8. 6,850	58	16	$4.90	_____	_____	_____
9. 785	64	31	$3.80	_____	_____	_____
10. 9,563	62	21	$3.70	_____	_____	_____

Malpractice insurance

Insurance that covers a failure in professional duty that results in injury, loss, or damage

Professionals need insurance to protect them from lawsuits. Doctors, lawyers, and other professionals carry **malpractice insurance** to pay the costs of lawsuits. Malpractice is a failure in professional duty that results in injury, loss, or damage. A doctor guilty of malpractice might have to pay a huge amount of money for a preventable injury. Malpractice insurance would pay a reasonable amount of the award plus the court fees. Professionals pass the cost of malpractice insurance on to their clients.

Humor on the Job

"Dan, I'll be out of the office most of the afternoon. I have a dentist appointment at 2:30."

"Ted, that's the best time to go to the dentist."

"What do you mean, Dan?"

"Tooth-hurtie."

| EXAMPLE | Dr. Thomas is a family doctor. She sees 500 patients a year. Her premium for malpractice insurance last year was $20,000. This year it is $30,000. How much does she need to increase the cost of an office visit to cover the increase in her malpractice insurance premium? |

Step 1   Find the increase in insurance premium.

$30,000   New premium
−20,000   Old premium
$10,000   Increase in premium

Move the decimal point the same number of places left or right in both the dividend and the divisor.

Step 2   Divide the increase by the number of patients.

$$\begin{array}{r} 20 \\ 500)\overline{10,000} \end{array} \quad \to \quad \begin{array}{r} 20 \\ 5)\overline{100} \end{array}$$

Dr. Thomas raises the cost of an office visit by $20 to cover the increase in her malpractice insurance premium.

PROBLEM SOLVING

Exercise C   Solve. Each doctor passes on the increased cost of malpractice insurance to patients. Round to the nearest cent.

1. Dr. Mitchell sees 620 patients a year. His malpractice insurance premiums increase $5,797. How much does he increase the cost of an office visit?

2. Dr. Burger does 200 operations a year. She paid $125,000 for malpractice insurance last year and $159,000 this year. How much does she increase the cost of an operation?

3. Dr. James sees 400 patients a year. Last year he charged $25 for an office visit. His malpractice premium increased $2,000. How much does an office visit now cost?

4. Dr. Westerly sees 500 patients a year. Last year she charged $65 per visit. She paid $21,350 for malpractice insurance last year and $27,900 this year. What is her charge per visit now?

Application

The Price Is Right

The top executives of Hardin Software Company are discussing pricing. Hardin sells educational software. Its best seller is *Hooked on Physics*, which sells for $29.95.

"Let's increase the price," suggests Leslie, the company president. "It's been at the same price for over a year. Inflation is running about 5% a year."

How to set the price of this software is a big issue for the company. *Hooked on Physics* produced about $300,000 of Hardin's revenues last year. This year it is expected to sell just as well.

"I don't like increasing the price," counters Eve, who heads the marketing group. "It would put the price over $30. I'm for keeping the price where it is."

"But look at the extra revenue we lose if we don't raise the price, Eve."

"That's true. But we could also lose revenue by raising the price, Leslie. We could lose customers."

Leslie doesn't seem to be listening. She is looking at her calculator. "Let's see. A 5% increase puts the price at $31.45. I think we should go with that."

"If you have to raise the price, why leave it at $31.45? Make it $31.95."

For Discussion

1. Estimate the number of units of *Hooked on Physics* sold last year.

2. Explain why Eve is against increasing the price.

3. Why do you think the product was originally priced at $29.95 instead of $30.00?

4. Which of the two executives understands pricing psychology better? Explain.

Write the letter of the best answer to each question.

1. A store owner charges $15.70 for a scarf. She raises the price by 20% to pay for increased costs. By how much does she increase the price of the scarf?

   a. $1.57   **b.** $2.00   **c.** $3.14   **d.** $5.70

2. Mr. Fitzgerald owns a clothing store. He sells pants for $45.80. He increases the price 10% to pay for increased costs. What do the pants sell for now?

   a. $50.38   **b.** $55.80   **c.** $46.80   **d.** $46.26

The table shows the average price of a loaf of bread in five cities. Use the table for problems 3–7.

City	BASE PERIOD Price	BASE PERIOD Index	CURRENT PERIOD Price	CURRENT PERIOD Index
A	$1.20	100	$1.80	150
B	$2.30	100	$3.80	165
C	$1.85	100	$2.59	140
D	$3.20	100	$3.84	120
E	$2.10	100	$3.57	170

3. Which city had the highest base price?

4. Which city had the lowest base price?

5. Which city had the greatest increase in price?

6. Which city has the highest current price?

7. Which city has the highest Consumer Price Index?

Solve problems 8–15.

8. A loaf of bread costs $2.29. The price is increased by the same percent as the 2.5% inflation rate. What is the price increase? Round to the nearest cent.

9. The yearly inflation rate is 4.8%. Mr. Daily increases the prices in his store by the inflation rate. What is the new price of skates that sold for $28.50? Round to the nearest cent.

10. The price of milk was $1.30 in the base year. The current price of milk is $2.08. What is the Consumer Price Index for milk?

11. A dozen eggs cost $.45 ten years ago in the base year. A dozen eggs now cost $.81. What is the Consumer Price Index for a dozen eggs?

12. Carl's harvests for the last four years were 92, 68, 80, and 86 bushels per acre. What is his average yield per acre?

13. Denise has catastrophic insurance that pays for 50% of her average crop yield for the last 4 years. The harvests for the last 4 years were 74, 80, 92, and 84 bushels per acre. For how many bushels per acre does the insurance pay?

14. Roger's catastrophic insurance guarantees payment for 60 bushels per acre. He harvested only 20 bushels per acre because of heavy rains. The insurance pays for 60% of the market value. The market price of his crop is $3.00 per bushel. How much money per acre does his insurance pay?

15. Dr. Watson sees 500 patients in her office each year. She charges $62 for an office visit. She paid $27,000 for malpractice insurance last year and $30,000 this year. She increases the price of an office visit just enough to cover the increase in her insurance premium. How much does she charge for an office visit now?

Test-Taking Tip | Check your answer by doing the problem again. Be sure to cover the answer. Then compare answers.

Chapter

12

Sales and Marketing

All businesses make sales and revenue projections. A successful business needs to plan how to sell its products to customers. A marketing plan may include advertising, conventions, exhibits, and entertainment. Each marketing plan must produce at least enough new sales to cover the marketing expenses.

In this chapter, you will learn about different types of marketing plans and evaluate their effectiveness. You will learn how revenues are used for the future growth of a company. You will use math skills to evaluate sales and marketing strategies.

Goals for Learning

▶ To determine the sales needed to cover operating expenses and have 10% left for the company's growth

▶ To calculate the number of inquiries that result in sales at a convention

▶ To compare the costs of a convention booth and entertainment to the revenues they are expected to bring

▶ To determine the number of employees needed in a convention booth

▶ To compare the cost of a promotion with the number of potential customers it will reach

▶ To choose the market channel most likely to reach the potential buyer

▶ To determine a good return on a marketing piece

Cost of goods sold

Cost of manufacturing or buying the product that is sold

Gross profit

Difference between sales and cost of goods sold

A company must sell enough goods to cover the **cost of goods sold** and operating expenses. The cost of goods sold is the cost to buy or manufacture the product that is sold. The difference between sales and cost of goods sold is **gross profit**.

EXAMPLE | Blaze Candle Company sells a candle for $6.75. The cost of goods sold for each candle is $4.50. The company's monthly operating expenses are $4,500. How many candles must be sold monthly to cover the operating expenses?

Step 1 Estimate.

$6.75 ≈ $7 $4.50 ≈ $5 $4,500 ≈ $5,000

Subtract the cost from the selling price.

$7 − $5 = $2

Divide the operating expenses by the difference.

$5,000 ÷ $2 = 2,500

Blaze Candle Company needs to sell **about 2,500** candles.

Step 2 Find the difference between the selling price and the cost of goods sold.

$ 6.75   Selling price
− 4.50   Cost of goods sold
$ 2.25   Gross profit per candle

Move the decimal point in the divisor first. Move the decimal point in the dividend the same number of places and in the same direction.

Step 3 Divide the operating expenses by the gross profit per candle.

$$\begin{array}{r} 20\ 00 \\ 2.25\overline{)4{,}500.00} \end{array}$$

The answer is close to the estimate. Blaze Candle Company must sell 2,000 candles each month to cover operating expenses.

Exercise A Find each company's gross profit per item. Then find the number of sales necessary to pay the cost of goods sold and operating costs.

Company	Monthly Operating Expenses	Selling Price per Item	Cost per Item	Gross Profit per Item	Number of Sales
1. Toy Carz	$8,100.00	$8.95	$4.45	_____	_____
2. Bubbles	$4,625.00	$2.10	$.85	_____	_____
3. Bulb Magic	$34,230.00	$3.71	$2.08	_____	_____
4. Bee Books	$23,250.00	$6.95	$3.85	_____	_____
5. Waves Etc.	$15,162.00	$11.25	$7.64	_____	_____
6. Style Friends	$20,615.00	$.62	$.27	_____	_____
7. Card City	$17,793.60	$1.66	$.34	_____	_____
8. Saw Tooth	$12,226.50	$21.38	$13.97	_____	_____
9. Mixed Nuts	$4,836.00	$.83	$.57	_____	_____
10. Squares	$20,643.50	$58.72	$36.99	_____	_____

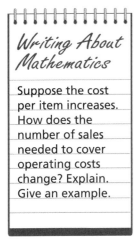

Writing About Mathematics

Suppose the cost per item increases. How does the number of sales needed to cover operating costs change? Explain. Give an example.

Businesses must pay expenses and earn a profit. A successful business also must grow. A successful company uses some of its profits for growth.

EXAMPLE Everyday Wear manufactures a jacket that sells for $18.62. Each jacket costs $4.95 to manufacture. Everyday Wear's monthly operating expenses are $7,980. How many jackets must be sold monthly to cover operating expenses and have 10% extra for future growth?

Step 1 Find the difference between the selling price and the cost of one jacket.

$18.62 Selling price per jacket
$- 4.95$ Cost per jacket
$13.67 Gross profit per jacket

Step 2 Find 10% of operating expenses for growth.
10% = .10

$7,980 × .10 = $798.00 Money for growth

Step 3 Add the money for growth to operating expenses.

$7,980 Operating expenses
$+ 798$ Money for growth
$8,778 Sales needed

Step 4 Divide sales needed by gross profit per jacket. Divide to one decimal place.

$$\begin{array}{r} 642.1 \\ 13.67\overline{)8,778.00\,0} \end{array}$$

Round up to 643 to cover operating expenses and 10% growth.

Everyday Wear must sell 643 jackets each month to cover operating expenses and have money for 10% growth.

Alternate Method for Step 2

Another way to find 10% of a number is to move the number's decimal point one place to the left.

$7,980 × 10% =
$7,980 × .1 = $798.0

Exercise B   Each company sells just enough to cover monthly operating expenses and have 10% for future growth. Complete the table to find the number of items sold. Round the number of sales up to the next whole number.

Company	Monthly Operating Expenses	Operating Costs Plus 10% Growth	Selling Price per Item	Cost per Item Sold	Gross Profit per Item	Number of Items Sold
1. A	$6,200	_____	$19.78	$9.78	_____	_____
2. B	$9,300	_____	$26.81	$23.40	_____	_____
3. C	$11,000	_____	$52.94	$16.24	_____	_____
4. D	$15,000	_____	$17.80	$2.38	_____	_____
5. E	$29,584	_____	$39.99	$21.35	_____	_____

TRY THIS...

What percent of the selling price per item is the cost per item sold?

Technology Connection

Percents

You can use a calculator to find what percent of the selling price per item is the cost per item sold.

Step 1	Key in the cost per item.
Step 2	Press ÷.
Step 3	Key in the selling price per item sold.
Step 4	Press %.

For example, suppose the selling price of a car battery is $64. The car battery costs $40. Use a calculator to find what percent of the selling price is the cost of the battery.

Press: 40 ÷ 64 %   The display on most calculators reads *62.5*.

The cost of the car battery is 62.5% of its selling price.

Conventions and Exhibits

Many businesses promote their products with booths and exhibits at conventions. Salespeople talk to potential customers. Businesses hope to make future sales from exhibiting and talking about their products at conventions.

EXAMPLES | Static Charge sells electronic equipment. It has a booth at an electronics convention. During the convention it has 2,400 inquiries about its products. After follow-up calls, 850 of the inquiries result in sales. What percent of the inquiries result in sales?

Step 1 Write the ratio of sales to inquiries as a decimal. Round to two decimal places.

$\dfrac{850}{2,400}$ Sales
Inquiries

$\dfrac{.354}{2,400 \overline{)850.000}} \approx .35$

Step 2 Write the decimal as a percent. $.35 = 35\%$

About 35% of the inquiries result in sales.

If 35% of inquiries result in sales, how many inquiries are needed for 1,000 sales?

Write and solve a proportion. Round to the nearest whole number.

$\dfrac{850}{2,400} = \dfrac{1,000}{\blacksquare}$ Sales
Inquiries

Find the cross products.

$850 \times \blacksquare = 1,000 \times 2,400 \qquad 850\blacksquare = 2,400,000$

Divide by 850.

$850\overline{)2,400,000}$ ⟶ $\dfrac{2,823.5}{85\overline{)240,000.0}} \approx 2,824$

Static Charge needs 2,824 inquiries to make 1,000 sales.

Exercise A   Solve. Round to the nearest whole percent or whole number.

1. Sea Fare has 3,600 inquiries about its products, with 612 of the inquiries resulting in sales. What percent of the inquiries result in sales?

2. Carton Carriers has 960 inquiries resulting in 336 sales. What percent of the inquiries result in sales? How many inquiries are needed to make 500 sales?

3. Del Saws has 2,230 inquiries resulting in 200 sales. What percent of the inquiries result in sales? How many inquiries are needed to make 500 sales?

4. A convention booth boasts that 56% of inquiries result in sales. How many inquiries would be needed for 640 sales? for 1,000 sales?

At a convention, companies pay for booth space, employee wages, and samples given away. Companies expect that sales resulting from the convention will more than cover the convention expenses.

EXAMPLE   Hilarious Hats pays $1,200 for booth space at a convention. It pays 8 employees $150 each to staff the booth. It gives away hats with the company's name and logo that cost $1,752. How many sales are needed to cover the costs of the convention if the average profit per hat is $1.75?

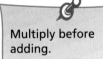

Multiply before adding.

Step 1   Find the convention costs.
$1,200 + (8 × $150) + $1,752 = $4,152

Step 2   Divide the costs by the profit per hat. Round up to cover the costs.
$4,152 ÷ $1.75 = 2,372.5714 ≈ 2,373

Hilarious Hats must sell 2,373 hats to cover the convention costs.

Exercise B Solve, given the average profit per sale. Round sales up.

1. A convention costs a company a total of $2,870. It earns a $3.50 profit on each sale. How many sales are needed to cover the convention costs?

2. Merry Machines pays a total of $4,860 in convention costs. The profit on each sale is $6.84. How many sales are needed to cover the convention costs?

3. Jolly J. pays $1,350 for a booth and $1,850 for mugs to give away. It pays 6 people $125 each to staff the booth. The profit per sale is $298. How many sales are needed to cover convention costs?

4. LL Co. pays $652 per day for a booth and gives away 2,000 pencils that cost $.23 apiece. It pays 8 people $125 each per day. The profit on each sale is $.64. How many sales are needed to cover the 2-day convention costs?

Companies want enough employees at a booth, but no more than are actually needed.

EXAMPLE LinCo expects 80 people an hour to visit its booth. Each visitor takes about 2 minutes of an employee's time. How many employees are needed at the booth each hour?

Step 1 Find the total number of minutes per hour with visitors.

80 people × 2 minutes = 160 minutes

Step 2 Divide by the minutes in an hour to find the number of employees needed. Round up.

160 minutes ÷ 60 minutes ≈ 2.6 = 3

LinCo needs 3 employees at the booth each hour.

Exercise C Find the number of employees needed each hour. Round up.

	Visitors per Hour	Time with Each Visitor	Employees Needed per Hour
1.	90	4.0 minutes	_____
2.	150	3.0 minutes	_____
3.	85	2.0 minutes	_____
4.	230	3.5 minutes	_____
5.	300	4.5 minutes	_____

Conventions often involve entertainment expenses.

EXAMPLE A salesperson takes 7 customers to dinner for $45.72 each, including tip. Each customer is given a key chain with the company's logo that costs $.89. What is the company's entertainment cost?

Step 1 Multiply the costs by the number of people.

Dinner for 8: $45.72 × 8 = $365.76   Key chains for 7: $.89 × 7 = $6.23

Step 2 Add the costs. $365.76 + $6.23 = $371.99

The company's entertainment cost is $371.99.

PROBLEM SOLVING

Exercise D Solve.

1. A company gives away 20 theater tickets. Each ticket costs $52 per person. How much is the entertainment expense?

2. A company takes 12 people to dinner for $38.17 per person, including tip. How much is the entertainment expense?

3. Pleasant Pastimes takes 34 people to dinner for $25.84 each. It gives away 15 theater tickets that cost $65 each. How much are the entertainment costs?

4. Misty Mirrors spends $3,559.75 for a banquet for 115 people and a vacation giveaway. The vacation giveaway costs $2,450. How much does the banquet cost per person?

Distribution

Number of readers of a magazine or newspaper

Marketing channel

A place to advertise

Companies need to find who their potential customers are and how to reach them. A **marketing channel** is a place to advertise. One marketing channel is popular magazines. Companies research which magazines their customers read. They ask how many readers the magazine has, which is called the **distribution**. Companies then spend their advertising budgets where potential sales revenues are greatest.

EXAMPLE

Alt Furniture sells chairs. It wants to advertise a chair. The cost of advertising in *One Magazine* is $265,000. *One Magazine* has a distribution of 2,400,000 readers. The company expects that $\frac{1}{50}$ of *One's* readers will buy the chair. What is the advertising cost for each chair sold by the advertisement?

Step 1   Find the number of sales.

$$\frac{1}{50} = 1 \div 50 = .02$$

2,400,000	Distribution
$\times$ .02	Fraction who buy, written as a decimal
48,000.00	Number of chairs sold

Step 2   Divide the advertisement cost by the number of chairs sold. Round to the nearest cent.

$$\begin{array}{r} 5.520 \approx 5.52 \\ 48,000 \overline{)265,000} \longrightarrow 48\overline{)265.000} \end{array}$$

Advertising in *One Magazine* costs $5.52 for each chair sold by the advertisement.

Exercise A Find the advertising cost per sale. Round to the nearest cent.

Magazine Distribution	Cost of Advertising	Fraction of Readers Who Buy	Advertising Cost per Sale
1. 500,000	$25,000	$\frac{1}{100}$	————
2. 200,000	$45,000	$\frac{1}{50}$	————
3. 940,000	$80,000	$\frac{1}{25}$	————
4. 585,000	$50,000	$\frac{3}{100}$	————
5. 2,100,000	$125,000	$\frac{1}{40}$	————

Profile

Shopping patterns of potential customers

Manufacturers want to sell their products to stores that will resell them to the greatest number of people.

Companies create **profiles**, which are the shopping patterns of their potential customers. They use these profiles to decide which stores are the best marketing channels for their products.

The table below shows the percent of shopping time each age and gender spends in different department stores.

Age	Gender	Store A	Store B	Store C	Store D	Store E	Store F	Store G
15–20	F	39%	0%	25%	20%	2%	9%	5%
15–20	M	4%	4%	2%	34%	11%	30%	15%
21–25	F	25%	10%	13%	28%	4%	15%	5%
21–25	M	10%	12%	5%	31%	9%	23%	10%
26–30	F	35%	4%	14%	25%	6%	10%	6%
26–30	M	3%	18%	5%	24%	22%	13%	15%
31–40	F	28%	7%	8%	39%	6%	3%	9%
31–40	M	12%	28%	3%	28%	12%	15%	2%
41–50	F	36%	8%	9%	31%	1%	4%	11%
41–50	M	21%	32%	1%	35%	6%	4%	1%

EXAMPLE	Imagine Video markets a new video game to 18-year-old men and women. Store D and Store F sell the video game. Which store attracts more potential buyers?

Step 1 Use the table on page 239 to find the percent of 18-year-olds shopping in each store.

Store D   Women: 20%   Men: 34%
Store F   Women: 9%   Men: 30%

Step 2 Add the percents for each store.

Store D: 20% + 34% = 54%
Store F: 9% + 30% = 39%

Step 3 Compare the percents.   54% > 39%

Store D attracts more potential customers than Store F for Imagine Video's new video game.

PROBLEM SOLVING

Exercise B   Use the table on page 239 to solve.

1. Clothes Closet manufactures skirts for women aged 31–40. Which store has the most potential buyers?

2. Bamm Hammers wants to sell to men aged 21–25. Which store has the most potential buyers?

3. A company wants to sell a product to men and women aged 31–40. At which store do most of their potential customers shop?

4. A software company wants to sell to men aged 26–30. It can sell at either Store D or any other two stores. Where should it sell its products?

Businesses evaluate whether marketing plans are effective by looking at the amount of profit from new sales.

> **EXAMPLE**   Krazy Kars spends a total of $18,000 on a marketing plan. It results in sales totaling $798,500. The profit is 25% of sales. The marketing plan is effective if it costs no more than 10% of the profit from the new sales. Is the marketing plan effective?

Step 1   Find the profit.

$25\% = .25$ $\$798,500 \times .25 = \$199,625$

Step 2   Find 10% of the profits from new sales. This is the most money that can be spent on an effective marketing plan.

$10\% = .10$ $\$199,625 \times .10 = \$19,962.50$

Step 3   Compare with the cost of the marketing plan.

$\$19,962.50 > \$18,000$

The cost of the marketing plan is less than 10% of profits from new sales. It is effective.

Exercise C The marketing plan is effective if it costs less than the given percent of profits from new sales. Write *Yes* or *No* to tell whether each marketing plan is effective.

	Cost of Marketing Plan	Sales	Profit as a Percent of Sales	Amount of Profit	Percent of Profit from New Sales	Maximum Amount for Effective Advertising	Effective?
1.	$8,000	$162,000	35%	_____	10%	_____	___
2.	$92,000	$4,900,000	40%	_____	8%	_____	___
3.	$16,400	$67,500	68%	_____	12%	_____	___
4.	$23,200	$186,300	95%	_____	5%	_____	___
5.	$13,800	$428,629	22%	_____	16%	_____	___
6.	$34,600	$1,648,000	18%	_____	20%	_____	___
7.	$29,500	$964,350	37%	_____	13%	_____	___
8.	$340,000	$1,965,000	44%	_____	4%	_____	___
9.	$500,000	$18,100,000	26%	_____	15%	_____	___
10.	$1,500,000	$42,620,000	80%	_____	5.6%	_____	___

Did You Know?

Many large companies advertise on television or in magazines. This allows them to reach more customers. Some of the largest companies in the United States actually spend over one billion dollars per year on advertising.

As the Cookie Crumbles

George and Melba Sweet manage a small company called The Cookie Jar, Inc. They started their company about a dozen years ago in their own kitchen. They quickly outgrew that arrangement. Now they have several full-time employees in a small plant across town.

Their newest item is oatmeal cookies, sold by the tin. The cookies come in two-pound and four-pound tins, priced at $12.95 and $19.95. The recipe is a family secret. They market the cookies to customers by direct mail.

"Melba, we need to perk up sales. These oatmeal cookies are great, but no one knows about them. Let's market the new cookies by direct mail to 5,000 potential customers."

"The cookies are already listed in our newest catalog, George. Why spend the money?"

"You have to spend money to make money. I've done some checking. Direct mailing costs about $3 per mailing. That covers producing a full-color piece about the cookies. And it includes postage, buying the list of potential customers, everything. I'll bet we get lots of orders."

"But they can't taste the cookies that way, George. I have a better idea. Let's produce a small package of sample cookies. Just two or three cookies, say $\frac{1}{4}$ pound. This way, we'll be giving away cookies, not pictures of cookies. We'll spend more money, but the orders will come rolling in, I think."

"Melba, that's expensive. You're probably talking about $7 per mailing."

"George, you have to spend money to make money."

For Discussion

1. Find the cost of 5,000 direct-mailings at $3 each. About how many free samples at $7 each can they ship for the same amount of money?

2. With whom do you agree more, Melba or George? Why?

3. Suppose George's promotion would produce 450 new orders. If the average order is worth about $35 in revenue, how much revenue would the promotion bring?

Write the letter of the best answer to each question.

1. Mark & Sons sells a marker for $3.29. The cost of each marker sold is $1.28. The operating expenses for one month are $3,962. How many markers must be sold to cover the operating expenses?

    a. 1,970   **b.** 1,972   **c.** 1,974   **d.** 1,980

2. Jumpin' Beans sells jelly beans for $1.87 per pound. The cost of each pound sold is $.23. The operating expenses for one month are $18,425. How many pounds of jelly beans must be sold to cover the monthly operating expenses?

    a. 11,000 pounds   **c.** 11,135 pounds
    b. 11,100 pounds   **d.** 11,235 pounds

The table below shows the percent of shopping time each age and gender spends in different department stores. Use the table for problems 3–4.

Age	Gender	Store A	Store B	Store C	Store D	Store E	Store F	Store G
15–20	F	41%	2%	19%	12%	8%	10%	8%
15–20	M	9%	8%	7%	15%	29%	20%	12%
21–25	F	31%	5%	20%	17%	8%	16%	3%
21–25	M	19%	24%	1%	6%	21%	28%	1%

3. Hair, Inc. plans to sell a new product for men and women aged 15–20. Which store has the greatest number of potential buyers?

4. A company sells sportswear for men and women aged 21–25. It sells in two stores. One store has the greatest number of potential male buyers. The other store has the greatest number of potential female buyers. Which two stores sell this sportswear?

Solve problems 5–10.

5. At a convention, Bugs Company has 920 inquiries about its batteries. These inquiries result in 617 sales. What percent of the inquiries result in sales? Round to the nearest whole percent.

6. Crash Computers pays $6,309 for a booth at a convention. It pays each of 10 workers $225 per day for 2 days. The profit on each computer sold is $175. How many sales are needed to cover the costs of the convention?

7. Tasty Nuts has a booth at a convention. An inquiry takes about 3.5 minutes of an employee's time. The average number of inquiries is 120 per hour. How many employees are needed in the booth each hour?

8. A company pays for dinner and theater tickets for 8 people. Dinner costs $42.75 per person, including tip. A theater ticket costs $58. How much are the entertainment costs?

9. A company spends $13,806 advertising a pillow in *Y Magazine. Y Magazine* has a distribution of 146,250 people. The company expects that $\frac{1}{25}$ of the readers will buy the pillow. What is the advertising cost for each pillow sold by the advertisement?

10. A company spends $11,200 on a marketing plan. It results in new sales totaling $356,900. The profit is 65% of sales. The marketing plan is effective if it costs no more than 5% of the profit from the new sales. Is the marketing plan effective?

Test-Taking Tip | Estimate percentages before calculating. For example, less than 50% of a number is less than half the number. More than 100% of a number is greater than the number.

Chapter

13

Mail-Order Business

Mail-order businesses sell mostly over the Internet and through catalogs. Many businesses with stores also use catalogs to sell items to customers who prefer shopping by mail. Mail-order businesses have large catalog, inventory, and shipping expenses. Their customer service relies on the phone, where timeliness and courtesy are very important.

In this chapter, you will learn about the different costs of mail-order businesses. You will use math skills to calculate the different costs of a mail-order business.

Goals for Learning

▶ To calculate the costs of catalog development and mailing

▶ To determine the costs of customer service systems and equipment

▶ To calculate and compare shipping costs for different carriers and delivery times

▶ To determine costs of handling, order fulfillment, and packaging

▶ To fill out order forms and calculate all ordering costs

▶ To compare the cost of inventory to the need for immediate order fulfillment

▶ To determine the costs of warehousing inventory

▶ To calculate the time needed to order products from manufacturers

Mass mailing
Sending a large number of the same items at the same time through the mail

Mail-order businesses use the Internet and catalogs to show their products to potential customers. The expense of developing a catalog includes costs for photography and writing descriptions of items for sale. There are expenses for the design and layout of each page. There are expenses for printing and publishing the catalogs. There may be extra charges for printing a different code on each catalog.

After catalogs are published, they are mailed. Businesses buy or develop mailing lists to reach potential customers. Catalogs are usually sent in a **mass mailing**. A mass mailing sends a large number of the same items at the same time. Mass mailings cost less than sending a few items at a time.

Businesses want to know the cost per catalog. This helps them evaluate whether this marketing channel is effective.

EXAMPLE Blueberries is a mail-order gift store. Its catalog has 90 pictures that cost $250 each. Each picture has a description that costs $45 each. Blueberries spends $125,600 to design and print the catalog. It spends $191,500 on a mass mailing. Blueberries mails 250,000 catalogs to potential customers. What is the cost to produce and mail each catalog?

Step 1 Find the cost of the pictures. $90 \times \$250 = \$22,500$
Find the cost of the descriptions. $90 \times \$45 = \$4,050$
Find the sum. $\$22,500 + \$4,050 = \$26,550$

Step 2 Find the total costs.

$\$26,550 + \$125,600 + \$191,500 = \$343,650$

Step 3 Find the cost per catalog. Round to the nearest cent.

$\$343,650 \div 250,000 = \$1.3746 \approx \$1.37$

It costs Blueberries $1.37 to produce and mail each catalog.

Exercise A   Find the cost per catalog. Round to the nearest cent.

	Catalogs Mailed	Number of Pictures and Descriptions	Cost per Picture	Cost per Description	Designing/ Printing Cost	Mailing Cost	Cost per Catalog
1.	200,000	85	$215	$38	$186,400	$157,000	_____
2.	300,000	62	$185	$42	$203,700	$217,500	_____
3.	280,000	110	$200	$50	$210,300	$185,490	_____
4.	400,000	95	$180	$55	$275,640	$286,350	_____
5.	600,000	120	$165	$48	$398,550	$486,250	_____
6.	500,000	230	$225	$58	$405,190	$352,941	_____
7.	850,000	105	$94	$65	$836,115	$628,372	_____
8.	1,200,000	230	$175	$75	$1,213,250	$923,450	_____
9.	2,000,000	72	$350	$100	$1,485,990	$1,438,261	_____
10.	2,800,000	286	$195	$85	$1,962,300	$1,981,867	_____

TRY THIS...

For problem 1, find the cost of the pictures and descriptions this way: First add the cost per picture and the cost per description. Then multiply the number of pictures and descriptions by the sum. Does 85 × ($215 + $38) = (85 × $215) + (85 × $38)? Repeat for problems 2–10.

800 number

Phone number that is free to the caller

Ordering from a catalog is easy and free. Customers call a free **800 number** to place an order. The call is paid for by the business. The cost to have an 800 number depends on the number of calls a business receives.

EXAMPLE   Simple Stuff asks its long-distance carrier for an 800 number. It can choose from two payment plans.

Plan A	Plan B
$25 per month, per phone	$5 per month, per phone
$.09 per minute	$.12 per minute
This plan charges for a fraction of a minute.	A fraction of a minute counts as a full minute.

Simple Stuff has 8 phones. The average call takes 4 minutes, 30 seconds. Which plan costs less if there are 600 calls per month?

Step 1   Find each monthly phone charge.

Plan A: $25 × 8 = $200   **Plan B:** $5 × 8 = $40

Step 2   Multiply the number of minutes by the cost per minute to find the cost of one call.

Plan A: Change seconds into a fraction of a minute. Write the fraction as a decimal.

30 seconds = $\frac{30}{60}$ minute = $\frac{1}{2}$ minute

$4\frac{1}{2}$ minutes × $.09 = 4.5 minutes × $.09 = $.405

Plan B: Round the seconds up to the next whole minute.

4 minutes, 30 seconds ≈ 5 minutes

5 minutes × $.12 = $.60

60 seconds = 1 minute

$\frac{1}{2}$ minute = .5 minute

Step 3   Multiply the number of calls by the cost per call to find the total cost of the calls.

Plan A: 600 × $.405 = $243   **Plan B:** 600 × $.60 = $360

Step 4   Add the monthly charge and the cost of the calls to find the total cost.

Plan A: $200 + $243 = $443   **Plan B:** $40 + $360 = $400

Step 5   Compare costs. $443 > $400

Plan B costs less if Simple Stuff receives 600 calls per month.

Exercise B   Use Plans A and B on page 250. Find each cost for one month. Round to the nearest cent.

	Phones	Calls	Average Call	Plan A Cost	Plan B Cost
1.	20	500	3 minutes, 30 seconds	_____	_____
2.	18	600	2 minutes, 30 seconds	_____	_____
3.	25	850	4 minutes, 45 seconds	_____	_____
4.	30	920	5 minutes, 15 seconds	_____	_____
5.	11	1,350	6 minutes, 5 seconds	_____	_____

Server

Large computer that connects many smaller computers

Employees taking orders use computers linked to a **server**. A server is a large computer that connects smaller computers.

> **EXAMPLE**   A mail-order business has 25 computers and a server. Each computer costs $1,428.72. The server costs $48,916.98. Equipment and network printers cost an additional $162,402.31. What is the cost for computer equipment?
>
> **Step 1**   Find the cost of 25 computers.
>
> $1,428.72 × 25 = $35,718
>
> **Step 2**   Find the total cost.
>
> $35,718 + $48,916.98 + $162,402.31 = $247,037.29
>
> The cost for computer equipment is $247,037.29.

   PROBLEM SOLVING

Exercise C   Solve.

1. A mail-order business orders 16 computers. Each costs $2,351.62. What is the cost of the computers?

2. Nancy's Clothing spends $53,863.68 for 32 computers for its mail-order business. How much does each computer cost?

3. A business buys 31 computers for $1,697.15 each and a server for $108,063.25. Programs, equipment, and printers cost $348,019.83. How much is the cost per call if the company expects 2,000,000 calls over the life of the equipment? Round to the nearest cent.

Ship
Send

Mail-order businesses send or **ship** items that are ordered. The buyer pays shipping costs. Some businesses charge a percentage of the sale for shipping.

EXAMPLE   Carla orders 8 plant hangers for $12.85 each and 6 plant stands for $22.50 each from a catalog. The shipping charge is the greater of $6\frac{1}{2}$% of the total cost or $14.50. How much does Carla pay for shipping?

Step 1   Find Carla's total purchases.

$8 \times $12.85 = 102.80 Plant hangers
$6 \times $22.50 = 135.00 Plant stands

$$102.80 + $135.00 = $237.80   Carla's total purchases

Step 2   Find $6\frac{1}{2}$% of the total purchases. Round to the nearest cent.

$237.80 \times 6\frac{1}{2}% = $237.80 \times 6.5% = $237.80 \times .065 = $15.457 \approx 15.46

Step 3   Compare. $15.46 > $14.50

Carla pays $15.46 for shipping.

PROBLEM SOLVING

Exercise A   Solve. Round to the nearest cent.

1. Mitch orders pots and pans that cost $408.50 from a kitchen catalog. The shipping charge is the greater of 6% of the total cost or $20. How much does Mitch pay for shipping?

2. Vicki orders a bike that costs $215.86 from a catalog. The shipping charge is the greater of 9% of the total cost or $15. How much does Vicki pay for shipping?

3. Loni orders 15 CDs. Each costs $19. The shipping charge is the greater of $8\frac{1}{2}$% of the total cost or $25. How much does Loni pay for shipping?

4. Pete orders 27 calculators. Each costs $29.85. The shipping charge is the greater of $7\frac{1}{2}$% of the total cost or $15. How much is the total cost including shipping?

Some shipping charges depend on the weight of the purchases and where they are being shipped. The company chooses the **carrier**, a business that delivers packages, that offers the best rate. Businesses offer customers faster delivery for an additional cost.

The table below shows rates for 2-day delivery service from Flushing, New York, to Temecula, California.

Carrier	Up to 1 Pound	More Than 1 Pound to 2 Pounds	More Than 2 Pounds to 3 Pounds	More Than 3 Pounds to 4 Pounds	More Than 4 Pounds to 5 Pounds
Carrier A	$3.50	$3.95	$5.15	$6.35	$7.55
Carrier B	$8.52	$9.83	$11.23	$12.73	$14.32
Carrier C	$10.40	$11.44	$12.74	$14.56	$16.38
Carrier D	$9.21	$10.63	$12.15	$13.77	$15.49

EXAMPLE Dale ordered in-line skates, knee guards, and a helmet from a mail-order catalog. His order weighs 2 pounds, 4 ounces. The company in Flushing, New York, ships to Dale in Temecula, California. Which carrier has the best rate?

Step 1 Find the column for 2 pounds, 4 ounces.
2 pounds < 2 pounds, 4 ounces < 3 pounds

Step 2 List the rate for each carrier from least to greatest.

Carrier A: $5.15
Carrier B: $11.23
Carrier D: $12.15
Carrier C: $12.74

Carrier A offers the best rate.

Did You Know?

Mailing a 1-ounce business letter at the post office cost 2 cents in 1921. Postage for the same letter was 3 cents in 1941, and 34 cents in 2001.

Many businesses choose a carrier that picks up packages when the business calls.

EXAMPLE   A mail-order business has a shipment of 6 packages. Each package weighs 1 pound, 12 ounces. How much would each carrier charge to ship them from Flushing, New York, to Temecula, California?

Step 1   Find the column for 1 pound, 12 ounces.
1 pound < 1 pound, 12 ounces < 2 pounds

Step 2   Find the shipping cost for each carrier. Use the shipping chart on page 253.

Carrier A: $3.95 × 6 = $23.70
Carrier B: $9.83 × 6 = $58.98
Carrier C: $11.44 × 6 = $68.64
Carrier D: $10.63 × 6 = $63.78

Carrier A charges $23.70. Carrier B charges $58.98.
Carrier C charges $68.64. Carrier D charges $63.78.

PROBLEM SOLVING

Exercise B   All packages are shipped from Flushing, New York, to Temecula, California, by Carrier B, C, or D. Use the shipping chart on page 253.

1. A mail-order business ships a package that weighs 4 pounds, 10 ounces. How much does it cost to ship using Carrier B?

2. Dazzle Enterprises ships 45 packages that weigh 3 pounds, 15 ounces each. How much does it cost to ship them using Carrier C?

3. A shipment has 21 packages weighing 2 pounds, 3 ounces each and 15 packages weighing 3 pounds, 8 ounces each. What is the cost of shipping by the least expensive carrier?

4. What is the difference in cost between shipping the packages in problem 3 by Carrier C and shipping them by Carrier B?

Most mail-order businesses offer faster delivery service for an additional cost. Carriers guarantee delivery by a given time on a given day. The cost of each delivery service varies with the weight of the package and how far it is shipped.

Costs to Ship 9 Pounds Between Zip Codes 60601 and 98101			
Guaranteed Delivery Time	Next-Day Service	Two-Day Service	Three-Day Service
8:00 A.M.	$68.91		
10:30 A.M.			
12:00 P.M.	$46.23	$29.71	$22.86
3:00 P.M.	$38.15		
4:30 P.M.	$35.91		
End of Day	$30.45	$25.78	$21.91

EXAMPLE   Fred Bovie's zip code is 60601. He orders 9 pounds of merchandise from a company whose zip code is 98101. He wants it shipped to his home. How much does next-day service by 10:30 A.M. cost? Use the chart above.

The cost is where the *10:30 A.M.* row and the *Next-Day Service* column meet.

Next-day service by 10:30 A.M. between zip codes 60601 and 98101 costs $51.19.

PROBLEM SOLVING

Exercise C   Use the chart above to solve.

1. Fred decides to use two-day service by 12:00 P.M. How much does shipping the 9-pound order cost?

2. If Fred's order is delivered the next day by 4:30 P.M., how much will it cost?

3. Fred changes his shipping time from three-day service by 12:00 P.M. to next-day service by 12:00 P.M. How much more money does he pay?

4. What is the difference in price between the most expensive and the least expensive delivery services?

After an order is received, an employee finds the items, packs them in a box, and labels the box. The customer's cost for processing and handling the order is usually included in a "shipping/handling" charge.

EXAMPLE

A company processes an order for 7 items. An employee finds the items and chooses a packing box. The box is 18 inches long by 12 inches wide by 16 inches high. Wrapping the items uses 1.5 square feet of packing material at $.42 per square foot. Handling the order takes the employee 30 minutes. The employee earns $18.90 per hour, including benefits. What is the total cost to process and handle the order?

The table shows the company's cost for packages of 10 boxes.

Length (inches)	Width (inches)	Height (inches)	Cost for 10 Boxes
12	12	12	$5.80
18	12	16	$8.10
20	20	20	$12.30
30	24	24	$18.70
36	24	24	$17.40

Step 1   Find the cost of the box.

Find the box size in the table.   18 inches by 12 inches by 16 inches

Divide to find the cost of one box.
$8.10 ÷ 10 = $.81

Step 2   Find the cost of the packing material.

1.5 square feet × $.42 per square foot = $.63

> Divide by 10 by moving the decimal point one place to the left.

Step 3   Find the cost of the employee's time.

30 minutes = $\frac{30}{60}$ hour = $\frac{1}{2}$ hour = .5 hour
$18.90 per hour × .5 hour = $9.45

Step 4   Find the total handling costs.

Box + Packing material + Employee's time = Total cost
↓   ↓   ↓   ↓
$.81 + $.63   + $9.45   = $10.89

The order costs $10.89 to process and handle.

Exercise A Use the table on page 256 to find the total cost of processing and handling. Round to the nearest cent.

	Box Size (inches)			Packing Material ($.42 per square foot)	Labor Time ($18.90 per hour)	Total Cost of Processing and Handling
	L	**W**	**H**			
1.	20	20	20	1.0 square foot	30 minutes	_____
2.	36	24	24	2.0 square feet	15 minutes	_____
3.	12	12	12	.5 square foot	15 minutes	_____
4.	18	12	16	1.5 square feet	10 minutes	_____
5.	36	24	24	2.5 square feet	5 minutes	_____

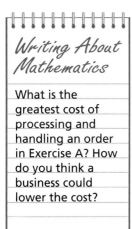

Writing About Mathematics

What is the greatest cost of processing and handling an order in Exercise A? How do you think a business could lower the cost?

Orders can be taken over the phone, by mail, or over the Internet. The same information is needed to complete an order.

EXAMPLE   Pamela Uri wants to order 1 blue and 2 red blouses in medium size. The catalog number is IZ1204. The blouses are on page 28 of the catalog. They cost $48.79 each. The sales tax is 7% of the total selling price. Shipping and handling is 8% of the selling price. Pamela wants to ship the blouses to her house at 10852 Dressy Lane, Omaha, Nebraska 68101. Her phone number is 601-555-2020. Complete the order form.

Step 1   Fill in Pamela's name, address, and phone number. To find *Total Price*, multiply *Quantity* by *Unit Price*.

$1 \times \$48.79 = \$48.79$ $2 \times \$48.79 = \$97.58$

Step 2   Find *Subtotal*. $\$48.79 + \$97.58 = \$146.37$

Step 3   Find *Sales Tax.* Round to the nearest cent.

$7\% \times \$146.37 = .07 \times \$146.37 = \$10.2459 \approx \$10.25$

Step 4   Find *Shipping/Handling.* Round to the nearest cent.

$8\% \times \$146.37 = .08 \times \$146.37 = \$11.7096 \approx \$11.71$

Step 5   Find *Total.*

$\$146.37 + \$10.25 + \$11.71 = \$168.33$

Name _Pamela Uri_	**Ship To:** _Pamela Uri_
Street or Route _10852 Dressy Lane_	**Street or Route** _10852 Dressy Lane_
City _Omaha_	**City** _Omaha_
State _NE_ **Zip Code** _68101_	**State** _NE_ **Zip Code** _68101_
Phone Number _(601) 555-2020_	**Phone Number** _(601) 555-2020_
E-Mail Address _____	

Catalog No.	Quantity	Page No.	Description	Size S, M, L	Color	Unit Price	Total Price
IZ1204	1	28	Blouse	M	Blue	$48.79	$48.79
IZ1204	2	28	Blouse	M	Red	$48.79	$97.58

Subtotal	$146.37
Sales Tax (7% of Subtotal)	$ 10.25
Shipping/Handling (8% of Subtotal)	$ 11.71
Total	$168.33

Exercise B   Pamela wants to order 2 blue sleeping bags from page 15 of the catalog. The item number is IZ4328. She wants the large size. Each sleeping bag costs $85.95. Complete the order form. Round to the nearest cent.

	Catalog No.	Quantity	Page No.	Description	Size S, M, L	Color	Unit Price	Total Price
1.								

2.	**Subtotal**	
3.	**Sales Tax (7% of Subtotal)**	
4.	**Shipping/Handling (8% of Subtotal)**	
5.	**Total**	

Back ordered

Temporarily out of stock

Customers expect that items in a catalog are currently available. A product is **back ordered** if it is temporarily out of stock. Customers may cancel orders that cannot be filled immediately. Mail-order businesses do not want the expense of keeping too large an inventory. However, they do not want the potential loss of sales from having too small an inventory.

EXAMPLE   About $\frac{2}{3}$ of a store's catalog sales are canceled when the items are back ordered. In May the back-ordered items are worth $48,962.16 in sales. How much money in sales is lost if $\frac{2}{3}$ of the orders are canceled?

Step 1   **Estimate.** $48,962.16 \approx $48,000$

$\frac{2}{3} = \frac{1}{3} + \frac{1}{3} = 2 \times \frac{1}{3}$

$\frac{1}{3} \times $48,000 = $16,000$ $2 \times $16,000 = $32,000$

About $32,000 of $48,962.15 in back-ordered sales is lost.

> To add fractions with the same denominator, add the numerators.

Step 2   Find the actual loss in sales.

$\frac{2}{3} \times 48,962.16 = \frac{2}{\cancel{3}_1} \times \frac{\cancel{48,962.16}^{16,320.72}}{1 \times 1} = \frac{2 \times 16,320.72}{1 \times 1} =$

$\frac{32,641.44}{1} = 32,641.44$

The store loses $32,641.44 of $48,962.16 in back-ordered sales.

PROBLEM SOLVING

Exercise A   Solve.

1. Thad's Things has $28,915.75 worth of sales back ordered. How much in sales will be lost if $\frac{2}{5}$ of the orders are canceled?

2. Melting Pot has $18,305.20 worth of sales back ordered. How much in sales will be lost if $\frac{3}{8}$ of the orders are canceled?

3. Open Air has $9,276.40 worth of sales back ordered. How much in sales will be lost if $\frac{3}{20}$ of the orders are canceled?

4. Lost Times lost $1,337.92 in sales because $4,013.76 worth of sales was back ordered. What fraction of sales was canceled?

Mail-order businesses need to keep enough items in inventory so they don't lose sales. However, storing inventory ties up money that could be used to make a profit on more popular items. Getting rid of inventory is one reason why businesses have sales.

The cost of inventory includes the cost of manufacturing or buying the items, and the warehouse space to store them. The cost includes insuring inventory against possible loss, and paying employees to put the inventory on shelves. Mail-order businesses compare the cost of inventory with their need to fill orders immediately.

EXAMPLE A mail-order business sells furniture. Storing furniture in its warehouse costs $.005 per cubic foot per day. A table that measures 5 feet long by 4 feet wide by 3 feet, 2 inches high is in inventory. How much does it cost to have the table in inventory for 30 days?

Step 1 Change all measurements to feet.
Write inches as a fraction of a foot. Simplify.

3 feet, 2 inches = $3\frac{2}{12}$ feet = $3\frac{1}{6}$ feet

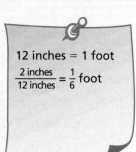

12 inches = 1 foot

$\frac{2 \text{ inches}}{12 \text{ inches}} = \frac{1}{6}$ foot

Step 2 Use the formula $V = lwh$ to find the volume.

$l = 5$ feet $w = 4$ feet $h = 3\frac{1}{6}$ feet

Write the numbers as fractions.

$l = \frac{5}{1}$ $w = \frac{4}{1}$ $h = 3\frac{1}{6} = \frac{19}{6}$

$V = \frac{5}{1} \times \frac{4}{1} \times \frac{19}{6} = \frac{20}{1} \times \frac{19}{6} = \frac{380}{6}$

Divide. Round up to the next whole number.

$$\begin{array}{r} 63 \\ 6\overline{)380} \\ -36 \\ \hline 20 \\ -18 \\ \hline 2 \end{array} \rightarrow 63\frac{2}{6} \approx 64 \text{ cubic feet}$$

$3\frac{1}{6} = 3 + \frac{1}{6} =$

$\frac{3 \times 6}{6} + \frac{1}{6} =$

$\frac{18}{6} + \frac{1}{6} = \frac{19}{6}$

Step 3 Find the cost per day for 64 cubic feet.
64 × $.005 = $.32

Step 4 Find the storage cost for 30 days.
30 × $.32 = $9.60

It costs $9.60 to store the table for 30 days.

The remainder 2 is the numerator of the fraction $\frac{2}{6}$. The divisor 6 is the denominator of the fraction $\frac{2}{6}$.

Exercise B For each cost per day, find the volume and cost of storage. Use the formula $V = lwh$. Round the volume up to the next whole cubic foot.

Cost per Cubic Foot per Day	Length	Width	Height	Volume	Cost for 30 Days
1. $.006	1 foot	2 feet	3 feet	_____	_____
2. $.003	2 feet	5 feet	6 feet	_____	_____
3. $.004	1 foot	1 foot	3 feet	_____	_____
4. $.300	2 feet, 6 inches	2 feet	1 foot	_____	_____
5. $.007	2 feet, 3 inches	6 inches	1 foot, 6 inches	_____	_____

Keeping a warehouse stocked reduces the number of back orders. Businesses keep track of inventory. They reorder before items are out of stock, allowing time for the manufacturer to process and ship their orders.

EXAMPLE | The warehouse manager of Tumble Toys takes 2 days to reorder 200 Atomic Atoms. The manufacturer needs 3 days to fill the order, then ships it by 2-day mail. The warehouse manager starts reordering on Tuesday. When will the Atomic Atoms arrive?

Step 1 Count the total number of workdays needed.

$2 + 3 + 2 = 7$ workdays

Step 2 Count off the workdays. Use a Monday–Saturday calendar.

Monday	Tuesday Order Started– Day 1	Wednesday Day 2	Thursday Day 3	Friday Day 4	Saturday Day 5
Monday Day 6	Tuesday Day 7	Wednesday	Thursday	Friday	Saturday

The Atomic Atoms will arrive on Tuesday of the following week.

Exercise C   Use the Monday–Saturday calendar on page 261 to solve.

1. A warehouse manager takes 3 days to reorder items. The manufacturer needs 3 days to fill the order. Shipping takes 4 more days. The manager starts reordering on Monday. When will the items arrive?

2. A warehouse manager takes 1 day to reorder items. The supplier needs 5 days to fill the order. Shipping takes 2 more days. The manager starts reordering on Thursday. When will the order arrive?

3. A warehouse manager takes 2 days to reorder items. The supplier needs 2 days to fill the order. Shipping takes 2 more days. The items arrive on Friday. When did he place the order?

4. A warehouse manager takes 3 days to reorder items. The manufacturer needs 6 days to fill the order. The manager starts reordering on Monday. The order arrives on Friday of the following week. How long did shipping take?

Technology Connection

Multiplying Fractions on a Fractions Calculator

You can use a fractions calculator to multiply fractions.

To find $5 \times 4 \times 3\frac{1}{6}$ on many calculators, enter the following keystrokes: 5 ⊠ 4 ⊠ 3 a 1 b/c 6 =

The display reads: $63\frac{2}{6}$

To show $63\frac{2}{6}$ as a decimal, press F↔D.

The display reads: 63.333333

Getting a Handle on Baskets

Taskett Baskets, Inc., has grown rapidly in the past few years. Marvin, who started the company, is a very clever buyer.

Once or twice a year he takes a trip to Indonesia and China. There, he buys baskets of every kind. The baskets are sold mostly to flower shops. They buy Taskett baskets by the dozens to use for flower arrangements.

Kerry is Marvin's sales director. She manages the salespeople who call on the larger flower shops. She also manages catalog sales. Taskett Baskets, Inc., sends out a very classy catalog.

"How was the buying trip, Marv?" asked Kerry.

"Great!" was Marvin's enthusiastic reply. "Look at these samples I brought back. This was the best buying trip ever. Let's print up more catalogs this time. This will be a big year for us!"

"Take it slow, boss. Those full-color catalogs are expensive to produce and to mail. And where else will we send them? We already send a catalog to every flower shop in the country."

"Can we send catalogs to gift shops as well as flower shops?" Marvin wished that Kerry shared his enthusiasm.

"I don't recommend it. Marv, be realistic. Most of our sales are made by our salespeople. Only a small percentage of sales are from the catalog alone. And gift shops? There must be a million of them. I think we'd be throwing good money after bad."

"You may be right, Kerry. We'll stick with what we know."

For Discussion

1. Why did Marvin want to print more catalogs?

2. What did Kerry mean by ". . . throwing good money after bad?"

Chapter 13 Review

Write the letter of the answer that best completes each sentence.

1. A catalog has 38 pictures and a description for each item. The pictures cost $175 each and the descriptions cost $45 each. The pictures and descriptions cost _____.

    a. $8,360   **b.** $9,585   **c.** $14,525   **d.** $299,250

2. MM's spends $487,900 for developing and mailing 240,000 catalogs. The cost per catalog, rounded to the nearest cent, is _____.

    a. $1.98   **b.** $2.01   **c.** $2.03   **d.** $2.05

Use the charts for problems 3–4.

Plan A
$15 per month, per phone
$.08 per minute
This plan charges for a fraction of a minute.

Plan B
$5 per month, per phone
$.15 per minute
A fraction of a minute counts as a full minute.

3. A mail-order business has 8 phones. The average call takes 3 minutes, 5 seconds. It received 500 calls last month. What would be the phone charge for each plan? Round to the nearest cent.

4. Stay In Touch has 13 phones. Each of 720 calls last month took an average of 2 minutes, 13 seconds. What would be the cost for each plan? Round to the nearest cent.

Solve problems 5–6.

5. A warehouse manager takes 3 days to reorder items. The manufacturer needs 5 workdays to fill the order. Shipping takes 2 more days. The manager starts reordering on Monday. When will the items arrive?

6. A company orders 23 new computers. Each costs $1,297.87. How much do the new computers cost?

The table shows rates for the same service. Use the table for problem 7.

Carrier	Up to 1 Pound	More Than 1 Pound to 2 Pounds	More Than 2 Pounds to 3 Pounds
Carrier A	$2.35	$3.15	$3.61
Carrier B	$7.59	$8.56	$9.62
Carrier C	$7.81	$8.59	$9.89
Carrier D	$6.62	$9.61	$10.01

7. Which carrier has the best rate for shipping a package that weighs 1 pound, 3 ounces: Carrier B, C, or D?

Solve problems 8–10.

8. A mail-order company receives an order for 12 tools. The shipping box costs $1.15. Packing the tools uses 5 square feet of wrapping material at $.15 per square foot. The employee who packs the box spends 15 minutes and earns $16.20 per hour. What is the cost of handling and processing the order?

9. A mail-order business has sales worth $18,209.88 on back order. How much money in sales will be lost if 26% of the customers cancel their orders? Round to the nearest cent.

10. A mail-order business pays $.007 per cubic foot per day to store inventory in a warehouse. A couch that measures 6 feet long by 4 feet wide by $3\frac{1}{2}$ feet high is in inventory. How much does it cost to have the couch in inventory for 30 days? Use $V = lwh$.

Test-Taking Tip   In business situations such as when a fraction of a minute counts as a full minute, numbers should always be rounded up. Read each problem carefully to know if the business situation requires rounding up.

Review of Basic Skills   1

Identifying the Place Value of Whole Numbers

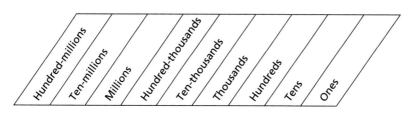

Example   Write the name of the place of the underlined digit.

6<u>5</u>,823	thousands
2,90<u>6</u>	tens
<u>4</u>,790,098	millions

Exercise   Write the name of the place for each underlined digit.

1) <u>2</u>3,456
2) 5<u>3</u>6
3) 5,1<u>2</u>6
4) 6<u>2</u>1
5) 150,<u>3</u>41
6) 780,<u>2</u>96
7) 3,10<u>3</u>,615
8) <u>8</u>2,605
9) <u>2</u>6
10) 7,4<u>0</u>5
11) <u>4</u>1,811
12) 9<u>6</u>3
13) 3<u>1</u>,005
14) <u>1</u>,815
15) 1,<u>0</u>07
16) <u>8</u>1,001
17) 56<u>7</u>
18) <u>3</u>14,152
19) <u>7</u>2,855
20) 6,2<u>9</u>3,000

Rounding Whole Numbers

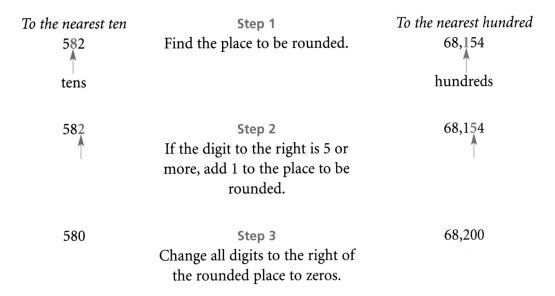

	Step 1	
To the nearest ten 582 tens	Find the place to be rounded.	*To the nearest hundred* 68,154 hundreds
	Step 2	
582	If the digit to the right is 5 or more, add 1 to the place to be rounded.	68,154
	Step 3	
580	Change all digits to the right of the rounded place to zeros.	68,200

Exercise   Round these numbers to the nearest:

		Ten	Hundred	Thousand
1)	26,311			
2)	40,592			
3)	7,098			
4)	415			
5)	89			
6)	49			
7)	2,900			
8)	3,200			
9)	6,004			
10)	129			

Adding Whole Numbers

Example   26 + 451 + 2 = ■

Solution
$$\left.\begin{array}{r} 26 \\ 451 \\ +\ \ 2 \end{array}\right\} \text{Addends}$$
479 ◄— Sum or total

Example   7 + 0 = ■

Solution
7 ◄— Addend
+0 ◄— Addend
7 ◄— Sum or total

Exercise   Write these addends in vertical form. Then add.

1) 235 + 62

2) 503 + 263

3) 211 + 623

4) 26 + 78 + 9

5) 395 + 75 + 37

6) 314 + 625 + 893

7) 512 + 726 + 89

8) 1,033 + 78 + 201

9) 1,515 + 301 + 201

10) 51 + 8,992 + 7

11) 72 + 6,203 + 45

12) 10,638 + 2,957

13) 6,203 + 89 + 1,458

14) 1,502 + 84 + 201

15) 302 + 895 + 102

16) 4,403 + 789 + 62

17) 5,067 + 29,835

18) 26 + 2,419 + 231

19) 45 + 671

20) 215 + 823

21) 305 + 876

22) 516 + 23 + 8

23) 3,007 + 926 + 85

24) 27 + 851 + 623

25) 351 + 603 + 1,151

26) 403 + 1,151 + 69

27) 62 + 89 + 5 + 301

28) 702 + 98 + 304

29) 1,346 + 62 + 891

30) 29,063 + 29 + 305

31) 62,301 + 89 + 901

32) 375 + 1,002 + 962

33) 1,302 + 63 + 115

34) 463 + 891 + 200

35) 135 + 60,039 + 12

36) 48 + 121 + 2,635

Subtracting Whole Numbers

Example   Subtract 26 from 235. The number following "from" is written first.

Solution

$$\begin{array}{r} 235 \\ -\ 26 \\ \hline 209 \end{array}$$ Minuend
Subtrahend
Difference

Check

$$\begin{array}{r} 26 \\ +209 \\ \hline 235 \end{array}$$

Exercise   Write these problems vertically. Then subtract.

1) $208 - 45$

2) $351 - 290$

3) $265 - 28$

4) $208 - 177$

5) $1,066 - 815$

6) $1,210 - 986$

7) $6,213 - 866$

8) $7,019 - 669$

9) $5,287 - 2,008$

10) $1,010 - 935$

11) $37,115 - 235$

12) $5,351 - 709$

13) $17,315 - 9,115$

14) $20,061 - 4,805$

15) $30,155 - 7,132$

16) $23,103 - 9,163$

17) $50,167 - 12,735$

18) $37,451 - 16,203$

19) $81,131 - 17,788$

20) $16,683 - 6,891$

21) $55,103 - 2,317$

22) $88,471 - 73,115$

23) $400 - 28$

24) $614 - 326$

25) $3,105 - 106$

26) $4,992 - 885$

27) $3,001 - 223$

28) $8,191 - 310$

29) $3,355 - 2,665$

30) $3,274 - 2,275$

31) $8,101 - 4,283$

32) $9,000 - 862$

33) $2,113 - 421$

34) $48,300 - 9,301$

35) $41,041 - 8,597$

36) $14,724 - 7,026$

37) $65,913 - 27,261$

38) $10,991 - 2,815$

39) $41,568 - 29,321$

40) $20,972 - 3,811$

41) $10,014 - 2,560$

42) $57,221 - 10,811$

43) $51,371 - 5,119$

44) $14,014 - 7,958$

Multiplying Whole Numbers (5)

Example $23 \times 6 = $ ■

Solution

$$\begin{array}{r} 23 \\ \times\ \ 6 \\ \hline 138 \end{array}$$ } Factors

Product

Example $46 \times 35 = $ ■

Solution

$$\begin{array}{r} 46 \\ \times\ \ 35 \\ \hline 230 \\ +1\,38 \\ \hline 1,610 \end{array}$$ } Factors

Product

Multiplying Whole Numbers With Zeros (6)

Example $267 \times 10 = $ ■

Solution

$$\begin{array}{r} 267 \\ \times\ \ 10 \\ \hline 2,670 \end{array}$$ ← One zero

← One zero

Example $342 \times 100 = $ ■

Solution

$$\begin{array}{r} 342 \\ \times\ \ 100 \\ \hline 34,200 \end{array}$$ ← Two zeros

← Two zeros

Exercise   Write these problems in vertical form. Then multiply.

1) 23×6

2) 403×5

3) 313×4

4) 26×45

5) 72×35

6) 567×10

7) 109×50

8) 815×400

9) 701×202

10) 511×120

11) $2,215 \times 63$

12) $6,057 \times 40$

13) $5,063 \times 41$

14) $2,267 \times 19$

15) $2,830 \times 110$

16) $5,011 \times 300$

17) $7,706 \times 250$

18) $1,127 \times 277$

19) $90,681 \times 22$

20) $15,012 \times 50$

21) $21,305 \times 100$

22) $89,000 \times 62$

23) $4,805 \times 1,001$

24) $57,119 \times 1,010$

25) $77,805 \times 601$

26) 38×9

27) 206×8

28) 231×11

29) 52×60

30) 391×20

31) 435×39

32) 623×67

33) 516×200

34) 870×270

35) 603×250

36) $4,120 \times 10$

37) $1,403 \times 27$

38) $8,010 \times 50$

39) $3,115 \times 28$

40) $4,100 \times 310$

41) $8,214 \times 200$

42) $5,066 \times 305$

43) $6,405 \times 115$

44) $40,363 \times 100$

45) $71,106 \times 602$

46) $28,015 \times 101$

47) $10,376 \times 203$

48) $72,011 \times 78$

49) $90,301 \times 201$

50) $53,103 \times 111$

Dividing Whole Numbers With Zero Remainders (7)

Example $576 \div 12 = \blacksquare$

Solution

$$
\begin{array}{r}
48 \\
12\overline{)576} \\
-48 \\
\hline
96 \\
-96 \\
\hline
0
\end{array}
$$

Check

$$
\begin{array}{r}
48 \\
\times\ 12 \\
\hline
96 \\
+48 \\
\hline
576
\end{array}
$$

Dividing Whole Numbers With Fractional Remainders (8)

Example $3,191 \div 25 = \blacksquare$

Solution

$$
\begin{array}{r}
127\frac{16}{25} \\
25\overline{)3,191} \\
-2\,5 \\
\hline
69 \\
-50 \\
\hline
191 \\
-175 \\
\hline
16
\end{array}
$$

Write the
remainder
over the
divisor

Check

$$
\begin{array}{r}
127 \\
\times\ \ 25 \\
\hline
635 \\
+2\,54 \\
\hline
3,175 \\
+\ \ 16 \\
\hline
3,191
\end{array}
$$
Remainder

Dividing Whole Numbers With Zeros in the Quotient (9)

Example $2,380 \div 14 = \blacksquare$

Solution

$$
\begin{array}{r}
170 \\
14\overline{)2,380} \\
-1\,4 \\
\hline
98 \\
-98 \\
\hline
00
\end{array}
$$

Check

$$
\begin{array}{r}
170 \\
\times\ \ 14 \\
\hline
680 \\
+1\,70 \\
\hline
2,380
\end{array}
$$

Example $4,864 \div 16 = \blacksquare$

Solution

$$
\begin{array}{r}
304 \\
16\overline{)4,864} \\
-4\,8 \\
\hline
064 \\
-64 \\
\hline
0
\end{array}
$$

Check

$$
\begin{array}{r}
304 \\
\times\ \ 16 \\
\hline
1,824 \\
+3\,04 \\
\hline
4,864
\end{array}
$$

Exercise A   Copy these problems and divide.

1) $138 \div 6$

2) $882 \div 9$

3) $1,030 \div 5$

4) $1,806 \div 6$

5) $1,631 \div 7$

6) $3,060 \div 4$

7) $1,404 \div 52$

8) $4,980 \div 60$

9) $5,040 \div 70$

10) $5,700 \div 95$

11) $6,510 \div 105$

12) $9,108 \div 18$

13) $30,954 \div 77$

14) $15,257 \div 73$

15) $9,646 \div 91$

16) $19,520 \div 32$

17) $30,310 \div 70$

18) $32,040 \div 40$

19) $45,150 \div 15$

20) $56,221 \div 11$

21) $44,520 \div 12$

22) $65,160 \div 36$

23) $51,090 \div 13$

24) $80,080 \div 40$

25) $12,524 \div 31$

26) $371 \div 7$

27) $3,159 \div 9$

28) $1,744 \div 8$

29) $3,018 \div 6$

30) $2,564 \div 4$

31) $6,033 \div 3$

32) $1,539 \div 27$

33) $4,100 \div 82$

34) $8,820 \div 90$

35) $3,375 \div 25$

36) $3,450 \div 15$

37) $19,418 \div 38$

38) $31,626 \div 63$

39) $19,530 \div 62$

40) $10,160 \div 80$

41) $34,310 \div 47$

42) $52,920 \div 60$

43) $8,866 \div 22$

44) $138,253 \div 23$

45) $738,500 \div 35$

46) $50,300 \div 10$

47) $103,200 \div 24$

48) $82,212 \div 51$

49) $90,900 \div 30$

50) $57,414 \div 14$

Exercise B Copy these problems and divide. Write any remainders as fractions.

1) 335 ÷ 6	**26)** 573 ÷ 6
2) 50 ÷ 8	**27)** 908 ÷ 9
3) 711 ÷ 9	**28)** 630 ÷ 9
4) 393 ÷ 6	**29)** 721 ÷ 8
5) 7,151 ÷ 8	**30)** 3,900 ÷ 9
6) 6,205 ÷ 15	**31)** 8,003 ÷ 15
7) 60,600 ÷ 15	**32)** 7,440 ÷ 22
8) 181,819 ÷ 18	**33)** 32,331 ÷ 16
9) 30,091 ÷ 25	**34)** 7,910 ÷ 19
10) 70,111 ÷ 80	**35)** 51,631 ÷ 25
11) 41,015 ÷ 32	**36)** 10,631 ÷ 81
12) 26,031 ÷ 26	**37)** 35,103 ÷ 34
13) 13,315 ÷ 25	**38)** 14,401 ÷ 72
14) 60,031 ÷ 81	**39)** 42,002 ÷ 60
15) 53,010 ÷ 52	**40)** 73,106 ÷ 73
16) 10,008 ÷ 50	**41)** 53,010 ÷ 38
17) 27,023 ÷ 62	**42)** 14,108 ÷ 80
18) 15,132 ÷ 25	**43)** 62,031 ÷ 20
19) 90,615 ÷ 23	**44)** 72,150 ÷ 80
20) 46,023 ÷ 23	**45)** 81,035 ÷ 90
21) 23,310 ÷ 70	**46)** 34,210 ÷ 81
22) 50,003 ÷ 85	**47)** 78,311 ÷ 30
23) 22,022 ÷ 60	**48)** 37,101 ÷ 51
24) 463,201 ÷ 71	**49)** 72,101 ÷ 82
25) 57,231 ÷ 500	**50)** 80,031 ÷ 198

Finding Values of Numbers With Exponents

Example   Find 3^4.

Solution $3^4 = 3 \times 3 \times 3 \times 3$ (4 times)
  $= 81$

Example   Find 2^3.

Solution $2^3 = 2 \times 2 \times 2$ (3 times)
  $= 8$

Exercise   Write the value of each expression.

1) 3^2
2) 5^3
3) 9^2
4) 19^2
5) 3^5
6) 8^2
7) 9^4
8) 18^2
9) 6^3
10) 2^6
11) 25^2
12) 7^2
13) 2^7
14) 26^2
15) 7^4
16) 30^2
17) 200^3
18) 70^2
19) 100^3
20) 80^3
21) 30^4
22) $1,000^2$
23) 46^2
24) 5^6
25) 10^4

26) 4^3
27) 4^2
28) 2^5
29) 7^3
30) 2^4
31) 11^2
32) 16^3
33) 5^4
34) 10^4
35) 15^2
36) 5^5
37) 8^4
38) 50^3
39) 5^3
40) 40^3
41) 77^2
42) 60^3
43) 92^2
44) 30^3
45) 80^2
46) 32^2
47) 16^2
48) 10^2
49) 8^3
50) 23^2

51) 5^2
52) 8^2
53) 9^3
54) 4^5
55) 6^2
56) 13^3
57) 12^2
58) 18^2
59) 28^2
60) 17^2
61) 24^2
62) 150^2
63) 300^4
64) 70^3
65) 22^2
66) 500^3
67) 15^3
68) 13^2
69) 42^2
70) 90^3
71) 10^3
72) 30^4
73) 63^2
74) 10^5
75) 3^3

Using the Order of Operations (Fundamental)

Rules

1. Evaluate expressions with exponents first.

2. Multiply and divide from left to right in order.

3. Add and subtract from left to right in order.

Example $2 \quad + \quad 3 \times 4 \quad - \quad 8 \div 4 \quad = \quad \blacksquare$

Solution $2 \quad + \quad \underline{3 \times 4} \quad - \quad \underline{8 \div 4} \quad =$

$$2 \quad + \quad 12 \quad - \quad 2 \quad = \quad 12$$

Example $2^3 \quad + \quad 3 \times 4 \div 2 \quad - \quad 48 \div 4^2 \quad = \quad \blacksquare$

$$8 \quad + \quad \underline{3 \times 4} \div 2 \quad - \quad 48 \div \underline{16} \quad =$$

$$\underline{12 \div 2} \qquad\qquad 3 \quad =$$

$$8 \quad + \quad 6 \quad - \quad 3 \quad = \quad 11$$

Exercise   Use the rules for the order of operations. Find the answers.

1) $3 + 8 \times 2 \div 4$

2) $5 + 9 \times 4 \div 12 - 2$

3) $8 - 8 \div 4 + 3 \times 2$

4) $13 - 16 \times 3 \div 12 - 1$

5) $9 + 6 \times 3 - 8 \times 2 \div 4$

6) $1 + 16 \times 3 \div 12 - 4$

7) $14 + 32 \div 16 - 4 \times 2$

8) $32 \div 16 + 9 \div 3 \times 2$

9) $5 - 16 \div 4 + 1 + 3$

10) $35 - 25 \times 4 \div 20 + 5$

11) $2^3 + 8 \times 2^2 + 3$

12) $8 - 6^2 \div 12 + 2 \times 5$

13) $15 + 8^2 \div 4 - 6$

14) $26 + 13^2 \div 13 - 20$

15) $9^2 + 32 \div 8 \times 4 - 6$

16) $3 + 2^3 \div 2^2 - 4$

17) $5 + 8 \times 9 \div 6^2 - 4$

18) $25 + 11^2 + 8 \times 2 - 3$

19) $39 \div 13 + 12^2 \div 6 - 5$

20) $52 + 12 \div 2^2 - 82 \div 2 + 3^2$

21) $35 + 2^5 \div 2^4 \times 3^2 - 2^3$

22) $18 \div 3^2 + 6 \times 8 \div 4^2 - 5$

23) $4 \times 3 \times 5 \div 10 + 8 \times 2^3 \div 2^4$

24) $9 - 16 \times 3 \div 12 + 8 \div 2^2 - 2^2$

Finding an Average

Example   Find the average for 98, 88, and 80.

Solution   Add the numbers. Divide the sum by the number of addends.

$$
\begin{array}{r}
98 \\
88 \\
+80 \\
\hline
266 \quad \text{3 addends}
\end{array}
\qquad\qquad
\begin{array}{r}
88\frac{2}{3} \\
3\,\overline{)\,266} \\
-24 \\
\hline
26 \\
-24 \\
\hline
2
\end{array}
$$

Answer   The average is $88\frac{2}{3}$.

Exercise   Compute the averages for each set of numbers.

1) 25, 63, 48, 52, 49, 38, 42, 67, 38

2) 98, 53, 42, 56, 72, 36, 72

3) 39, 40, 39, 62, 53, 86, 29, 34

4) 95, 83, 39, 42, 88, 77, 75, 42, 67

5) 88, 62, 42, 53, 96, 35, 35

6) 53, 60, 72, 43, 35, 39, 53

7) 52, 65, 83, 96, 35, 100, 92, 53

8) 91, 62, 39, 50, 42, 88, 53, 60, 83, 72

9) 36, 50, 42, 53, 46, 82, 80, 50, 52, 39

10) 81, 90, 92, 90, 83, 43, 46, 72, 53

11) 100, 103, 96, 105, 105, 97, 102, 120

12) 36, 42, 85, 92, 30, 33, 88, 29, 62, 50

13) 109, 156, 95, 108, 90, 83, 45, 80, 90, 98, 93, 96

14) 40, 42, 43, 40, 41, 42, 43, 48, 44, 42, 45, 42

15) 40, 38, 37, 35, 42, 43, 36, 49, 48, 53, 42, 39, 34

16) 21, 20, 23, 28, 25, 23, 20, 25, 24, 29, 28, 24, 22, 20

17) 52, 50, 59, 62, 63, 55, 54, 58, 60, 50, 52, 53, 57, 52, 51

18) 56, 50, 53, 65, 73, 72, 80, 95, 81, 87, 70, 82, 96, 68

19) 23, 12, 94, 71, 44, 39, 62, 57, 68, 25, 53, 22, 19, 80

Comparing Fractions (13)

Example   Compare $\frac{3}{4}$ and $\frac{5}{8}$.

Solution

24   20

$$\frac{3}{4} \;\;\times\;\; \frac{5}{8}$$

Because   Because

$4 \times 5 = 20$ $3 \times 8 = 24$

24 is greater than 20; therefore, $\frac{3}{4}$ is greater than $\frac{5}{8}$.

Changing Fractions to Higher Terms (14)

Example   Write $\frac{5}{6}$ as a fraction with 30 as the new denominator.

Solution   **Step 1** $\frac{5}{6} = \frac{\blacksquare}{30}$

Step 2   Divide 30 by 6. $\longrightarrow$ $6\overline{)30}$ with 5 on top

Step 3   Multiply $\frac{5}{6}$ by $\frac{5}{5}$. $\longrightarrow$ $\frac{5 \times 5}{6 \times 5} = \frac{25}{30}$

Answer $\frac{5}{6} = \frac{25}{30}$

Exercise   Express these fractions in higher terms.

1) $\frac{3}{4} = \frac{\blacksquare}{48}$

2) $\frac{1}{3} = \frac{\blacksquare}{21}$

3) $\frac{2}{3} = \frac{\blacksquare}{15}$

4) $\frac{5}{6} = \frac{\blacksquare}{18}$

5) $\frac{7}{8} = \frac{\blacksquare}{56}$

6) $\frac{3}{5} = \frac{\blacksquare}{20}$

7) $\frac{1}{7} = \frac{\blacksquare}{49}$

8) $\frac{5}{12} = \frac{\blacksquare}{24}$

9) $\frac{3}{7} = \frac{\blacksquare}{21}$

10) $\frac{4}{12} = \frac{\blacksquare}{36}$

11) $\frac{4}{9} = \frac{\blacksquare}{45}$

12) $\frac{3}{3} = \frac{\blacksquare}{18}$

13) $\frac{2}{11} = \frac{\blacksquare}{121}$

14) $\frac{15}{16} = \frac{\blacksquare}{48}$

15) $\frac{3}{10} = \frac{\blacksquare}{30}$

16) $\frac{12}{14} = \frac{\blacksquare}{70}$

17) $\frac{9}{12} = \frac{\blacksquare}{144}$

18) $\frac{5}{15} = \frac{\blacksquare}{45}$

19) $\frac{2}{8} = \frac{\blacksquare}{96}$

20) $\frac{1}{6} = \frac{\blacksquare}{72}$

21) $\frac{17}{24} = \frac{\blacksquare}{120}$

Renaming Fractions to Simplest Terms

Example   Rename $\frac{14}{16}$ to simplest terms.

Solution $\frac{14 \div 2}{16 \div 2} = \frac{7}{8}$

Choose a number that can be divided into the denominator and the numerator.

Answer $\frac{14}{16} = \frac{7}{8}$

Example   Rename $\frac{24}{30}$ to simplest terms.

Solution $\frac{24 \div 3}{30 \div 3} = \frac{8}{10}$

The division process may occur more than once if the divisor is not large enough in the first step.

$\frac{8 \div 2}{10 \div 2} = \frac{4}{5}$

Answer $\frac{24}{30} = \frac{4}{5}$

Exercise   Rename these fractions in simplest terms.

1) $\frac{24}{48}$

2) $\frac{10}{230}$

3) $\frac{45}{99}$

4) $\frac{5}{25}$

5) $\frac{13}{39}$

6) $\frac{56}{58}$

7) $\frac{63}{81}$

8) $\frac{6}{54}$

9) $\frac{16}{112}$

10) $\frac{39}{52}$

11) $\frac{12}{60}$

12) $\frac{16}{64}$

13) $\frac{18}{36}$

14) $\frac{22}{121}$

15) $\frac{53}{106}$

16) $\frac{18}{72}$

17) $\frac{5}{15}$

18) $\frac{55}{242}$

19) $\frac{10}{52}$

20) $\frac{48}{96}$

21) $\frac{28}{56}$

Renaming Improper Fractions as Mixed Numbers or Whole Numbers (16)

Example   Rename $\frac{13}{5}$.

Solution   Divide the numerator by the denominator.

$$\begin{array}{r} 2 \\ 5\overline{)13} \\ -10 \\ \hline 3 \end{array} \quad \longleftarrow \text{Remainder}$$

Answer $\frac{13}{5} = 2\frac{3}{5}$ $\quad \longleftarrow$ Write the remainder over the divisor.

Example   Rename $\frac{42}{16}$.

Solution

$$\begin{array}{r} 2 \\ 16\overline{)42} \\ 32 \\ \hline 10 \end{array}$$

$$2\frac{10}{16} = 2\frac{5}{8}$$

Answer $\frac{42}{16} = 2\frac{5}{8}$

Writing Mixed Numbers in Simplest Terms (17)

Example   Write $12\frac{4}{6}$ in simplest terms.

Solution $12\frac{4}{6} = 12 + \frac{4}{6} = 12 + \frac{2}{3} = 12\frac{2}{3}$

Answer $12\frac{4}{6} = 12\frac{2}{3}$

Exercise   Rename these improper fractions as either mixed numbers or whole numbers.

1) $\frac{13}{5}$

2) $\frac{18}{3}$

3) $\frac{19}{6}$

4) $\frac{14}{3}$

5) $\frac{23}{4}$

6) $\frac{12}{2}$

7) $\frac{38}{5}$

8) $\frac{66}{11}$

9) $\frac{56}{11}$

10) $\frac{19}{5}$

11) $\frac{52}{32}$

12) $\frac{55}{8}$

13) $\frac{28}{6}$

14) $\frac{32}{4}$

15) $\frac{90}{3}$

16) $\frac{63}{8}$

17) $\frac{50}{6}$

18) $\frac{58}{7}$

19) $\frac{52}{10}$

20) $\frac{37}{3}$

21) $\frac{120}{10}$

22) $\frac{73}{8}$

23) $\frac{13}{2}$

24) $\frac{51}{4}$

25) $\frac{82}{9}$

26) $\frac{23}{5}$

27) $\frac{52}{8}$

28) $\frac{32}{15}$

Renaming Mixed Numbers as Improper Fractions

Example   Write $2\frac{3}{4}$ as an improper fraction.

Solution   **Step 1**   Multiply the whole number by the denominator.

$$2 \times 4 = 8$$

Step 2   Add the numerator to the product from Step 1.

$$3 + 8 = 11$$

Step 3   Write the sum over the old denominator.

$$\frac{11}{4}$$

Answer $2\frac{3}{4} = \frac{11}{4}$

Exercise   Rename these mixed numbers as improper fractions.

1) $3\frac{2}{5}$

2) $6\frac{2}{5}$

3) $5\frac{1}{6}$

4) $7\frac{2}{12}$

5) $2\frac{1}{6}$

6) $9\frac{1}{2}$

7) $4\frac{1}{9}$

8) $8\frac{2}{11}$

9) $5\frac{2}{3}$

10) $8\frac{1}{3}$

11) $6\frac{10}{13}$

12) $16\frac{2}{3}$

13) $7\frac{3}{8}$

14) $15\frac{2}{3}$

15) $13\frac{9}{14}$

16) $9\frac{2}{3}$

17) $5\frac{11}{10}$

18) $20\frac{2}{3}$

19) $16\frac{5}{21}$

20) $11\frac{1}{8}$

Multiplying Fractions

Example $\frac{5}{6} \times \frac{3}{4} = \blacksquare$

Solution $\frac{5 \times 3}{6 \times 4} = \frac{15}{24}$

$\frac{15}{24} = \frac{5}{8}$

Answer $\frac{5}{8}$

Example $7 \times \frac{4}{5} = \blacksquare$

Solution $\frac{7 \times 4}{1 \times 5} = \frac{28}{5}$

$\frac{28}{5} = 5\frac{3}{5}$

Answer $5\frac{3}{5}$

Exercise   Multiply. Write your answers in simplest terms.

1) $\frac{1}{2} \times \frac{2}{3}$

2) $\frac{3}{5} \times \frac{5}{6}$

3) $\frac{7}{8} \times \frac{6}{13}$

4) $\frac{2}{9} \times \frac{3}{5}$

5) $\frac{6}{7} \times \frac{1}{2}$

6) $\frac{3}{11} \times \frac{2}{5}$

7) $\frac{2}{7} \times \frac{2}{9}$

8) $\frac{1}{6} \times \frac{1}{5}$

9) $\frac{5}{11} \times \frac{1}{4}$

10) $\frac{1}{6} \times \frac{2}{9}$

11) $\frac{5}{6} \times \frac{1}{4}$

12) $\frac{3}{11} \times \frac{2}{12}$

13) $\frac{4}{5} \times \frac{2}{9}$

14) $\frac{4}{7} \times \frac{1}{8}$

15) $\frac{3}{16} \times \frac{13}{21}$

16) $\frac{5}{21} \times \frac{7}{10}$

17) $\frac{5}{24} \times \frac{3}{13}$

18) $\frac{6}{28} \times \frac{7}{12}$

19) $\frac{2}{3} \times \frac{5}{6}$

20) $\frac{12}{21} \times \frac{7}{8}$

21) $\frac{13}{32} \times \frac{8}{26}$

22) $\frac{24}{25} \times \frac{5}{16}$

23) $\frac{1}{12} \times \frac{2}{7}$

24) $\frac{2}{17} \times \frac{3}{4}$

25) $\frac{10}{13} \times \frac{39}{100}$

26) $\frac{12}{18} \times \frac{9}{32}$

27) $\frac{2}{15} \times \frac{45}{50}$

28) $\frac{5}{11} \times \frac{55}{75}$

29) $\frac{4}{5} \times \frac{2}{13}$

30) $\frac{2}{11} \times \frac{3}{10}$

31) $\frac{3}{14} \times \frac{28}{30}$

32) $\frac{7}{13} \times \frac{39}{63}$

33) $\frac{24}{36} \times \frac{1}{3}$

Multiplying Mixed Numbers

Example $3\frac{2}{3} \times 1\frac{1}{2} = \blacksquare$

Solution $3\frac{2}{3} \times 1\frac{1}{2} = \blacksquare$ ◄——— Change to improper fractions.

$$\frac{11}{\cancel{3}_1} \times \frac{\cancel{3}^1}{2} = \frac{11}{2}$$

$$\frac{11}{2} = 5\frac{1}{2}$$

Answer $5\frac{1}{2}$

Exercise   Multiply these mixed numbers. Write your answers in simplest terms.

1) $2\frac{1}{2} \times \frac{1}{3}$

2) $\frac{1}{2} \times 1\frac{1}{5}$

3) $\frac{2}{7} \times 1\frac{1}{3}$

4) $\frac{1}{5} \times 1\frac{1}{7}$

5) $3\frac{1}{5} \times \frac{3}{4}$

6) $5\frac{2}{3} \times \frac{1}{5}$

7) $\frac{5}{7} \times 2\frac{3}{8}$

8) $1\frac{1}{2} \times \frac{15}{18}$

9) $4\frac{5}{7} \times \frac{7}{11}$

10) $2\frac{3}{5} \times 1\frac{1}{5}$

11) $2\frac{3}{7} \times 2\frac{1}{2}$

12) $5\frac{1}{7} \times 2\frac{1}{5}$

13) $5\frac{1}{6} \times 1\frac{1}{5}$

14) $1\frac{5}{6} \times 1\frac{1}{3}$

15) $1\frac{2}{7} \times 2\frac{1}{8}$

16) $6\frac{1}{2} \times 2\frac{3}{4}$

17) $2\frac{2}{5} \times 1\frac{3}{4}$

18) $4\frac{1}{2} \times 1\frac{1}{4}$

19) $3\frac{3}{7} \times 2\frac{1}{3}$

20) $5\frac{2}{9} \times 1\frac{1}{8}$

21) $5\frac{1}{4} \times 2\frac{1}{7}$

22) $6\frac{2}{5} \times 1\frac{1}{7}$

23) $13\frac{1}{3} \times 2\frac{1}{4}$

24) $1\frac{5}{9} \times 1\frac{3}{4}$

25) $3\frac{2}{5} \times 2\frac{2}{4}$

26) $5\frac{2}{5} \times 1\frac{1}{9}$

27) $5\frac{1}{3} \times 1\frac{1}{8}$

28) $5\frac{3}{9} \times 1\frac{1}{6}$

29) $1\frac{2}{8} \times 3\frac{1}{2}$

30) $3\frac{1}{2} \times 5\frac{1}{6}$

31) $2\frac{4}{5} \times 2\frac{1}{7}$

32) $4\frac{1}{5} \times 1\frac{5}{7}$

33) $3\frac{7}{8} \times 1\frac{1}{2}$

Dividing Fractions

Example $\dfrac{4}{7} \div \dfrac{1}{2} = \blacksquare$

Solution $\dfrac{4}{7} \div \dfrac{1}{2} = \blacksquare$ ←——— Invert the divisor. Then multiply.

$\dfrac{4}{7} \times \dfrac{2}{1} = \dfrac{8}{7}$

$\dfrac{8}{7} = 1\dfrac{1}{7}$

Answer $1\dfrac{1}{7}$

Exercise   Divide. Write your answers in simplest terms.

1) $\dfrac{2}{5} \div \dfrac{2}{7}$

2) $\dfrac{5}{6} \div \dfrac{1}{3}$

3) $\dfrac{2}{7} \div \dfrac{1}{8}$

4) $\dfrac{4}{5} \div \dfrac{1}{6}$

5) $\dfrac{2}{7} \div \dfrac{5}{6}$

6) $\dfrac{3}{8} \div \dfrac{1}{2}$

7) $\dfrac{4}{5} \div \dfrac{5}{6}$

8) $\dfrac{8}{9} \div \dfrac{4}{5}$

9) $\dfrac{5}{6} \div \dfrac{2}{5}$

10) $\dfrac{5}{11} \div \dfrac{2}{22}$

11) $\dfrac{8}{11} \div \dfrac{5}{11}$

12) $\dfrac{5}{12} \div \dfrac{5}{6}$

13) $\dfrac{3}{8} \div \dfrac{5}{12}$

14) $\dfrac{2}{11} \div \dfrac{3}{22}$

15) $\dfrac{8}{13} \div \dfrac{24}{26}$

16) $\dfrac{3}{9} \div \dfrac{1}{5}$

17) $\dfrac{11}{12} \div \dfrac{24}{30}$

18) $\dfrac{5}{7} \div \dfrac{48}{49}$

19) $\dfrac{1}{2} \div \dfrac{5}{7}$

20) $\dfrac{5}{7} \div \dfrac{5}{14}$

21) $\dfrac{8}{9} \div \dfrac{3}{6}$

22) $\dfrac{3}{4} \div \dfrac{6}{7}$

23) $\dfrac{13}{14} \div \dfrac{3}{7}$

24) $\dfrac{8}{15} \div \dfrac{2}{5}$

25) $\dfrac{1}{2} \div \dfrac{1}{2}$

26) $\dfrac{2}{3} \div \dfrac{1}{7}$

27) $\dfrac{3}{7} \div \dfrac{15}{21}$

28) $\dfrac{5}{10} \div \dfrac{2}{6}$

29) $\dfrac{4}{7} \div \dfrac{5}{14}$

30) $\dfrac{2}{3} \div \dfrac{14}{21}$

31) $\dfrac{18}{20} \div \dfrac{15}{40}$

32) $\dfrac{22}{27} \div \dfrac{11}{18}$

33) $\dfrac{16}{30} \div \dfrac{8}{15}$

Dividing Mixed Numbers

Example $2\frac{3}{4} \div 3\frac{1}{3} = \blacksquare$

Solution $2\frac{3}{4} \div 3\frac{1}{3} = \blacksquare$ ◄── Rename mixed numbers as improper fractions.

$\frac{11}{4} \div \frac{10}{3} = \blacksquare$ ◄── Invert the divisor and multiply.

$\frac{11}{4} \times \frac{3}{10} = \frac{33}{40}$

Answer $\frac{33}{40}$

Exercise Divide. Write your answers in simplest terms.

1) $1\frac{1}{2} \div \frac{1}{2}$

2) $3\frac{2}{3} \div \frac{1}{9}$

3) $1\frac{1}{5} \div \frac{2}{5}$

4) $2\frac{1}{6} \div \frac{3}{12}$

5) $\frac{3}{12} \div 3\frac{1}{6}$

6) $\frac{13}{15} \div 1\frac{3}{5}$

7) $1\frac{2}{5} \div \frac{14}{15}$

8) $3\frac{1}{2} \div \frac{5}{6}$

9) $1\frac{1}{2} \div 1\frac{2}{5}$

10) $\frac{1}{2} \div 1\frac{1}{2}$

11) $1\frac{1}{12} \div 2\frac{1}{6}$

12) $2\frac{2}{3} \div 3\frac{5}{9}$

13) $2\frac{1}{2} \div 3\frac{1}{7}$

14) $1\frac{5}{7} \div \frac{6}{7}$

15) $2\frac{5}{8} \div \frac{21}{24}$

16) $3\frac{5}{7} \div \frac{13}{14}$

17) $5\frac{2}{5} \div \frac{3}{4}$

18) $4\frac{1}{3} \div \frac{26}{27}$

19) $5\frac{3}{7} \div \frac{1}{3}$

20) $3\frac{2}{9} \div \frac{1}{8}$

21) $5\frac{2}{5} \div \frac{9}{10}$

22) $8\frac{2}{3} \div \frac{1}{7}$

23) $6\frac{1}{7} \div \frac{7}{18}$

24) $5\frac{1}{5} \div 1\frac{1}{2}$

25) $2\frac{3}{4} \div 1\frac{1}{6}$

26) $1\frac{1}{7} \div 1\frac{1}{6}$

27) $1\frac{1}{8} \div 1\frac{1}{9}$

28) $13\frac{2}{3} \div \frac{1}{9}$

29) $3\frac{2}{3} \div \frac{22}{27}$

30) $3\frac{6}{7} \div 1\frac{1}{4}$

31) $5\frac{2}{7} \div 7\frac{2}{5}$

32) $2\frac{1}{6} \div 1\frac{1}{2}$

33) $1\frac{1}{12} \div 2\frac{1}{6}$

Adding Mixed Numbers With Like Denominators

Example $3\frac{2}{7} + 1\frac{3}{7} = \blacksquare$

Solution

$$3\frac{2}{7}$$
$$+1\frac{3}{7}$$
$$\overline{\quad 4\frac{5}{7}}$$

Step 1	Write in the vertical form.
Step 2	Add the numerators.
	$2 + 3 = 5$
Step 3	Keep the denominator.
Step 4	Add the whole numbers.

Answer $4\frac{5}{7}$

Exercise   Add. Write your answers in simplest terms.

1) $\frac{2}{5} + \frac{2}{5}$

2) $\frac{5}{7} + \frac{1}{7}$

3) $\frac{8}{12} + \frac{3}{12}$

4) $\frac{5}{8} + \frac{1}{8}$

5) $\frac{2}{7} + \frac{5}{7}$

6) $\frac{8}{11} + \frac{4}{11}$

7) $1\frac{1}{6} + 2\frac{3}{6}$

8) $2\frac{5}{8} + \frac{1}{8}$

9) $5\frac{3}{10} + \frac{2}{10}$

10) $5\frac{1}{6} + \frac{1}{6}$

11) $8\frac{1}{12} + \frac{3}{12}$

12) $5\frac{1}{6} + \frac{3}{6}$

13) $8\frac{5}{11} + 1\frac{2}{11}$

14) $9\frac{1}{10} + 3\frac{3}{10}$

15) $8\frac{2}{5} + 3\frac{4}{5}$

16) $6\frac{2}{9} + \frac{5}{9}$

17) $8\frac{2}{12} + 6$

18) $11\frac{12}{21} + 2\frac{3}{21}$

19) $5 + 2\frac{1}{7}$

20) $7\frac{1}{7} + 13\frac{1}{7}$

21) $13\frac{12}{21} + 1\frac{3}{21}$

22) $8\frac{6}{13} + \frac{6}{13}$

Adding Fractions With Unlike Denominators (24)

Example $\dfrac{7}{15} + \dfrac{2}{5} = \blacksquare$

Solution

$\dfrac{7}{15} = \dfrac{7 \times 1}{15 \times 1} = \dfrac{7}{15}$

$+ \dfrac{2}{5} = \dfrac{2 \times 3}{5 \times 3} = + \dfrac{6}{15}$ Add the numerators.

$\dfrac{13}{15}$

Rename the fractions
with like
denominators.

Answer $\dfrac{13}{15}$

Adding Mixed Numbers With Unlike Denominators (25)

Example $5\dfrac{5}{8} + 2\dfrac{7}{12} = \blacksquare$

Solution

$5\dfrac{5}{8}$ $\dfrac{5}{8} = \dfrac{5 \times 3}{8 \times 3} = \dfrac{15}{24}$ $5\dfrac{5}{8} = 5\dfrac{15}{24}$

$+ 2\dfrac{7}{12}$ $\dfrac{7}{12} = \dfrac{7 \times 2}{12 \times 2} = \dfrac{14}{24}$ $+ 2\dfrac{7}{12} = 2\dfrac{14}{24}$

$7\dfrac{29}{24} = 8\dfrac{5}{24}$

Rename the fractional portion
with like denominators.

Rename $7\dfrac{29}{24}$.

$7 + \dfrac{29}{24} = 7 + 1\dfrac{5}{24} = 8\dfrac{5}{24}$

Answer $8\dfrac{5}{24}$

Exercise Find common denominators and add. Write your answers in simplest terms.

1) $\frac{3}{7} + \frac{1}{3}$

2) $\frac{5}{6} + \frac{1}{3}$

3) $\frac{8}{12} + \frac{1}{8}$

4) $\frac{4}{17} + \frac{3}{34}$

5) $\frac{6}{11} + \frac{3}{4}$

6) $\frac{8}{15} + \frac{1}{6}$

7) $\frac{2}{15} + \frac{3}{45}$

8) $\frac{5}{8} + \frac{5}{6}$

9) $\frac{7}{9} + \frac{5}{27}$

10) $2\frac{1}{6} + \frac{2}{9}$

11) $12\frac{3}{10} + \frac{1}{15}$

12) $5\frac{6}{72} + \frac{1}{8}$

13) $8\frac{5}{16} + 2\frac{1}{8}$

14) $15\frac{2}{17} + 1\frac{1}{3}$

15) $26\frac{5}{7} + 2\frac{4}{21}$

16) $10\frac{6}{11} + 2\frac{5}{121}$

17) $8\frac{3}{36} + 2\frac{1}{12}$

18) $9\frac{5}{18} + 2\frac{5}{54}$

19) $5\frac{1}{2} + 2\frac{1}{17}$

20) $7\frac{3}{36} + 2\frac{1}{12}$

21) $3\frac{5}{18} + 1\frac{5}{54}$

22) $10\frac{1}{2} + 12\frac{1}{17}$

Subtracting Mixed Numbers With Like Denominators

Example $14\frac{5}{11}$

$-6\frac{2}{11}$

$8\frac{3}{11}$

Step 1   Subtract 2 from 5.

$5 - 2 = 3$

Step 2   Keep the denominator.

Step 3   Subtract the whole number portions.

$14 - 6 = 8$

Answer $8\frac{3}{11}$

Exercise   Subtract. Write your answers in simplest terms.

1) $\frac{5}{8} - \frac{2}{8}$

2) $\frac{6}{13} - \frac{2}{13}$

3) $\frac{4}{15} - \frac{1}{15}$

4) $\frac{12}{17} - \frac{2}{17}$

5) $\frac{8}{9} - \frac{5}{9}$

6) $\frac{6}{7} - \frac{3}{7}$

7) $\frac{8}{19} - \frac{2}{19}$

8) $2\frac{3}{5} - \frac{2}{5}$

9) $8\frac{7}{8} - \frac{3}{8}$

10) $5\frac{6}{10} - 4\frac{1}{10}$

11) $15\frac{12}{13} - 4\frac{1}{13}$

12) $7\frac{7}{10} - 5\frac{2}{10}$

13) $18\frac{15}{16} - 5\frac{7}{16}$

14) $12\frac{5}{8} - 2\frac{2}{8}$

15) $17\frac{3}{4} - 5\frac{2}{4}$

16) $31\frac{5}{18} - 2$

17) $39\frac{16}{21} - 5\frac{6}{21}$

18) $14\frac{5}{6} - 2\frac{2}{6}$

19) $22\frac{3}{10} - 5\frac{3}{10}$

20) $9\frac{35}{40} - 6\frac{10}{40}$

21) $3\frac{1}{7} - \frac{1}{7}$

22) $16\frac{3}{8} - 12\frac{1}{8}$

Subtracting With Unlike Denominators

Example

$$18 \frac{2}{3}$$

$$\frac{2}{3} = \frac{2 \times 7}{3 \times 7} = \frac{14}{21}$$

$$-5 \frac{1}{7}$$

$$\frac{1}{7} = \frac{1 \times 3}{7 \times 3} = \frac{3}{21}$$

$$18 \frac{2}{3} = 18 \frac{14}{21}$$

$$-5 \frac{1}{7} = 5 \frac{3}{21}$$

$$13 \frac{11}{21}$$

Rename the fractional portions with like denominators.

Subtract the numerators and the whole numbers.

Answer $13 \frac{11}{21}$

Exercise Find common denominators and subtract. Write your answers in simplest terms.

1) $13 \frac{4}{5} - 5 \frac{2}{3}$

2) $9 \frac{7}{8} - 3 \frac{1}{3}$

3) $5 \frac{5}{6} - 2 \frac{1}{3}$

4) $18 \frac{4}{8} - 5 \frac{2}{24}$

5) $15 \frac{10}{24} - 5 \frac{1}{6}$

6) $3 \frac{5}{8} - 1 \frac{2}{6}$

7) $10 \frac{13}{14} - 3 \frac{1}{2}$

8) $36 \frac{2}{5} - 5 \frac{1}{6}$

9) $11 \frac{8}{9} - 5 \frac{2}{8}$

10) $16 \frac{9}{13} - 2 \frac{2}{3}$

11) $8 \frac{15}{17} - 2 \frac{2}{3}$

12) $28 \frac{10}{32} - 5 \frac{1}{8}$

13) $18 \frac{2}{7} - 16 \frac{1}{28}$

14) $31 \frac{5}{12} - 4 \frac{3}{48}$

15) $16 \frac{7}{13} - 5 \frac{2}{39}$

16) $32 \frac{5}{12} - 8 \frac{2}{24}$

17) $28 \frac{1}{6} - 3 \frac{1}{9}$

18) $3 \frac{1}{3} - 1 \frac{1}{7}$

19) $56 \frac{3}{11} - 5 \frac{1}{9}$

20) $15 \frac{32}{33} - 8$

21) $8 \frac{15}{16} - 2 \frac{3}{24}$

22) $23 \frac{8}{15} - 6 \frac{9}{20}$

Subtracting With Renaming

Example   12

$- \quad 3\frac{1}{7}$

Solution

Step 1   Rename.

$12 = 11 + 1$

$12 = 11 + \frac{7}{7}$

$12 = 11\frac{7}{7}$

Step 2   Subtract.

$12 \quad = \quad 11\frac{7}{7}$

$- \quad 3\frac{1}{7} = \quad 3\frac{1}{7}$

$8\frac{6}{7}$

Answer $8\frac{6}{7}$

Example $21\frac{1}{5}$

$- \quad 4\frac{3}{5}$

Solution

Step 1   Rename.

$21\frac{1}{5} = 21 + \frac{1}{5}$

$= 20 + 1 + \frac{1}{5}$

$= 20 + \frac{5}{5} + \frac{1}{5}$

$= 20\frac{6}{5}$

Step 2   Subtract.

$21\frac{1}{5} \quad = \quad 20\frac{6}{5}$

$- \quad 4\frac{3}{5} \quad = \quad 4\frac{3}{5}$

$16\frac{3}{5}$

Answer $16\frac{3}{5}$

Exercise Find common denominators and subtract. Write your answers in simplest terms.

1) $13\frac{2}{5} - 5\frac{6}{7}$

2) $18\frac{1}{5} - 2\frac{3}{5}$

3) $14\frac{3}{10} - 2\frac{1}{2}$

4) $26\frac{5}{7} - 5\frac{13}{14}$

5) $10\frac{5}{12} - 6\frac{3}{4}$

6) $24\frac{1}{11} - 5\frac{6}{22}$

7) $8\frac{2}{9} - 3\frac{4}{5}$

8) $6\frac{1}{12} - 3\frac{1}{2}$

9) $13\frac{1}{7} - 6\frac{3}{8}$

10) $14 - 2\frac{5}{11}$

11) $28\frac{2}{13} - 6\frac{7}{8}$

12) $12 - 8\frac{3}{7}$

13) $25\frac{5}{6} - 1\frac{9}{10}$

14) $9\frac{2}{15} - 4\frac{4}{5}$

15) $42\frac{1}{5} - 3\frac{3}{8}$

16) $53\frac{6}{9} - 4\frac{17}{18}$

17) $13\frac{5}{11} - 1\frac{21}{22}$

18) $30 - 6\frac{15}{19}$

19) $18\frac{1}{9} - 3\frac{2}{3}$

20) $33\frac{12}{40} - 8\frac{9}{10}$

21) $5\frac{5}{13} - 2\frac{30}{39}$

22) $16\frac{7}{10} - 4\frac{49}{50}$

23) $7\frac{1}{18} - 2\frac{2}{3}$

24) $13\frac{1}{11} - 3\frac{4}{22}$

25) $36 - 8\frac{3}{7}$

26) $13\frac{1}{4} - 5\frac{3}{5}$

27) $27\frac{5}{13} - 6\frac{25}{26}$

28) $14\frac{1}{6} - 3\frac{5}{8}$

29) $18\frac{2}{9} - 6\frac{3}{4}$

30) $6\frac{27}{30} - 5\frac{13}{15}$

31) $7\frac{8}{11} - 1\frac{21}{34}$

32) $6\frac{1}{5} - 4\frac{7}{8}$

33) $4\frac{1}{2} - 2\frac{7}{12}$

34) $16\frac{5}{9} - 3\frac{17}{18}$

35) $14\frac{3}{17} - 2\frac{5}{34}$

36) $2 - 1\frac{5}{11}$

37) $45\frac{4}{9} - 5\frac{4}{5}$

38) $32\frac{5}{16} - 5\frac{15}{32}$

39) $8\frac{3}{14} - 2\frac{6}{7}$

40) $29\frac{1}{10} - 3\frac{10}{15}$

41) $13\frac{5}{16} - 8\frac{23}{24}$

42) $4\frac{2}{7} - 2\frac{4}{5}$

43) $13\frac{15}{35} - 1\frac{6}{7}$

44) $10\frac{2}{3} - 8\frac{8}{9}$

45) $15\frac{11}{20} - 4\frac{4}{5}$

Identifying Place Value With Decimals (29)

Example Write the place value of the underlined digits.
   1) 23.0671   Hundredths
   2) 105.1062   Ten-Thousandths

Ten Thousands	Thousands	Hundreds	Tens	Ones		Tenths	Hundredths	Thousandths	Ten-Thousandths
			2	3	.	0	6	7	1
		1	0	5	.	1	0	6	2

Comparing Decimals (30)

Example Compare 2.38 and 2.4. Use the symbols < or >.

Solution Insert zeros to give each decimal the same number of places.
   1) 2.38 and 2.4
   2) 2.38 and 2.40 (After inserting a zero.)
   Since 38 is less than 40, then 2.38 < 2.40.

Example Compare 19.2 and 8.8943.

Solution Since the whole number 19 is greater than 8, then 19.2 > 8.8943.

Exercise Write the place name for each underlined digit.

1) 35.0<u>6</u>

2) .52<u>6</u>03

3) 5.681<u>1</u>

4) 1.0<u>6</u>11

5) .58<u>1</u>11

6) .40101<u>5</u>

7) .00<u>2</u>731

8) <u>2</u>76.03

9) 2.0<u>8</u>35

10) .2850<u>1</u>

11) 12.3005<u>2</u>

12) 52.083<u>1</u>

13) .306<u>1</u>11

14) .56<u>0</u>891

15) 1.0065<u>1</u>

16) 60.00<u>7</u>9

17) 14.000<u>8</u>1

18) 156.0<u>1</u>23

19) 133.0<u>1</u>

20) 15.0<u>1</u>911

21) 1.99<u>1</u>15

22) 8.567<u>2</u>3

23) 12.03587<u>6</u>

24) <u>8</u>,315.67

Rounding Decimals

Example   Round 2.7017 to the nearest thousandth.

Solution   2.7017 ◄─── Number (7) to the right of the thousandth place is 5 or more, so add 1 to the thousandths place and drop all digits to the right.

Answer   2.7017 ≈ 2.702 (≈ means "about equal to.")

Example   Round 8.1649 to the nearest hundredth.

Solution   8.1649 ◄─── Number (4) to the right of the hundredth place is less than 5, so drop the 4 and 9.

Answer   8.1649 ≈ 8.16

Exercise   Round each decimal to the places named.

		Tenths	Hundredths	Thousandths
1)	2.063	_____	_____	_____
2)	.0891	_____	_____	_____
3)	1.0354	_____	_____	_____
4)	.15454	_____	_____	_____
5)	32.70391	_____	_____	_____
6)	7.63	_____	_____	_____
7)	19.808964	_____	_____	_____
8)	34.00354	_____	_____	_____
9)	2.061155	_____	_____	_____
10)	139.4181891	_____	_____	_____

Adding Decimals

Example   23 + .62 +1.9 = ▮

Solution   23.

        .62 ◄— Line up all the

      + 1.9   decimal points.

      25.52

        23.00 ◄— Inserting zeros

         .62   may help.

      + 1.90

      25.52

Answer   25.52

Exercise   Write these problems in vertical form. Then add.

1) 2.3 + 6 + 8.41

2) .413 + 9.6 + .2

3) 17 + .205 + 1.6

4) 2 + .63 + .5 + 1.1

5) 3.5 + 8.21 + .006

6) 8 + .15 + 1.61 + 2

7) 81.7 + 10.73 + 1.673

8) .02 + .603 + 8 + .11

9) 13.06 + 1.5 + 9 + .41

10) 2.71 + .031 + 8 + 9.9

11) 39.4 + 3 + 8.27 + .1

12) 5 + 8.4 + .07 + 6

13) 42 + .126 + .1 + .23

14) 6.28 + .28 + 5.4

15) 7.6 + 1 + .212

16) .561 + 4.7 + 215

17) 81.4 + 6.7 + 8.41

18) 50.51 + 2.6 + 9.15

19) 42.6 + .57 + 23.5

20) 39.6 + .003 + 1.81

21) 95.1 + 1.63 + 101.1

22) 8 + 1.53 + .007

23) .203 + .72 + .025

24) 1.56 + 1.231 + .07

25) 13 + .92 + 6.7

26) 83 + 9.6 + 1.305

27) 5.03 + .607 + .19

28) 18.95 + 1.4 + .071

29) 39.9 + 14.62 + 2.3

30) 2.3 + 1.78 + .663

31) 8.702 + 3.7 + .63

32) 3.0101 + .62 + 4

33) 2.7 + .063 + 1.77

34) 12.8 + .14 + .03 + 3

35) 1.9 + 5.621 + .03

36) 4.7 + .726 + 89.1

37) 1.7 + 2.31 + .631

38) 6.7 + .815 + 2

39) .37 + 2.9 + 8

40) 6.09 + .261 + 9.2

41) 23 + 1.003 + 5.4

42) 5.21 + .53 + 15.6

43) 63 + 1.92 + 88.8

44) .38 + 7.02 + .115

45) 5 + .27 + 1.919

46) 1 + .006 + .0071 + 1.8

47) 11.001 + 1.1 + 6.27

48) 3.9 + 1.06 + .081

Subtracting Decimals

Example $12 - 1.68 = ■$

Solution

$$\begin{array}{r} 12.00 \\ -\ 1.68 \\ \hline 10.32 \end{array}$$

12.00 ← Line up the decimal points and insert zeros.

Answer 10.32

Exercise Write these problems in vertical form. Then subtract.

1) 6.59 − .48
2) 36 − 2.3
3) 19.83 − 2.3
4) 33.89 − .32
5) 5.2 − .156
6) 31.4 − 8
7) 38.5 − 1.67
8) 7.6 − .67
9) .091 − .0197
10) 1.1 − .99
11) 7.7 − 2.63
12) 36.5 − 1.83
13) 6.7 − 2.34
14) 1.6 − 1.08
15) .89 − .098
16) 2.31 − .9
17) .011 − .00201
18) .3 − .234
19) 1.03 − .89
20) 75 − .108
21) 8.7 − 2.31
22) 1 − .9
23) 8.3 − .99
24) 45.1 − .06
25) .101 − .0982
26) 53.72 − 1.8
27) 9.01 − .6
28) 2.171 − .18
29) 5.6 − .42
30) 2.1 − .8
31) 9 − .62
32) 12 − 4.35
33) 1 − .08
34) .1 − .0356
35) .35 − .19
36) 5.51 − .6
37) 19.5 − .34
38) 2.81 − .931
39) 11.23 − 9.9
40) 31.3 − .61
41) 4.35 − .6
42) .68 − .086
43) .1 − .06
44) 1.63 − .89
45) 7.5 − 6
46) 3 − .4
47) 5.52 − .66
48) 6 − .9
49) .32 − .0832
50) 1 − .662

Multiplying Decimals

Example $.26 \times 1.3 = \blacksquare$

Solution

$$
\begin{array}{r}
.26 \quad \longleftarrow \text{ 2 places plus} \\
\times \ 1.3 \quad \longleftarrow \text{ 1 place equals} \\
\hline
78 \\
+26 \\
\hline
.338 \quad \longleftarrow \text{ 3 places}
\end{array}
$$

Example $.321 \times .002 = \blacksquare$

Solution

$$
\begin{array}{r}
.321 \quad \longleftarrow \text{ 3 places plus} \\
\times \quad .002 \quad \longleftarrow \text{ 3 places equals} \\
\hline
.000642 \quad \longleftarrow \text{ 6 places}
\end{array}
$$

Exercise   Write these problems in vertical form. Then multiply.

1) $.2 \times .3$

2) $.7 \times 1.2$

3) $1.9 \times .3$

4) 2.6×8

5) $.26 \times .2$

6) $.62 \times .3$

7) $.81 \times 1.2$

8) $.42 \times 6.3$

9) $.92 \times .21$

10) $.65 \times .07$

11) 1.23×1.2

12) $.128 \times .52$

13) $5.8 \times .006$

14) $.081 \times .02$

15) $.96 \times .73$

16) $8.03 \times .67$

17) $.126 \times .73$

18) $25.3 \times .62$

19) $.5 \times 6$

20) $1.3 \times .8$

21) $2.3 \times .5$

22) $4.3 \times .8$

23) $3.5 \times .7$

24) $.85 \times 3$

25) $.26 \times 1.5$

26) $1.8 \times .18$

27) $4.8 \times .06$

28) $.31 \times .09$

29) $3.62 \times .05$

30) $.402 \times .11$

31) $.71 \times .62$

32) $1.62 \times .71$

33) $52.6 \times .36$

34) $4.2 \times .008$

35) $703 \times .02$

36) $.91 \times .083$

Scientific Notation

Example   Express 2,800 in scientific notation.

Solution $2,800 = 2.800 \times 10^3$ ◄——— 3 places

　　　　　　　　or

　　　　　　　2.8×10^3

Example   Express 0.00039 in scientific notation.

Solution $0.00039 = 3.9 \times 10^{-4}$ ◄——— 4 places

　　　　　　(Use the negative sign ($^{-4}$) when the decimal point is moved to the left.)

Exercise   Write these numbers in scientific notation.

1) 3,600	**23)** 510
2) 35,100	**24)** 8,702
3) 46,000	**25)** 92,300
4) 75,100	**26)** 18,000
5) 6,530	**27)** 980,000
6) 391,000	**28)** 5,600,000
7) 1,725,000	**29)** 7,810,000
8) 5,301,000	**30)** 1,000,000
9) 87,100,000	**31)** 45,000,000
10) 267,000,000	**32)** 9,720,000
11) 100,000	**33)** 5,300,000,000
12) 1,700,000,000	**34)** 961,000,000
13) 34,000,000	**35)** 171,800,000
14) 306.2	**36)** 48.39
15) 12.721	**37)** 150.82
16) .0000623	**38)** .0000031
17) .00002	**39)** .000175
18) .1602	**40)** .003
19) 623.05	**41)** .00231
20) .000000005	**42)** .000000453
21) .00000101	**43)** .000119
22) .00663	**44)** .0024

Dividing Decimals by Whole Numbers (36)

Example .168 ÷ 14 = ■

Solution

```
       .012
  14 ).168     Place the decimal
     −14       point in the quotient
      28       directly above the
     −28       one in the dividend.
       0
```

Example 68.6 ÷ 28 = ■

Solution

```
        2.45
  28 ) 68.60    Adding a zero
     −56        may terminate
      12 6      the answer.
     −11 2
       1 40
      −1 40
         0
```

Dividing Decimals by Decimals (37)

Example 8.04 ÷ .6 = ■

Solution

```
        13.4
  .6 ) 8.0 4
     −6
      2 0
     −1 8
      2 4
     −2 4
        0
```

Step 1 Move the decimal point in the divisor to the right.

Step 2 Move the decimal point in the dividend the same number of places to the right.

Step 3 Divide and bring the decimal point straight up into the quotient.

Renaming Decimals as Fractions (38)

Example Rename .13 as a fraction.

Solution $.13 = \frac{13}{100}$

Example .026 = ■

Solution $.026 = \frac{26}{1,000}$ or $\frac{13}{500}$

Renaming Fractions as Decimals (39)

Example   Rename $\frac{13}{25}$ as a decimal.

Solution $\frac{13}{25} = \frac{13 \times 4}{25 \times 4} = \frac{52}{100}$

> Choose a multiplier that will give you a denominator that is a power of 10. (10, 100, 1,000, 10,000...)

$$= .52 \text{ OR}$$

$$
\begin{array}{r}
.52 \\
25\overline{)13.00} \\
-12\,5 \\
\hline
50 \\
-50 \\
\hline
0
\end{array}
$$

> Dividing the numerator by the denominator will also give the decimal equivalent.

Exercise   Copy these problems and divide. Rename decimals as fractions.

1) $4.7 \div 2$

2) $.78 \div 3$

3) $1.448 \div .8$

4) $2.88 \div .9$

5) $10.2 \div 1.2$

6) $11.55 \div 2.1$

7) $4.545 \div .9$

8) $2.807 \div .7$

9) $.351 \div .09$

10) $4.004 \div .22$

11) $.777 \div .15$

12) $13.7046 \div .91$

13) $.0615 \div 1.5$

14) $.00902 \div .41$

15) $.01952 \div 3.2$

16) $.00206 \div .002$

17) $32.92 \div .4$

18) $.12741 \div .31$

19) $.08833 \div .11$

20) $.0084 \div .007$

21) $6.2432 \div 1.6$

22) $36.8 \div 8$

23) $3.51 \div 9$

24) $7.23 \div 3$

25) $2.412 \div .6$

26) $8.32 \div 3.2$

27) $10.44 \div 2.9$

28) $.159 \div .15$

29) $.266 \div .07$

30) $2.173 \div 4.1$

Why Is a Retirement Plan Needed?

Since the estimated age of retirement is 65, a person needs a retirement plan to provide income after retiring. It is estimated that a person will need between 60%–80% of preretirement income (the amount of money earned the year before retirement) to maintain the set standard of living. A retirement plan allows a person to continue to receive monthly payments after retirement. It is recommended to start saving as soon as possible to be able to meet your retirement needs.

What Is a Retirement Plan?

A retirement plan can be made up of many investments. It also includes any pension plans from an employer. It can be established either by an individual or employer at any brokerage or financial company.

The U.S. government provides tax breaks to people who contribute to retirement plans and agree not to withdraw the money until retirement. One tax break is allowing the invested money to grow on a tax-deferred basis. This means that a person does not pay tax on any of the profits until retirement. Another tax break is that employer-sponsored 401(k) contributions are taken out before taxes. An employee is then taxed at a lower rate. These two tax breaks can save a lot of money for employees each year.

Types of Retirement Investment Plans

Pension Plan   Some employers offer a pension plan to employees. There are many kinds of pension plans. One example is the defined-benefit plan. Companies provide retired employees a monthly payment based on a pension formula. This is employer paid, so employees do not have to contribute anything to receive these benefits. Another example is the defined contribution plan. This is also known as a 401(k). Employees contribute to a 401(k) and many companies will match a percentage of those contributions.

Many employers require employees to be with the company for a certain period of time before becoming eligible for the pension plan. Companies may also have a vesting period. This is a number of years of employment that must be completed to be eligible for pension benefits like the defined-benefit plan.

401(k)s   A 401(k) is a defined contribution plan provided by employers. Employees pay money into the plan and the employer and plan provider do all of the paperwork. Some companies match a percentage of the contribution that employees make to their plans.

The money is taken out before taxes, so it lowers how much of an employee's income is taxed.

A 401(k) is made up of many investment options that are chosen by the employer. These options may include mutual funds, stock in the company, and other investments. The employee chooses which options to invest in. An employee will be penalized for withdrawing any of the money before the age of $59\frac{1}{2}$, except under specific circumstances.

403(b)s The difference between the 401(k) and the 403(b) is that the 401(k) covers private-sector employees. The 403(b) covers employees of public schools and certain tax-exempt organizations. Like the 401(k), the 403(b) participants are offered several investment options. The contributions are also taken out on a pre-tax basis like the 401(k).

IRAs An IRA is an Individual Retirement Account opened up by an individual to save funds for retirement. It can be opened through a bank, mutual fund company, insurance company, or a brokerage firm. A person can contribute up to $2,000 a year from earned income to an IRA. People can choose from many investment options including stocks, bonds, mutual funds, CDs, and money markets.

There are two types of IRAs. The first type is the traditional IRA. Someone who owns a traditional IRA does not pay taxes on any gains until retirement. Then, when money is withdrawn from the account, taxes must be paid on the amount taken out. However, the contributions made to the IRA before retirement can be tax deductible depending upon income level.

The other type of IRA is the Roth IRA. One difference between the two IRAs is that the Roth IRA has an income limit. Anyone making an adjusted gross income under $95,000 and any married couple making a combined total under $150,000 adjusted gross income qualifies for a Roth IRA. Another difference is that the money withdrawn from the Roth IRA at retirement is tax-free. However, contributions made before retirement are not tax deductible.

Types of Retirement Investments

Stocks Buying a stock is buying a piece of ownership in a company. This can be done as an individual or as part of a group. An investment club is a group of people who put their money together to invest in stocks. They research and choose the stocks that they want to invest in. They also make decisions about when to sell and when to buy based on their own investment research and education.

All stockholders take a risk. They can lose the invested money if the company does not do well. They can increase the invested money if the company does do well. If a company's stock is very high, a stockholder could sell some of the stock and receive the profits. Always know how much you can afford to lose and become educated about investments before playing the stock market.

Certificates of Deposit (CD) A Certificate of Deposit is purchased when a person lends a bank a specific amount of money for a certain amount of time. The loan earns interest at a certain rate during that time frame. At the end of that time, the person receives the loaned amount of money back as well as the interest. The FDIC (Federal Deposit Insurance Corporation) insures Certificate of Deposits so a person is guaranteed not to lose money. However, the return rate of money is not as much as other investment types available. It is a low risk, low return investment. It also ties up money for a certain amount of time with penalties if taken out early.

Savings Account   A savings account is a place to store money for emergency use. Banks offer savings accounts at varying, but also very low, interest rates. Often times the interest rate is lower, and with taxes, the owner is losing money. A minimum balance is usually required.

Money Market Account   A money market account has a slightly higher interest rate than a savings account. However, it is as easy to access as a savings account. It is also FDIC insured. A minimum beginning deposit is usually required.

Bonds   A bond is a loan that a person makes to the U.S., state, or local government, or to a big company. Like a CD, an amount of money is lent for a certain amount of time to either the government or a company. The borrower guarantees to pay interest on the money at a set interest rate. A U.S. savings bond can be purchased at any bank. It is also easy to cash in before the maturity date. There are a variety of bonds, so an investor should research carefully before buying one.

Mutual Funds   A mutual fund is a single portfolio of stocks, bonds, and cash managed professionally by an investment company. Mutual funds allow people to spread their investments over a variety of options. Like the stock market, investors lose and gain money as the market falls and climbs. So, the risk level is still there.

A person buys shares in a mutual fund that is managed by a fund manager, who invests the money. The fund manager will try to have many investments so that the other investments would balance out possible losses from the stock market. This is called a diversified portfolio. It contains a percentage of stocks, bonds, and cash equivalents (money markets, CDs, etc.).

A person can decide what percentages go to each investment. This is a good idea, depending on how close retirement is. For a 25-year-old investor, a large percentage of investment may be in stocks, because the losses can be regained over time. For a 55-year-old investor, only a small percentage should be in stocks, with the most being in bonds to hold onto what has already been built up.

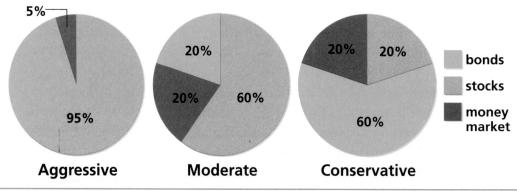

Retirement Planning: Estimated Retirement Planning Table

The left column going down shows the age at which a $100 monthly investment begins.

The top row going across indicates how much interest an investment is earning, depending on the type of investment.

To figure out an estimate of how much money an individual will have at age 65, place one finger on the age at which investing will start and one finger on the investment rate. Move fingers across and down until the two fingers meet.

Age	Interest Rate						
	4%	6%	8%	9%	10%	15%	20%
20	$233,232.26	$389,839.20	$680,577.81	$911,361.73	$1,229,405.42	$5,914,474.28	$30,069,043.90
22	$208,746.74	$340,130.42	$576,722.84	$760,342.21	$1,009,334.46	$4,465,629.78	$20,874,846.85
24	$186,440.47	$296,218.66	$488,009.81	$633,556.51	$827,780.64	$3,370,411.40	$14,490,297.80
26	$166,133.05	$257,450.37	$412,262.86	$527,152.37	$678,043.58	$2,544,569.94	$10,056,878.25
28	$147,658.46	$223,244.66	$347,617.29	$437,887.95	$554,586.56	$1,916,889.34	$6,978,395.53
30	$130,863.93	$193,085.30	$292,475.13	$363,035.66	$452,834.48	$1,444,057.59	$4,840,827.63
32	$115,608.92	$166,513.49	$245,467.08	$300,300.25	$369,006.94	$1,086,788.40	$3,356,659.91
34	$101,764.14	$143,121.58	$205,419.83	$247,750.55	$299,980.31	$816,888.58	$2,326,230.06
36	$89,210.71	$122,547.41	$171,328.08	$203,761.74	$243,173.67	$613,040.67	$1,610,884.29
38	$77,839.30	$104,469.21	$142,330.52	$166,966.85	$196,454.62	$459,126.16	$1,114,335.79
40	$67,549.43	$88,601.22	$117,689.31	$136,215.86	$158,061.41	$342,957.69	$769,719.27
42	$58,248.72	$74,689.62	$96,772.39	$110,541.37	$126,538.57	$255,320.39	$530,601.01
44	$49,852.29	$62,509.05	$79,038.37	$89,129.65	$100,683.76	$189,246.98	$364,735.86
46	$42,282.16	$51,859.42	$64,023.60	$71,296.28	$79,503.76	$139,469.66	$249,731.79
48	$35,466.68	$42,563.10	$51,331.02	$56,465.66	$62,178.20	$102,005.69	$170,039.26
50	$29,340.09	$34,462.48	$40,620.67	$44,153.74	$48,029.52	$73,843.95	$114,860.35
52	$23,842.00	$27,417.68	$31,601.49	$33,953.54	$36,498.18	$52,708.01	$76,696.95
54	$18,916.97	$21,304.62	$24,024.36	$25,522.90	$27,122.13	$36,876.96	$50,342.38
56	$14,514.14	$16,013.24	$17,676.07	$18,574.21	$19,519.89	$25,049.91	$32,181.26
58	$10,586.87	$11,445.98	$12,374.17	$12,865.76	$13,376.55	$16,243.53	$19,703.27
60	$7,092.36	$7,516.33	$7,962.62	$8,194.43	$8,432.19	$9,714.64	$11,165.45
62	$3,991.98	$4,147.64	$4,307.94	$4,389.62	$4,472.33	$4,901.59	$5,357.70
64	$1,248.00	$1,272.00	$1,296.00	$1,308.00	$1,320.00	$1,380.00	$1,440.00

There are many kinds of electronic calculators. Each calculator is a little different from others. Some have more keys than others. The keys may be placed differently. You may have to press the keys in a certain order. Most calculators, however, are very similar.

Here is a calculator that has the basic functions you find on most calculators.

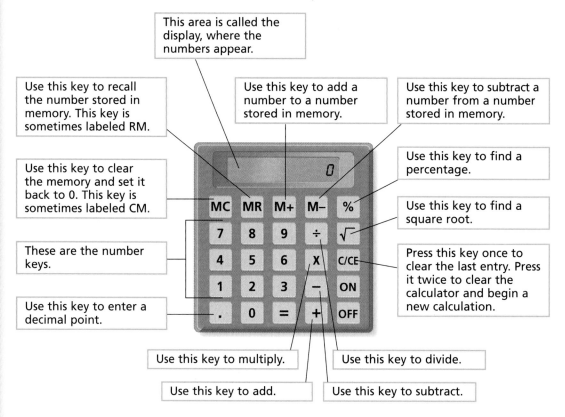

This area is called the display, where the numbers appear.

Use this key to recall the number stored in memory. This key is sometimes labeled RM.

Use this key to clear the memory and set it back to 0. This key is sometimes labeled CM.

These are the number keys.

Use this key to enter a decimal point.

Use this key to add a number to a number stored in memory.

Use this key to subtract a number from a number stored in memory.

Use this key to find a percentage.

Use this key to find a square root.

Press this key once to clear the last entry. Press it twice to clear the calculator and begin a new calculation.

Use this key to multiply.

Use this key to add.

Use this key to divide.

Use this key to subtract.

You can use a calculator to help you do arithmetic quickly and accurately. In many cases, you key the calculation the same way you would write it on paper.

Press $2 3$ $+$ $6 1$ $=$
The display will read 84.
$23 + 61 = 84$

Press $1 2$ $\times$ $1 2$ $=$
The display will read 144.
$12 \times 12 = 144$

Press $9 8$ $-$ $1 8$ $=$
The display will read 80.
$98 - 18 = 80$

Press $6 3$ $\div$ 9 $=$
The display will read 7.
$63 \div 9 = 7$

It's a good idea to look at the display after you key in each number. It helps to check that you haven't pressed a wrong key by mistake.

The $\sqrt{}$ key will give you the square root of a number.

Example   What is the square root of 81?
          Press *8 1* $\sqrt{}$
          The display will read *9*.

The % key will help you find a percentage. The % key works differently on different kinds of calculators. You may need to press = after % on some calculators. The examples show how the key works on most calculators.

Examples   What is 25 percent of 44?   What is 20 percent less than 65?
          Press *4 4* × *2 5* %   Press *65* − *2 0* %
          The display will read *11*.   The display will read *5 2*.

          What is 10 percent more than 50?
          Press *5 0* + *1 0* %
          The display will read *55*.

If you are going to use the same number, or constant, in a series of calculations, you can store it in memory. Remember to clear the memory by pressing MC before you begin.

Examples   What is 18 times 4? 18 times 12? 18 times 31?

          Press *1 8* M+ C/CE
          The display reads *0*. The number 18 is stored in memory.
          Press MR × *4* = The display reads *72*.
          Press MR × *1 2* = The display reads *216*.
          Press MR × *3 1* = The display reads *558*.

You can add to or subtract from the number in memory by using the M+ and M− keys. Remember to clear the memory by pressing MC before you begin.

Press	Display	Number in Memory
2 2	*22*	0
M+	*22*	22
6	*6*	22
M+	*6*	28
2 0	*20*	28
M−	*20*	8

Decimal, Percent, and Fraction Conversion

Renaming Decimals as Percents

Example   Rename .75 as a percent.

Solution   .75

.75 = 75%

Step 1	Move the decimal point two places to the right.
Step 2	Then insert a percent symbol.

Example   Rename .5 as a percent.

Solution   .5 = .50

.5 = 50%

Renaming Percents as Decimals

Example   Rename 80% as a decimal.

Solution   80% = 80.%

80% = .80

Step 1	Move the decimal point two places to the left.
Step 2	Then drop the percent symbol.

= .8 ◄——— You can always drop zeros at the end of a decimal.

Renaming Fractions as Decimals

Example   Rename $\frac{7}{20}$ as a decimal.

Solution   **Method 1**

$\frac{7}{20} = \frac{7 \times 5}{20 \times 5} = \frac{35}{100}$

$= .35$

Choose a multiplier that makes the denominator a power of 10 (10, 100, 1,000, . . .)

Method 2

$\frac{7}{20} = 20\overline{)7.00}$

$\begin{array}{r} .35 \\ 20\overline{)7.00} \\ -6\,0 \\ \hline 1\,00 \\ -1\,00 \\ \hline \end{array}$

Divide the numerator by the denominator.

Decimal, Percent, and Fraction Conversion

Renaming Decimals as Fractions

Example   Rename .025 as a fraction.

Solution   First, read the decimal: "25 thousandths"

Then write the fraction, and simplify.

$$.025 = \frac{25}{1{,}000} = \frac{25 \div 25}{1{,}000 \div 25} = \frac{1}{40}$$

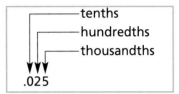

Renaming Fractions as Percents

Example   Rename $\frac{9}{25}$ as a percent.

Solution   *Method 1*

Write as an equivalent fraction with denominator 100.

$$\frac{9}{25} = \frac{9 \times 4}{25 \times 4} = \frac{36}{100} = 36\%$$

> *Percent* means *per 100.*
> So, 36 hundredths is 36%.

Method 2

$$\frac{9}{25} = .36 = 36\%$$

> **Step 1**   Rewrite the fraction as a decimal.
>
> **Step 2**   Rewrite the decimal as a percent.

Renaming Percents as Fractions

Example   Rename 2% as a fraction.

Solution $2\% = \frac{2}{100}$ ◄— *Percent* means *per 100.*

$= \frac{1}{50}$ ◄— Simplify.

Geometry

Area of a rectangle = $l \times w$ (p. 182)

$A = lw$

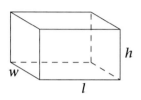

Volume of a rectangular prism = $l \times w \times h$ (p. 260)

$V = lwh$

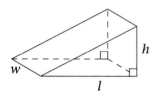

Volume of half a rectangular prism = $\dfrac{l \times w \times h}{2}$ (p. 200)

$V = \dfrac{lwh}{2}$

Business

Gross pay − Deductions = Net pay (p. 10)

Commission = Sales × Rate of commission (p. 24)

Price − Cost = Profit (p. 64)

Interest = Rate of interest × Time for which money is loaned (p. 118)

$I = PRT$

Profit = Revenue − Expenses (p. 131)

Cost of production = Fixed costs + Variable costs (p. 158)

Inventory turnover = $\dfrac{\text{Cost of goods sold}}{\text{Value of inventory}}$ (p. 168)

Net sales = Revenue from sales − Sales returns and allowances (p. 170)

Gross profit = Net sales − Cost of goods sold (p. 170)

Net income = Gross profit − Operating expenses (p. 170)

CIF = Cost of goods + Insurance on goods + Freight to ship goods (p. 208)

*M*ultiplication Table

X	2	3	4	5	6	7	8	9	10	11	12
2	4	6	8	10	12	14	16	18	20	22	24
3	6	9	12	15	18	21	24	27	30	33	36
4	8	12	16	20	24	28	32	36	40	44	48
5	10	15	20	25	30	35	40	45	50	55	60
6	12	18	24	30	36	42	48	54	60	66	72
7	14	21	28	35	42	49	56	63	70	77	84
8	16	24	32	40	48	56	64	72	80	88	96
9	18	27	36	45	54	63	72	81	90	99	108
10	20	30	40	50	60	70	80	90	100	110	120
11	22	33	44	55	66	77	88	99	110	121	132
12	24	36	48	60	72	84	96	108	120	132	144

Measurement Conversion Factors

Metric Measures

Length
1,000 meters (m) = 1 kilometer (km)
100 centimeters (cm) = 1 m
10 decimeters (dm) = 1 m
1,000 millimeters (mm) = 1 m
10 cm = 1 decimeter (dm)
10 mm = 1 cm

Area
100 square millimeters (mm^2) = 1 square centimeter (cm^2)
10,000 cm^2 = 1 square meter (m^2)
10,000 m^2 = 1 hectare (ha)

Volume
1,000 cubic meters (m^3) = 1 cubic centimeter (cm^3)
100 cm^3 = 1 cubic decimeter (dm^3)
1,000,000 cm^3 = 1 cubic meter (m^3)

Capacity
1,000 milliliters (mL) = 1 liter (L)
1,000 L = 1 kiloliter (kL)

Mass
1,000 kilograms (kg) = 1 metric ton (t)
1,000 grams (g) = 1 kg
1,000 milligrams (mg) = 1 g

Temperature Degrees Celsius (∞C)
0°C = freezing point of water
37°C = normal body temperature
100°C = boiling point of water

Customary Measures

Length
12 inches (in.) = 1 foot (ft)
3 ft = 1 yard (yd)
36 in. = 1 yd
5,280 ft = 1 mile (mi)
1,760 yd = 1 mi
6,076 feet = 1 nautical mile

Area
144 square inches (sq in.) = 1 square foot (sq ft)
9 sq ft = 1 square yard (sq yd)
43,560 sq ft = 1 acre (A)

Volume
1,728 cubic inches (cu in.) = 1 cubic foot (cu ft)
27 cu ft = 1 cubic yard (cu yard)

Capacity
8 fluid ounces (fl oz) = 1 cup (c)
2 c = 1 pint (pt)
2 pt = 1 quart (qt)
4 qt = 1 gallon (gal)

Weight
16 ounces (oz) = 1 pound (lb)
2,000 lb = 1 ton (T)

Temperature Degrees Fahrenheit (∞F)
32°F = freezing point of water
98.6°F = normal body temperature
212°F = boiling point of water

Time
60 seconds (sec) = 1 minute (min)
60 min = 1 hour (hr)
24 hr = 1 day

Measurement Conversion Factors

To change	To	Multiply by	To change	To	Multiply by
centimeters	inches	.3937	meters	feet	3.2808
centimeters	feet	.03281	meters	miles	.0006214
cubic feet	cubic meters	.0283	meters	yards	1.0936
cubic meters	cubic feet	35.3145	metric tons	tons (long)	.9842
cubic meters	cubic yards	1.3079	metric tons	tons (short)	1.1023
cubic yards	cubic meters	.7646	miles	kilometers	1.6093
feet	meters	.3048	miles	feet	5,280
feet	miles (nautical)	.0001645	miles (statute)	miles (nautical)	.8684
feet	miles (statute)	.0001894	miles/hour	feet/minute	88
feet/second	miles/hour	.6818	millimeters	inches	.0394
gallons (U.S.)	liters	3.7853	ounces avdp	grams	28.3495
grams	ounces avdp	.0353	ounces	pounds	.0625
grams	pounds	.002205	pecks	liters	8.8096
hours	days	.04167	pints (dry)	liters	.5506
inches	millimeters	25.4000	pints (liquid)	liters	.4732
inches	centimeters	2.5400	pounds advp	kilograms	.4536
kilograms	pounds avdp	2.2046	pounds	ounces	16
kilometers	miles	.6214	quarts (dry)	liters	1.1012
liters	gallons (U.S.)	.2642	quarts (liquid)	liters	.9463
liters	pecks	.1135	square feet	square meters	.0929
liters	pints (dry)	1.8162	square meters	square feet	10.7639
liters	pints (liquid)	2.1134	square meters	square yards	1.1960
liters	quarts (dry)	.9081	square yards	square meters	.8361
liters	quarts (liquid)	1.0567	yards	meters	.9144

401(k) plan (fôr ō wun kā plan) program in which employees can postpone receiving some of their salary until retirement (p. 43)

800 number (āt hun′drəd num′bər) phone number that is free to the caller (p. 250)

A

Accounting period (ə koun′ting pir′ē əd) period of time covered by an income statement (p. 170)

Actuary (ak′chü er′ ē) person who calculates premiums and benefits using statistics and probabilities (p. 40)

Airfare (âr′fâr) cost of a plane ticket (p. 100)

A.M. (ā em) the hours before noon (p. 12)

Annual wage (an′yü əl wāj) money earned by an employee in one year (p. 9)

Annually (an′yü əl ē) once a year (p. 21)

Apportioned Plate (ə pôr′shənd plāt) license plate that allows a vehicle to operate in several states (p. 206)

Asset (as′et) item of value owned by a company (p. 125)

Automated teller machine (ATM) (ȯ′tə māt′əd tel′ər mə shēn′) (ā tē em) computer terminal that allows 24-hour access to bank accounts (p. 106)

Average cost method (av′ər ij kȯst meth′əd) a method of calculating the value of an inventory using the average cost of all items in the inventory (p. 166)

Axis (Axes) (ak′sis) (ak′sēz′) line of reference on a graph (p. 93)

B

Back ordered (bak ȯr′dərd) temporarily out of stock (p. 259)

Balance (bal′əns) the value of a financial account (p. 43)

Bar graph (bär graf) graph that uses bars to compare amounts or sizes (p. 93)

Base year (bās yir) the earlier year, in calculating percent change (p. 173)

Beneficiary (ben′ə fish′ē er′ē) person(s) named to receive money when the insured dies (p. 137)

Benefit (ben′ə fit) portion of medical expenses covered by an insurance company (p. 34)

Bimonthly (bī munth′lē) every two months (p. 21)

Biweekly (bī wēk′lē) every two weeks (p. 21)

Bodily injury (bod′l ē in′jər ē) physical injury to a person (p. 183)

Bonus (bō′nəs) money given an employee in addition to earned wages or salary (p. 28)

Budget (buj′it) plan for managing income and expenses, usually for a set period of time (p. 70)

C

Carrier (kar′ē ər) a business that picks up and delivers packages or letters (p. 253)

Cash advance (kash ad vans′) money that must be repaid (p. 106)

Cash flow (kash flō) amount of money that a company receives and pays out in the same time period (p. 129)

Cash flow statement (kash flō stāt′mənt) form used to track cash flow over a period of time (p. 129)

Cash value (kash val′yü) money available to an owner who ends a whole life insurance policy (p. 188)

Casualty insurance (kazh′ü əl tē in shûr′əns) insurance coverage that pays for injuries to others and for the repair or replacement of damaged or destroyed property (p. 180)

Catastrophic loss (kat′ə strof′ik lȯs) a major loss caused by a natural disaster (p. 220)

a	hat	e	let	ī	ice	ȯ	order	ù	put	sh	she		a	in about
ā	age	ē	equal	o	hot	oi	oil	ü	rule	th	thin		e	in taken
ä	far	ė	term	ō	open	ou	out	ch	child	₣H	then	ə	i	in pencil
à	care	i	it	ȯ	saw	u	cup	ng	long	zh	measure		o	in lemon
													u	in circus

Charge (chärj) purchase using a credit card (p. 106)

CIF (sē ī ef) abbreviation for the sum of the cost of goods and the insurance and freight charges for shipping the goods (p. 208)

Collision (kə lizh′ən) damage to the insured's car caused by a car accident (p. 183)

Commission (kə mish′ən) payment of a percentage of total sales (p. 24)

Compound interest (kom′pound in′tər ist) interest paid on both the principal plus any interest added to date (p. 121)

Comprehensive (kom′pri hen′siv) damage to the insured's car not caused by a collision (p. 183)

Consumer Price Index (CPI) (kən sü′mər prīs in′deks) measurement of the change in price of certain goods and services compared to a base period (p. 218)

Contribution (kon′trə byü′shən) Social Security tax paid to a Social Security account (p. 40)

Co-payment (kō pā′mənt) fixed amount or percentage the insured pays for certain medical services (p. 34)

Cost of goods sold (kôst ov gudz sōld) cost of manufacturing or buying the product that is sold (pp. 168, 230)

Cost of living increase (kôst ov liv′ing in′krēs) wage increase to help workers keep the same standard of living during inflation (p. 90)

Cost of production (kôst ov prə duk′shən) expense of manufacturing a product (p. 158)

Coverage (kuv′ər ij) specific services paid by the insurance policy (p. 34)

Credit card (kred′it kärd) card used to buy items and pay for them at a later time, often with interest (p. 106)

Deductible (di dukt′ə bəl) money the insured pays before benefit coverage begins (p. 36)

Deduction (di duk′shən) money withheld from gross pay (p. 10)

Defer (di fər′) postpone receiving part of one's salary until retirement by putting it into a 401(k) account (p. 43)

Dependent (di pen′dənt) person supported by a worker (p. 89)

Depreciation (de prē′shē ā′shən) distribution of the cost of an asset over its useful life (p. 150)

Discount (dis′kount) reduce the selling price of an item by a fixed amount or a percentage (p. 60)

Distribution (dis′trə byü′shən) number of readers of a magazine or newspaper (p. 238)

Donation (dō nā′shən) contribution made without expectation of goods or services in return (p. 70)

Double bar graph (dub′əl bär graf) a graph that displays data using two sets of bars (p. 160)

Double occupancy (dub′əl ok′yə pən sē) space for two people (p. 103)

Double time (dub′l tīm) payment of 2 times the regular hourly rate (p. 14)

Economy hotel (i kon′ə mē hō tel′) thrifty lodging with fewer services and conveniences (p. 103)

Endowment policy (en dou′mənt pol′ə sē) life insurance policy that has a guaranteed cash value at the end of its term (p. 186)

Exercise options (ek′sər sīz op′shənz) take advantage of stock options by actually buying the stock (p. 46)

Export (ek′spôrt) sell to another country (p. 209)

Fixed cost (fikst kôst) cost that remains the same however many units are produced (p. 158)

Gross pay (grōs pā) full earnings before deductions (p. 10)

a	hat	e	let	ī	ice	ô	order	u̇	put	sh	she		a	in about
ā	age	ē	equal	o	hot	oi	oil	ü	rule	th	thin	ə	e	in taken
ä	far	ė	term	ō	open	ou	out	ch	child	ᵺ	then		i	in pencil
â	care	i	it	ȯ	saw	u	cup	ng	long	zh	measure		o	in lemon
													u	in circus

Gross profit (grōs prof´it) difference between net sales and cost of goods sold; difference between sales and cost of goods sold (pp. 170, 230)

Horizontal (hôr´ə zon´tl) sideways (p. 93)

Horizontal analysis (hôr´ə zon´tl ə nal´ə sis) comparison of the same income statement categories for different accounting periods (p. 173)

Hourly rate (our´lē rāt) amount of money paid for each hour of work (p. 8)

Import (im´pôrt) buy from another country (p. 209)

In stock (in stok) on hand (p. 56)

Income statement (in´kum´ stāt´mənt) statement of income and expenses showing a profit or loss during a given period of time (p. 170)

Inflation (in flā´shən) increase in the price of consumer goods and services (p. 90)

Insured (in shùrd´) person whose costs are covered by an insurance policy (p. 34)

Interest (in´tər ist) fee charged on the unpaid balance of a charge account; fee charged to a borrower for the use of money loaned (pp. 106, 118)

International business (in´tər nash´ə nəl biz´nis) business conducted across national borders (p. 208)

International Fuel Tax Agreement (IFTA) (in´tər nash´ə nəl fyü´əl taks ə grē´mənt) (ī ef tē ā) organization of most U.S. states and Canadian provinces that is responsible for distributing fuel taxes fairly (p. 204)

Interstate commerce (in´tər stāt´ kom´ərs) business conducted across state lines (p. 204)

Inventory (in´vən tôr´ē) products available for sale (p. 63)

Inventory turnover (in´vən tôr´ē tėrn´ō´vər) number of times inventory is replaced during a given period of time (p. 167)

Inventory valuation (in´vən tôr´ē val´yü ā´shən) the process of determining the value of an inventory (p. 166)

Labor force (lā´bər fôrs) all people who are capable of working (p. 82)

Labor union (lā´bər yü´nyən) organization of workers in the same industry (p. 90)

Layoff (lā´ôf´) firing workers, often temporarily (p. 129)

Liability (lī´ə bil´ə tē) financial responsibility (p. 188)

Liability insurance (lī´ə bil´ə tē in shùr´əns) insurance coverage that pays money to anyone injured or to anyone whose property is damaged by the insured (p. 180)

Life expectancy table (līf ek spek´tən sē tā´bəl) statistics that predict how long a person is expected to live, based on date of birth and gender (p. 38)

Life insurance (līf in shùr´əns) insurance coverage that pays money to a beneficiary when the insured dies (p. 37)

Line of credit (līn ov kred´it) arrangement with a bank allowing a company the right to borrow up to a specific amount of money (p. 125)

Living wage (liv´ing wāj) annual wage needed to provide necessary things (p. 9)

Lodging (loj´ing) place to stay while traveling (p. 103)

Luxury hotel (luk´shər ē hō tel´) expensive lodging with more services and conveniences (p. 103)

Malpractice insurance (mal prak´tis in shùr´əns) insurance that covers a failure in professional duty that results in injury, loss, or damage (p. 223)

a	hat	e	let	ī	ice	ô	order	ù	put	sh	she		a	in about
ā	age	ē	equal	o	hot	oi	oil	ü	rule	th	thin	ə	e	in taken
ä	far	ė	term	ō	open	ou	out	ch	child	ᴛH	then		i	in pencil
â	care	i	it	ȯ	saw	u	cup	ng	long	zh	measure		o	in lemon
													u	in circus

Marketing (mar′kə ting) all business activity that gets goods and services from the producer to the customer (p. 162)

Marketing channel (mar′kə ting chan′l) a place to advertise (p. 238)

Mass mailing (mas mā′ling) sending a large number of the same items at the same time through the mail (p. 248)

Medical (med′ə kəl) treatment of injuries to the driver and passengers of the insured's car (p. 183)

Miles per gallon (mpg) (mīlz pər gal′ən) (em pē jē) number of miles that can be driven on 1 gallon of fuel (p. 204)

Minimum wage (min′ə məm wāj) least hourly rate that a worker can legally be paid (p. 20)

N

Negative cash flow (neg′ə tiv kash flō) the cash flow during a period when expenses are greater than revenue (p. 129)

Net income (net in′kum′) difference between gross profit and operating expenses (p. 170)

Net sales (net sālz) difference between sales revenue and amount for returned and defective merchandise (p. 170)

Nonprofit business (non prof′it biz′nis) company that puts all its profit back into the company to further its cause (p. 70)

O

Operating expense (op′ə rāt ing ek spens′) administrative costs not directly related to manufacturing or marketing a product (p. 142)

Out-of-pocket expense (out′ ov pok′it ek spens′) total amount an insured pays for medical expenses (p. 36)

Output (out′put′) number of units produced (p. 158)

Overhead (ō′vər hed′) expenses that are not costs of production or sales, such as rent, utilities, and insurance (p. 216)

Overtime (ō′vər tīm′) working time beyond a regular 40-hour week (p. 14)

P

Payroll (pā′rōl′) total wages paid to employees (p. 129)

Peak hour (pēk our) time when stores have the most customers (p. 62)

Pension (pen′shən) retirement income paid by a former employer (p. 42)

Pension plan (pen′shən plan) money placed in a special account to be paid to employees when they retire (p. 42)

Percentage (pər sen′tij) an amount calculated by multiplying a percent by a number (p. 17)

Piecework (pēs′wėrk′) work paid according to the number of units completed (p. 18)

P.M. (pē em) the hours after noon (p. 12)

Pollutant (pə lüt′nt) unhealthy or unnatural material introduced into the environment (p. 196)

Positive cash flow (poz′ə tiv kash flō) the cash flow during a period when revenue is greater than expenses (p. 129)

Poverty level (pov′ər tē lev′əl) family income that is not enough to provide basic needs (p. 89)

Premium (prē′mē əm) amount paid for insurance coverage (p. 34)

Principal (prin′sə pəl) amount of money loaned (p. 18)

Product payment cost (prod′əkt pā′mənt kôst) cost associated with processing cash, checks, or credit transactions (p. 133)

Production schedule (prə duk′shən skej′ūl) plan showing how many goods to manufacture each day or week (p. 54)

Profile (prō′fīl) shopping patterns of potential customers (p. 239)

Profit (prof′it) amount of money earned after paying all expenses (p. 45)

Profit sharing (prof′it shâr′ing) benefit that gives a portion of a company's profits to its employees (p. 45)

a	hat	e	let	ī	ice	ȯ	order	u̇	put	sh	she		a	in about
ā	age	ē	equal	o	hot	oi	oil	ü	rule	th	thin	ə	e	in taken
ä	far	ė	term	ō	open	ou	out	ch	child	ᴛʜ	then		i	in pencil
â	care	i	it	ȯ	saw	u	cup	ng	long	zh	measure		o	in lemon
													u	in circus

Property damage (prop´ər tē dam´ij) damage to somebody else's property (p. 183)

Quarterly (kwôr´tər lē) every quarter of a year, or every three months (p. 21)

Raise (rāz) amount of pay increase or percent pay increase (p. 86)

Rate (rāt) percent of interest charged for money loaned (p. 118)

Rate of commission (rāt ov kə mish´ən) the percent used to compute commissions (p. 24)

Ratio (rā´shē ō) number relationship between two or more things (p. 43)

Receipt (ri sēt´) proof of purchase (p. 109)

Receivable (ri sē´və bəl) money owed to a company for goods and services sold on credit (p. 125)

Reimburse (rē´ im bėrs´) pay back (p. 109)

Retail store (rē´tāl stôr) business that sells items to the general public (p. 62)

Retire (ri tīr´) voluntarily stop full-time work permanently (p. 40)

Revenue (rev´ə nü) total income earned by a company (p. 58)

Rider (rī´dər) a change to the original policy (p. 186)

Round trip (round trip) a trip to a place and back, often over the same route (p. 100)

Salary (sal´ər ē) payment of a fixed amount of money at regular intervals (p. 21)

Sales force (sālz fôrs) employees who sell a company's products or services (p. 80)

Semiannually (sem´ē an´yü əl ē) every 6 months (p. 86)

Semimonthly (sem´i munth´lē) twice a month (p. 21)

Server (sėr´vər) large computer that connects many smaller computers (p. 251)

Service business (sėr´vis biz´nis) company whose focus is service instead of a product (p. 66)

Share (shâr) equal parts into which a corporation's capital stock is divided (p. 46)

Ship (ship) send (p. 252)

Simple interest (sim pəl in´tər ist) constant fee charged for the use of money loaned (p. 118)

Single occupancy (sing´gəl ok´yə pən sē) space for one person (p. 103)

Slope (slōp) fraction describing the steepness of a line, in which the numerator is the vertical change and the denominator is the horizontal change (p. 200)

Social Security (sō´shəl si kyùr´ə tē) federal program that provides retirement benefits to all U.S. citizens over age 62 who have paid into the program (p. 40)

Square foot (ft²) (skwâr fùt) a measure of the area of a square with 1-foot sides (p. 146)

Staff (staf) all the people employed by a company (p. 78)

Statement (stāt´mənt) monthly record of all changes in a financial account (p. 106)

Stock (stok) part of a corporation that can be divided into shares and sold (p. 46)

Stock option (stok op´shən) share of stock offered at a guaranteed price for a limited time (p. 46)

Suite (swēt) group of rooms occupied as a unit (p. 103)

Take-home pay/net pay (tāk´hōm´pā) amount a worker receives after deductions are subtracted from gross pay (p. 10)

Tariff (tar´if) tax on goods entering from another country (p. 208)

Term (tėrm) period of time that insurance coverage is in effect (p. 189)

Territory (ter´ə tôr´ē) geographic area where a salesperson sells the company's products or services (p. 80)

a	hat	e	let	ī	ice	ô	order	ù	put	sh	she	⎧ a	in about
ā	age	ē	equal	o	hot	oi	oil	ü	rule	th	thin	e	in taken
ä	far	ė	term	ō	open	ou	out	ch	child	₮H	then	ə ⎨ i	in pencil
â	care	i	it	ȯ	saw	u	cup	ng	long	zh	measure	o	in lemon
												⎩ u	in circus

Time (tīm) period for which the money is loaned (p. 118)

Time and a half (tīm and ə haf) payment of 1.5 times the regular hourly rate (p. 14)

Time card (tīm kärd) record of the number of hours an employee works each day (p. 12)

Tip (tip) extra money given for good service (p. 16)

Turnover (tėrn´ō´vər) number of employees who leave a company and are replaced (p. 84)

U

Unemployed (un´em ploid´) not working at a paying job (p. 82)

Unemployment insurance (un´em ploi´mənt in shür´əns) insurance coverage that pays money to employees who are laid off (p. 144)

Unemployment rate (un´em ploi´mənt rāt) percent that compares the number of workers who do not have a job to the labor force (p. 82)

V

Value (val´yü) the amount of money a share of stock is worth if it is sold (p. 46)

Variable cost (vâr´ē ə bəl kôst) cost that changes with the number of units produced (p. 158)

Vertical (vėr´tə kəl) up and down (p. 93)

Volume (vol´yəm) measure in cubic units of space inside a container (p. 200)

W

Wage (wāj) money paid for hourly work (p. 8)

Whole life (hōl līf) life insurance that has a cash value (p. 188)

Workers' compensation (wėr´kərz kom´pən sā´shən) insurance coverage that pays money to employees who cannot work because of job-related injuries (p. 144)

Y

Yield (yēld) amount of crops produced per acre (p. 220)

a	hat	e	let	ī	ice	ô	order	u̇	put	sh	she	ə	a	in about
ā	age	ē	equal	o	hot	oi	oil	ü	rule	th	thin		e	in taken
ä	far	ė	term	ō	open	ou	out	ch	child	ᴛʜ	then		i	in pencil
â	care	i	it	ȯ	saw	u	cup	ng	long	zh	measure		o	in lemon
													u	in circus

Index

Risks, 215–226
    financial, 216–220
    legal, 220–224
Rounding
    always up, 62, 68, 79, 200, 265
    to hundredths place, 22
    money, 106
    of sales goals, 58–59
    up or down, 39

S

Salaries
    calculating, 21–22
    monthly gross pay, 22
    as operating expense, 142–145
    pay periods for, 21
    plus commission, 26
Sales
    commissions and, 24–27
    conventions/exhibits for, 234–237
    cost of, 162–164
    cost/price of products, 230–231
    goals for, 58–59
    growth and, 232–233
    inventory and, 260
    by mail-order, 247
    marketing for, 234–243
    profits from, 241–242
    shipping and, 252–255
    staff for, 80–81
Schedules
    for peak hours, 62–63
    for production, 54–55
    for reordering, 261
Server, 251
Service businesses, 66–69
Shipping costs, 252–255
Slope, 200
Social Security
    contribution to, 40–41
    monthly benefits from, 41–42
Spreadsheets, 87
Staff, 76–82
Statements
    of cash flow, 129–132
    for credit cards, 106–109
    of income, 170–173
Stock on hand, 56–57
Stocks options, 46–48
Subtraction
    of decimals, 11
    of fractions, 12
Supplies, 66–68

T

Tariffs, 208–210
Term of insurance policy, 189
Territories, 80–81
Time
    accounting periods, 170, 173
    A.M./P.M., 12
    changing months/years, 31, 122, 127
    months in a year, 180
    pay periods, 21
    peak hours in retail, 62
    period of loan, 118
    production schedules and, 54–55
    scheduling reorders, 261
    semiannual raises, 86
    wages and, 12–15
    weeks in year, 20
Time card, 12
Tips, 14, 16–17
Toll free number, 250
Transportation
    airfare, 100–102
    company cars for, 150–152
Travel, business, 99–113
    airfare, 100–102
    credit cards for, 106–109
    lodgings for, 103–105
    reimbursement forms, 109–112
Turnover
    of employees, 84–85
    of inventory, 166–167

U

Unemployment insurance, 144–145
Unemployment rates, 82–83

V

Valuation of inventory, 166–168
Variable costs, 158
Volume, 200, 261

W

Wages, 7–31
    bonuses, 28–29
    commissions, 24–27
    cost of living and, 90–93
    deductions from, 10–11
    education and, 91–93
    estimating annual income, 9–10, 20
    gross pay, 10–11, 22
    hourly pay, 8, 12
    labor unions and, 90–91
    manufacturing vs. retail, 65

minimum wage, 18–19
necessary for living, 9–10
net pay, 10–11
as operating expenses, 142–145
for overtime, 14
pay periods for, 21
for piecework, 18–19
poverty level and, 89–90
raises, 29, 86–88
salary, 21–22
take home pay, 10–11
time card, 12
tips, 16–17
Web sites
for available jobs, 23
for converting square numbers, 202
design of, 69
to find value of dollar, 219
for insurance definitions, 181
for marketing, 248
for marketing plans, 164
for Social Security benefits, 41
Wheelchairs, 200–203
Whole life insurance, 188–190
Whole numbers, 198
Workers' Compensation, 144–145

Y

Yield per acre, 220